EXAMPLES ILLUSTRATING AACR 2

ANGLO-AMERICAN CATALOGUING RULES

SECOND EDITION

by **ERIC J. HUNTER, MA, FLA, AMIET,** *Senior Lecturer*

and **NICHOLAS J. FOX, BA,** *Research Assistant*

of the Department of Library and Information Studies,
Liverpool Polytechnic

Compiled on behalf of the Cataloguing and Indexing
Group of The Library Association

with financial assistance from

The British Library Bibliographic Services Division

THE LIBRARY ASSOCIATION

LONDON

12988

Published by The Library Association, 7 Ridgmount Street, London
WC1, England, and printed in the United States of America for the
publishers by R.R. Donnelley & Sons Co., Chicago. All rights reserved.
No part of this book may be reproduced in any form without the
prior permission of the publishers.

British Library Cataloguing in Publication Data

Hunter, Eric Joseph
    1. Anglo-American cataloguing rules, 1978
    2. Descriptive cataloguing — Problems, exercise, etc.
    I. Title II. Fox, Nicholas J. III. Library Association
    025.3'2   Z694

    ISBN 0-85365-951-6

CONTENTS

ACKNOWLEDGMENTS

The authors gratefully acknowledge the help and/or advice willingly given by the following people:

R.M. Andrews, Pendlebury Library of Music, University of Cambridge

K.G.B. Bakewell, Dept. of Library and Information Studies, Liverpool Polytechnic

Joan M. Bibby, Dept. of Library and Information Studies, Liverpool Polytechnic

R.M. Brunt, Dept. of Library and Information Studies, Queens University of Belfast

I.C. Butchart, New College Library, Durham

Joyce E. Butcher, Bibliographical Services Division, British Library

R.A. Christophers, Reference Division, British Library

J.C. Downing, Bibliographic Services Division, British Library

J. Faughey, Dept. of Librarianship, Newcastle-upon-Tyne Polytechnic

D.J. Ferris, Bibliographic Services Division, British Library

M.J. Gorman, University of Illinois

Ellen J. Gredley, School of Librarianship, Polytechnic of North London

G.E. Hamilton, Library Association Library

Frances Hendrix, Preston Polytechnic Library

A.E. Jeffreys, University Library, Newcastle-upon-Tyne

H.L. de Mink, Inter Documentation Company

E.A. (Liz) Roberts, Manchester Public Library

V. de P. Roper, Dept. of Library and Information Studies, Liverpool Polytechnic

E.H. Seagroatt, Dept. of Library and Information Studies, Liverpool Polytechnic

M.R. Shifrin, Central Library Resources Service, Inner London Education Authority

R.A. Wall, Loughborough University of Technology Library

Mention should also be made of the members of the Library Association Cataloguing and Indexing Group Working Party on Cataloguing Examples, in particular G.E. Hamilton, for the help given in preparing the earlier sampler which illustrated the first edition of AACR.

Facsimiles of title pages and illustrations of other media are reproduced by kind permission of:

Boosey & Hawkes Music Publishers Ltd., London

Butterworth & Co. Ltd., London

Caedmon Records, New York

Cassell & Co. Ltd., London

Educational Productions Ltd., Wakefield, Yorkshire

Gatehouse Prints, Robin Hood's Bay, Yorkshire

George Allen & Unwin Ltd., London

Hamilton Historical Board, Hamilton, Ontario

Hamlyn Publishing Co., London

Her Majesty's Stationery Office, London

Inter Documentation Company BV, Leiden, Netherlands

Macdonald & Co. Ltd., London

Manchester University Press

Martin Secker & Warburg Ltd., London

National Library of Canada, Ottawa

Open University, Milton Keynes

Raphael Tuck & Sons Ltd., Blackpool

Readex Microprint Corporation, New York

Regional Municipality of Hamilton-Wentworth, Ontario

Routledge & Kegan Paul Ltd., London

Selective Marketplace Ltd., London

Sir Isaac Pitman & Sons Ltd., London

Society for Promoting Christian Knowledge, London

Staples Printing Group Ltd., London

Thames & Hudson Ltd., London

University of Nottingham, Dept. of Adult Education

Video Arts Ltd., London

INTRODUCTION

Firstly, we stress that there is no intention in this work of presenting an official view of how particular rules in AACR 2 are to be interpreted. Some rules deliberately provide for more than one interpretation. Indeed, section 0.7 of AACR 2 explains that there are a number of rules which are designated as *alternative rules*, or as *optional additions*, and some other rules or parts of rules are introduced by the word *optionally*. Further, it will always be possible to produce convincing arguments for favouring at least two *different* rules for deciding the same point when cataloguing certain items. In fact, if this collection provokes discussion of alternative solutions to a problem, one of its objectives will be achieved.

The work may be used in several ways:

i   To find an example illustrating a particular and previously identified AACR 2 rule.

ii   To find an example illustrating a particular cataloguing problem.

iii As a medium to browse through to discover how AACR 2 approaches various cataloguing difficulties.

The examples are arranged in one alphabetical sequence of main entries filed in accordance with the second edition of the *ALA rules for filing catalog cards*. The entries are numbered consecutively for indexing purposes.

A wide range of media is covered but there must obviously be a greater emphasis on the more usual library materials (e.g. the printed monograph) as compared with the, at present, less common ones (e.g. the machine-readable data file).

AACR 2 recognises that many libraries no longer find it necessary to distinguish between the main entry and other entries but Part II of the rules is still based upon the proposition that one main entry is made for each item described and that this is supplemented by added entries.

Each main entry in this sampler is followed by a tracing showing the headings for any necessary added entries. These tracings do not relate to any standard method of presentation but are simply given in a form which we consider to be the most suitable for this work. Selected examples of added entries, illustrating the various circumstances in which they should be made, are included in Appendix 1.

After the tracing, a brief indication is given of the problems involved in the cataloguing of the item concerned, together with the numbers of the relevant rules which are illustrated. Detailed indexes of these problems and rules precede the main entry section.

It will be clear that certain rules must have been used repeatedly in formulating the examples, e.g. rule 1.1B1 (transcription of the title proper). To note, and index, a rule every time that it has been used would be both unnecessary and uneconomic. Rules are therefore noted, and indexed, selectively according to the illustrative purpose of each example.

However, the initial 11 examples illustrate basic layouts for a variety of media, arranged in the order of Chapters 2-12 of Part I of AACR 2. Each of these examples includes a reasonably comprehensive statement of the rules used in its production and, for Example no.1, a complete statement of every rule which has been involved in producing the entry is given.

To help reveal the nature of some items and to make clear why the entries for particular items take the form that they do, illustrations — mostly reproductions of the chief sources of information — are provided. We hope that these may prove useful when, for example, the entry for a printed monograph is conditioned by the typography of the title page or the entry for a sound recording by the information that appears (or does not appear) on the label. These reproductions (title page facsimiles, etc.) appear with the entries that they illustrate. The initial 11 examples are all accompanied by such visuals.

Entry layout

The layout of each main entry follows a standard pattern and the areas into which the description of an item may be divided are given in the order laid down in AACR 2, i.e.

> HEADING
> Title and statement of responsibility. —
> Edition. — Material (or type of publication)
> specific details. — Publication, distribution, etc.
> Physical description. — (Series).
> Note(s).
> Standard number.

A general material designation may be included following the title proper. As this is *optional*, such designations are not included in these examples. However, a short explanation of general material designations will be found preceding the main entry section.

Each area, other than the first area, must be preceded by a full stop, space, dash, space (. —) unless the area begins a new paragraph. Whether paragraphing is adopted, and to what extent it is adopted, will depend upon the in-house style of the individual cataloguing agency. The 'in-house' style of this sampler agrees with that of its predecessor (see below) in that paragraphing is used for the physical description area, the note(s) area and the standard number area. The paragraphing of the physical description area has the advantage of making the specific material designation more prominent. Selected examples showing the appearance of entries when paragraphing is not employed will be found in Appendix 3.

The amount of information given in each example is a maximum set, i.e. a third level of description. For those cataloguing agencies not requiring this amount, AACR 2 indicates (in rule 1.0D) the elements that are to be included in less detailed second and first levels.

The heading for each entry is capitalised to bring it into prominence although AACR 2 does not prohibit the use of lower case if preferred. No designations of function are required in main entry headings. (Some designations *may* be added to headings for added entries as indicated in Appendix 1).

Usually, the references that would be required from variant forms of an entry heading will be reasonably obvious. Where this is not so, a note concerning them is given. As with added entries, selected examples of references are provided (Appendix 2).

The entries are shown as they would appear if a standard typewriter (with the addition of a dash (—) and square brackets) were used to produce them. However, as AACR 2 states (0.14), examples must not be *prescriptive* and it should be stressed that AACR 2 does not link description to a typed or printed 'card' format. The rules acknowledge the fact that the computer has enabled cataloguing agencies to produce variously formatted records from one machine-readable data base.

Scope of the work

Despite the fact that this sampler illustrates a vast number of rules, the authors make no claim for exhaustivity, nor anything approaching it. Some sections of AACR 2 have been represented very selectively, for instance 22.21-22.28 (Special rules for names in certain languages) and 25.18B-25.18M (Sacred scriptures for religions other than Christianity). Nevertheless, the cataloguer will find included here suggested solutions to a high percentage of the everyday difficulties which he or she is likely to encounter.

The previous sampler, published in 1973, illustrated the British Text of the 1967 edition of *Anglo-American cataloguing rules*. That was a less substantial work, containing 217 examples. Just over 50% of these have been retained in the present work, and we hope this will be helpful to those cataloguers who may find it necessary to compare and contrast the two editions of the rules.

E.J.H.
N.J.F.
Liverpool 1979

PROBLEM AND GENERAL INDEX

All references are to numbers in the main entry sequence of this volume except where page numbers are quoted.

Although broadly compatible with Bakewell's excellent index to AACR 2 itself, the approach adopted in this sampler must, by its very nature, be somewhat different, as will be seen if entries such as: Accompanying materials; Music; Serials; and Three-dimensional artefacts and realia are compared in the two works.

Inevitably, indexing is not exhaustive in that a particular problem cannot be linked to every example that includes a solution. The date of publication, distribution, etc., for instance, *must* appear in some form in every example. More specifically, there are a number of examples where an approximate date has been supplied but only a representative selection of these will be found in the index.

AACR 2 deals with *conditions* of authorship and *not* individual cases (e.g. particular institutions) or types of publication (e.g. books of quotations or encyclopedias). Cases and types of publication mentioned here are merely illustrative of how AACR 2 rules are to be interpreted.

Chief sources of information: serials *(continued)*

> first issue not available, 15
> sound recordings, 5, 160, 302
> three-dimensional artefacts and realia, 9, 363

Chiefs of state, 347

Christian names *see* Forenames; Given names, etc.

Chronological designation of serials *see* Numeric and/or alphabetic, chronological, or other designation (serials)

Church bodies *see* Religious bodies

Church music, 75

Churches
    additions to names, 362
    Catholic Church *see* Catholic Church
    Church of England, 69
    established, 69
    liturgical works, 65, 75
    local, 362
    Methodist Church, 68

Cine mode (filmstrips, microfilms, etc.), 134, 185

Cinefilms *see* Motion pictures and videorecordings

Cities, towns, etc.
    added to corporate names, 77, 139, 167, 311, 350, 362
    governments, 288
        with similar names, 256

Classical Greek works
    uniform titles, 27

Coats of arms
    illustrative matter (printed monographs), 124, 171

Coins, 348

Collaborations *see* Mixed responsibility, works of; Shared responsibility, works of

Collaborators
    added entries *see under* Added entries

Collation *see* Physical description area

Collections
    added entries *see under* Added entries
    of extracts from a work or works *see under* Extracts
    of items of varying character, 163, 352
    of laws governing more than one jurisdiction, 138
    of letters, 87
    of manuscripts, 87, 320
    of music, 24, 234
    of translations, 147
    of treaties, 215
    produced under editorial direction, 323
    with collective title, 75, 92, 215, 229, 234, 235, 331, 375
    without collective title, 31, 43, 66, 84, 159, 160, 180, 199, 202, 203
    see also Collective title; Complete works; Contents notes; Selections; "With" notes

Collective title
    and titles of individual works on title page, 235, 321, 331
    as title proper, 75, 92, 215, 229, 234, 235, 331, 375
    lack of
        individually titled works by different persons, 84, 160, 199
        individually titled works by the same person, 31, 43
        sound recordings, 66, 159, 160, 180, 202, 203
    music, 75
    sound recordings, 234, 375

Colour characteristics
    graphic materials, 7, 213, 332
    motion pictures and videorecordings, 6, 76
    three-dimensional artefacts and realia, 34, 73, 179, 248, 357

Coloured illustrations *see under* Illustrations

Columns, notes on, 287

Commentaries
    commentary emphasised, 60, 128, 145
    presented as edition of work with accompanying annotations, 162
    selected passages of text only, 128
    text not included
        not considered as commentary, 263

"Commission", word implying administrative subordination, 188

---

[1]
The rules on contents notes are, perhaps, a little
inconsistent.

Rule 1.7B18 (the general rule) includes examples
of both full and partial contents but no instructions.

Rule 2.7B18 (printed monographs) instructs that
a note is to be made of the contents of an item
either *selectively* or fully.

Rule 5.7B18 (music), 6.7B18 (sound recordings)
and 7.7B18 (motion pictures) appear to direct
that a note of the separately titled works contained in an item *must* be given. This is not
always practical (see, for instance, example no.234).
These rules do, however, include a further
instruction: 'Make notes on additional or partial
contents when appropriate.'

Chapter 13 of AACR 2 recognises that individual
cataloguing agencies must decide their own policies with regard to analysis and rule 13.3 states
that an entry *may* contain a display of parts in
the note area.

In this sampler, full contents notes will be found
in examples no. 5, 6, 80, 164, 229, 235, 321, 323,
331, 345, 354, 373, 375. Otherwise partial contents notes are considered sufficiently illustrative
of the rules.

Contents notes *(continued)*

Corporate bodies: headings for *(continued)*

Designations
added to corporate names, 66, 318
added to personal names, 173
of function
in added entry headings, p.170
serials *see* Numeric and/or alphabetic,
chronological, or other designation

Detail, levels of, p.viii

Diameter
charts, 308
medals, 220
sound discs, 5
tape reels, 240

Diaries, 42, 277

Digests, 338

Dimensions
format of early printed monographs, 50,
52, 58
inappropriate, 49, 205
not recorded if standard, 122, 240, 302, 352,
380, 381
of containers, 34, 111, 297
word added to indicate which dimension is
being given, 73, 179, 208, 220, 245,
308, 372
see also Gauge; Height; Size; Width; and
specific materials, e.g. Globes; Medals;
Microscope slides; Realia; Three-dimensional
artefacts and realia

Dioceses, 65

Dioramas, 247

Direct or indirect subheading *see under*
Subordinate bodies

Discs, sound, 43, 66, 70, 89, 159, 160, 180,
187, 225, 249, 276, 285, 318, 375
as accompanying materials, 64
with accompanying materials, 285
see also Sound recordings

Discussions, 40

Dissertations, 381

Distinguishing terms, etc. *see under* Corporate
names; Governments; Personal names

Distributor
added in square brackets to name of
publisher, distributor, etc., 6, 89, 259
notes on, 219

Distributor, place of *see* Place of publication,
distribution, etc.

"Division", word implying administrative subordination, 312

Dolby processed sound recordings, 302

Drawings, technical, 88

Duplicating masters, 246, 364

Duration
motion pictures and videorecordings, 6, 257
music, 105, 144, 351, 361
sound recordings, 5, 70, 159, 240
omission, 318

Early printed monographs, 50, 52, 58, 124
definition, 50
sources of information, 50, 124
see also Works created before 1501

Ecclesiastical officials, 264, 377

Edition
date of, 1, 31, 226
reissues, 232, 286
notes on, 157, 214, 219, 260, 359
see also Edition statement

Edition statement
statement of responsibility relating to an
edition, 22, 104, 206, 226
subsequent edition statements, 232
transcription, 22, 132, 168, 192, 243, 306
see also Edition

Editorial direction, works produced under, 24,
53, 81, 108, 227, 235, 258, 262, 281, 322, 376

Editors
added entries *see under* Added entries
of works of single personal authorship, 106
serials, 16, 241

Joint committees, 177

Joint pseudonyms, 253

'Jr', surnames followed by, 181

Jurisdictions no longer existing, U.K. place names, 82, 256, 288

Key (music), 207
    added to uniform titles, 207, 361

Key-titles (serials), 55

Kings, 13

Kits, 163, 196, 201, 298, 352

Koran
    uniform titles, 182

Labels (machine-readable data files)
    as sources of information, 8

Labels (sound recordings)
    as sources of information, 5, 160

Language
    added to uniform titles, 27, 50, 51, 130, 267
        Bible, 44, 45, 46
    notes on, 46, 57, 112, 157, 173, 243, 244
    of description
        chief source of information in more than
            one language or script, 112, 157
        title proper, 46, 216, 276
    of headings
        corporate bodies, 178
        personal names, 27, 74
            given names, 173
    uniform titles
        basic story found in many versions, 147
        music, 130
        sacred scriptures, 182
        works created after 1501, 131
        works created before 1501, 86

Large print books, 306

Laws, etc., 32, 138, 215, 327, 333, 334, 340, 341, 345, 383

Laws, etc. *(continued)*
    capitalisation, 333, 334
    governing more than one jurisdiction, 215
    governing one jurisdiction, 138, 333, 334, 345
    of ancient jurisdiction, 162
    uniform titles, 162, 333, 334, 345
        dealing with one subject, 138
    see also Constitutions; Courts

Leaves
    pagination recorded in terms of, 3, 13, 77, 139
    plates as *see* Plates in pagination
    unnumbered, 13

Lectures, series of, 237, 330

Legal documents, manuscript
    lack of title, 228
    location of original, 228

Legal materials *see* Constitutions; Courts; Laws, etc.; Treaties

Legislative bills, 340, 341

Legislative bodies
    with more than one chamber, 340, 341, 346

Legislative enactments *see* Bills; Laws, etc.

Legislative subcommittees of U.S. Congress, 346

Length of performance *see* Duration

Lesson cards, 186, 295, 368

Lettered pages, 230

Letters, initial *see* Initials

Letters, manuscript, 3
    collections, 87

Levels of description, p.viii

Libraries, 55, 82, 83, 192
    subordinate bodies, 197, 239, 352

Library's holdings, notes on
    serials, 155

Librettos, 135

"Limited"
    not required in headings for corporate
        bodies, 54, 303
    required in headings for corporate bodies,
        143, 312, 363

Limited editions, notes on, 157, 214

Lining papers containing illustrations, 19,
    48, 215

Literary works
    sound recordings of, 5, 285

Liturgical music, 75

Liturgical works, 65

Local bylaws, 138

Local churches, 362

Local government reorganisation in the U.K.,
    82, 256

Local place names added to corporate names,
    139, 362

Location
    accompanying materials, notes on, 64, 122,
        325
    originals of art reproductions, notes on, 370
    originals of manuscripts, notes on, 3, 185, 228

Logical records, machine readable data files
    number of, 260

Loops, film, 257

Loose-leaf printed monographs, 219

Lord added to personal names, 206, 212

Machine-readable data files, 8, 197, 260, 304
    availability, notes on, 8
    data files, 260
    object programs, 304
    program files, 8, 197
    sources of information, 8
    specific material designation, 8, 197

Maiden names
    middle name of married woman maiden
        surname, 200

Main entries, p.vii, 169

Manufacture, date of *see under* Date(s)

Manufacturer
    recorded in publication, distribution, etc.
        area, 73, 179, 289, 363

Manuscripts, 3, 87, 228, 230, 320
    collections, 87, 320
    handwritten, 3, 228, 230
    holographs, 3, 230
    letters, 3, 87
    sources of information, 3
    wills, 228

Maps, 2, 120, 204, 299, 350, 378
    collections, 378
    illustrative matter (printed monographs),
        61, 74, 83, 125
    Ordnance Survey, 378
    see also Cartographic materials

Marks of omission *see* Omission, marks of

Married women
    using maiden name and husband's surname,
        200

Material of which object is made or upon which
    item is printed
    cartographic materials, 54, 299
    three-dimensional artefacts and realia, 73,
        107, 179, 220, 248, 348, 357

Medals, 220

Medium (art originals), 176, 360

Medium of performance (music), 38, 100, 105,
    130, 361
    in uniform titles, 38

Meetings *see* Conferences

Members of a group, ensemble, etc. (sound
    recordings), 43

Methods of reproduction (art reproductions), 329

Metric measurements, 5

Mezzosoprano, abbreviation for, 130

Microfiches, 10, 94, 192
  see also Microforms

Microfilms, 185, 239, 381
  compared with filmstrips, 185
  see also Microforms

Microforms, 10, 94, 140, 185, 192, 239, 381
  original item, notes on, 10, 94, 140, 239
  sources of information, 10
  specific material designation, 10, 381

Microopaques, 140
  see also Microforms

Microreproductions, 94, 140
  original item, notes on, 94, 140
  see also Facsimiles

Microscope slides, 107

Middle English, 267

Military forces, 335, 336, 343

Miniature books
  size, 44, 150

Miniature scores (music), 100, 105, 207

Ministries, government, 99, 210, 288, 317, 325

Mis-spelled words in chief source of
  information, 24

Misprints in chief source of information, 24

Mixed authorship see Mixed responsibility,
  works of

Mixed material items, 163, 196, 298, 352

Mixed responsibility, works of, 72, 121, 125,
  129, 284, 327
  see also Shared responsibility, works of

Mock-ups, 223

Models, 363

Monarchs, 13

Monographic series see Series

Monographs see Early printed monographs;
  Printed monographs

Months
  abbreviations, 28

Motion pictures and videorecordings, 6, 76,
  256, 257, 292, 358
  duration less than five minutes, 257
  film loops, 257
  film reels, 6, 256, 292, 358
  sources of information, 6
  specific material designation, 6, 76
  videorecordings, 76

Multilevel description, 24, 113, 116, 169, 183,
  186

Multimedia items, 163, 196, 201, 298, 352
  see also Accompanying materials

Multipart items, 182, 298, 364

Multipartite treaties, 328

Multiple series statements, 78, 164, 177, 188,
  319, 328

Multi-volumed printed monographs see under
  Volumes

Museums, 56, 266
  subordinate bodies, 269

Music, 4, 24, 37, 38, 57, 100, 105, 109, 130,
  135 (libretto), 144, 207, 234, 251, 261, 265,
  268, 361
  abbreviations for voices, 130
  adaptations, 261
  arrangements, 37, 130, 144, 361
  ballets, musical settings for, 105
  church music, 75
  collections, 24, 234
  composer, entry under, 37, 130, 251, 268
  contents, notes on, 24
  copyright dates, 4, 100, 265
  duration of performance, 144
  generic terms, titles consisting of, 4, 207
  illustrative matter (printed monographs), 81, 234

Pagination, 1
    changing from Roman to Arabic, 254
    complex, 214
    each numbered sequence recorded, 226
    estimated, 277
    inappropriate, 35
    in opposite directions, 112, 199
    irregularities in numbering, 214
    lettered, 230
    music, 4, 24, 109
    part of larger sequence, 189
    plates *see* Plates in pagination
    recorded in terms of leaves, 3, 139
    recorded whether numbered in item or not, 3
    tête bêche, 112, 199
    unnumbered, 71, 129, 199, 221, 307, 364
    volume which contains both leaves and
        pages, 175, 272
    works in more than one volume, 219, 277

Paintings, 176, 360
    reproductions, 229, 370

Pamphlets
    as accompanying materials, 49, 63, 111, 285
    see also Printed monographs

"Panel", word implying administrative
    subordination, 33

Papers (manuscripts), 87, 320

Parallel texts, 46, 112, 162, 199

Parallel title, 86, 107, 208, 215
    music, 57
    serials, 216
    series, 215
    statements of responsibility for, 216

Parentheses, use of
    in description
        material (or type of publication) specific
            details area (serials), 11, 16, 155
        mathematical data area (cartographic
            materials), 359
        physical description area, 5, 8, 10, 30,
            37, 49
        publication, distribution, etc. area, 73, 289
        series area, 29, 319, 322
        standard number area, 22, 163
    in headings
        corporate names, 66, 77, 78, 191
    in uniform titles, 334

Partial contents, notes on, 37, 187, 298
    see also Contents notes

Parts (music), 109

Parts of works
    item consisting of consecutively numbered
        parts, 244
    item issued in weekly parts, 219
    item which is section of another item, 182
    uniform titles, 244
    see also Extracts; Selections

Peepshow books, 35

Peers and peeresses *see* Titles of honour, nobility,
    address, etc.

Performance, duration of *see* Duration

Performance, medium of *see* Medium of
    performance

Performers
    sound recordings
        entry under, 43, 66, 89, 187, 225, 249,
            302, 380
        named in a note, 66, 70, 89, 159, 180,
            276, 285, 302, 318
        statement of responsibility, 5, 43, 66,
            225, 249
    see also Cast (motion pictures, sound record-
        ings, etc.)

Periodicals *see* Serials

Personal authors, 1
    artists as, 72, 221
    composers as, 4, 37, 130, 251, 268
    photographers as, 13, 129, 309
    place of origin, 161
    probable, 231, 299
    serials, 198
    works erroneously or fictitiously attributed
        to, 52
    see also Mixed responsibility, works of;
    Personal names; Shared responsibility, works
    of; Statements of responsibility

Personal names
    headings for
        additions to, 13, 42, 86, 137, 161, 162,
            173, 174, 212, 237, 274, 278, 279,

Personal names: headings for: additions to
(continued)

305, 306, 324
consisting of initials, 98
distinguishing between names which are
the same, 136, 137, 181, 277, 278,
279, 305, 306
no dates or distinguishing terms available, 87, 88
entry element, 1, 293
entry under phrase, 52, 124, 254, 283
entry under proper name, if known, even
if characterising phrase appears in chief
source of information, 254
established English language form of name
not in Roman alphabet, 27, 180
form determined by way in which it appears
in author's works, 91, 361
form determined by way in which it appears
in reference sources, 14, 361
in different language forms, 74
name by which person is commonly known
or identified, 40, 70, 91, 132, 209,
225, 249
omissions from, 5, 181
phrase denoting place of origin, 161
references *see under* References
Roman, 50, 243, 244
romanisation, 149, 324
vernacular term of honour or address added
to names of persons of religious vocation,
274
well-established English form, 27, 50
with prefixes, 93, 105, 130, 131, 322, 356,
357
without surname, 12, 161
see also Forenames; Given names, etc.;
Hyphenated personal names; Maiden names;
Pseudonyms; Surnames; Titles of honour,
nobility, address, etc.; Words or phrases

Persons, headings for *see* Personal names

Phonorecords *see* Sound recordings

Photographers as personal authors, 13, 129, 309

Photographs, 13, 309

Phrases *see* Words or phrases

Physical description area

Physical description area *(continued)*

accompanying material in *see under*
Accompanying materials
notes on, 6, 23, 34, 36, 87, 111, 112,
129, 136, 156, 246, 255, 260, 287,
297, 352, 354, 372
see also Description; and specific elements,
e.g. Illustrations; Size; and particular
materials, e.g. Music; Serials; Sound
recordings

Piano scores, 265, 361

Picture cards (teaching materials), 368

Pictures, 354
inappropriate as specific material
designation, 301, 368
see also Art originals; Motion pictures and
videorecordings; etc.

Pieces, 297, 298
used for items of varying character assembled
together, 196, 255

Place names
abbreviations, 156, 296
added to headings
corporate bodies
branch that carries out activities in
particular locality, 117
conferences, 77, 167, 311
distinguishing between bodies of same
name, 191, 256
if body could be confused with those of
the same or similar names, 139, 350
local churches, 362
personal names, 161
added to place of publication, 292, 296
as headings for corporate bodies, 32, 383
changes of name, 82, 256
jurisdiction no longer existing (U.K.), 82,
256, 288

Place of manufacture, 73, 179, 289, 363

Place of origin of personal authors, phrase
denoting, 161

Place of printing
early printed monographs, 50, 52

1
AACR 2 defines (Appendix D) a plate as a leaf
containing illustrative matter. However, it must
be stressed that plates are recorded as part of
the pagination and *not* as illustrations.

Printed monographs *(continued)*

consisting of text and detachable graphics, 246
consisting principally of artist's illustrations for a text, 326
consisting wholly of illustrations, 13
early printed monographs *see* Early printed monographs
in more than one volume *see under* Volumes
large print books, 306
multipart sets, 298
parallel texts, 46, 112, 119
parallel titles, 86, 107, 208, 215
published in weekly parts, 219
revisions *see under* Revisions
sources of information, 1, 48
tête bêche works, 112, 199
text for which artist has provided illustration, 121, 125, 156, 246
translations *see under* Translations
with accompanying materials, 64, 110, 122, 163, 315, 325
with variant titles
uniform titles *see* Uniform titles
see also particular types of work, e.g. Encyclopedias (which are included merely as illustrations of how AACR 2 rules are to be interpreted); conditions of responsibility, e.g. Editorial direction, works produced under; Shared responsibility, works of; etc.; and specific problems, e.g. Pagination; Place of publication; etc.

Printer
early printed monographs
as publisher, 50, 58

Printing, date of
see Date(s) of printing

Printing process (graphics), 114

Prints, art, 114

Prints, study *see* Study prints

Probable authorship, 231, 299

Probable date of publication, 249

Probable place of publication, 249

Probable publisher, 367

Proceedings (conferences) *see* Conferences

Process (art prints), 114

Producers (filmstrips, motion pictures and videorecordings), 6, 292, 353

Production companies (motion pictures and videorecordings), 292

Program files (machine-readable data files), 8, 197

Programmed texts, 199

Programmes of events, 158

Programming languages (machine-readable data files), 8, 197

Programs, computer, 8, 197, 304

Projection (cartographic materials), 359

Projection speed (motion pictures and video-recordings), 6

'Prominently stated', meaning of, 282

Promulgation, dates of (single modern laws) added to uniform titles, 334

Proper names *see* Corporate bodies; Personal names; Place names; Surnames

Protocols, etc., 78

Pseudonyms, 14, 91
person known by more than one name, 19
person predominantly identified by, 104
person with more than one pseudonym, 224, 275
shared, 253

Publication date *see* Date(s) of publication, distribution, etc.

Publication, distribution, etc. area, 1
details in more than one language, 215
no publication details, 58, 204
notes on, 22, 219, 236, 241, 290
omitted for naturally occurring objects, 245
only date given for art originals, 176, 360
see also individual elements, e.g. Date(s) of

Publication, distribution, etc. area *(continued)*

    publication, distribution, etc.; Place of
    publication, distribution, etc.; Publisher,
    distributor, etc.; and specific materials, e.g.
    Printed monographs

Publisher, distributor, etc.
    added entries *see under* Added entries
    change of, notes on, 222
    function, 89, 269, 298, 330
    given in shortest form in which it can be under-
      stood and identified, 18, 25, 48, 300,
      321, 378
    in title and statement of responsibility area, 18
    in title proper, 235
    more than one, 74, 103, 112, 126, 201, 219,
      226, 290, 330
    none given, 58, 115
    not applicable, 9, 88
    which includes subordinate body, 290
    words indicating role included, 50, 52

Publishers' numbers, notes on *see under* Numbers

Publishers' signs (early printed monographs),
    50, 52

Punched cards (machine-readable data files), 8

Punctuation
    edition area, 206
    element ending with mark of omission, 23
    following question mark, 76
    material (or type of publication) specific
      details area, 15, 194, 195
    note area, 94
    physical description area, 1, 13, 196
    publication, distribution, etc. area, 1, 11,
      155, 194, 195
    series area, 138, 168, 319
    title and statement of responsibility area,
      1, 12, 31, 42, 79, 84, 135, 146, 158,
      225, 280
      alternative titles, 209
      items lacking collective title, 31, 66
    see also Omission, Marks of; Parentheses;
    Question marks; Square brackets; and
    specific materials, e.g. Serials

Puzzles, 248, 372

Qualifications

Qualifications *(continued)*

    added to publisher's numbers, 187
    added to standard numbers, 22, 163

Qualifications, academic, etc. *see* Academic
    degrees, honours, etc.

Question marks
    full stop retained after, 76
    use of, 367

Queens, 13

Quotations, books of, 286

Quotations, notes which are *see under* Notes

Radio and television programmes
    related works, 81

Radiographs, 242

Rank, titles of *see* Titles of honour, nobility,
    address, etc.

Realia, 9, 289, 316, 349

Recordings, sound *see* Sound recordings

Records, logical (machine-readable data files)
    number of, 260

Records of a corporate body
    collections, 320

Reduction ratio (microforms), 10, 94, 140, 381

Reels
    film, 6, 256, 292, 358
    microfilm, 239, 381
    sound tape, 240

References
    (Only examples which include a particular
    note about references or which relate to the
    illustrative references included in Appendix 2
    (marked *) are indexed)
    explanatory references
      corporate bodies
        acronyms, 123
        changes of name, 82, 139, 288, 317

References: explanatory references *(continued)*

    personal names, 174
      prefixed, 262
      pseudonyms
        joint pseudonyms, 253
  in lieu of added entries, p.181
  name-title references
    initials, 98
    titles of parts of a work catalogued
      separately, 168
    uniform titles, 51, 90
    works of a person entered under two
      different headings, 19
  see references
    corporate bodies
      different forms of heading, 177, 188,
        191, 337, 338, 345
      different forms of name, 35, 65, 97,
        108, 142, 178, 216, 217, 282, 326
      initials, 36, 217
      different names, 333, 382
    personal names
      different entry elements, 52, 283
        compound names
          hyphenated names, 330
          prefixes, 93
      different forms of name, 132, 244
        language, 74
      different names
        change of name, 200, 340
        phrases, 52, 254, 273
        pseudonyms, 104, 224, 275
        real name to better known form, 40,
          187, 209
        titles of nobility, 42, 62, 212
    titles, p.177
    uniform titles, 25, 46, 145
  see also references
    corporate bodies
      related bodies, 166
    personal names
      works of one person entered under two
        different headings, 275

Regiments, 336

Reissues, 232, 286

Related works
  added entries *see under* Added entries
  described dependently
    multilevel description, 116

Related works *(continued)*

  described independently, 81, 170, 189,
    224, 227
  special issue of serial, 80
  see also Adaptations; Radio and television
  programmes; Revisions; Translations; etc.

Relationship, words indicating, following surnames, 181

Relief models, 54

Religious bodies, 17, 69
  see also Catholic Church; Churches;
  Religious officials

Religious officials, 264, 377

Religious vocation, persons of
  additions to names, 274

Reporters (court cases), 58

Reports
  of court proceedings, 58
  of interviews and exchanges, 40
  recording collective thought of corporate
    body, 18, 69, 177, 188, 191, 233, 270,
    288, 337

Representative fraction (scale, cartographic
  materials), 2

Reprints, 131, 232, 286
  see also Facsimiles; Microreproductions

Reproduction methods
  art reproductions, 329

Reproductions, 309, 316, 370
  in different material, 316
  notes on original, 309, 370
  see also Art reproductions; Facsimiles;
  Microreproductions

Responsibility, statement of *see* Statement of
  responsibility

Restricted access *see* Access, restrictions on

Restrictions on showing of film, notes on, 257

Revisions
   entry under original author, 206, 226
   entry under reviser, 20

Roman Catholic Church *see* Catholic Church

Roman names, 50, 243, 244

Roman numerals
   added to names of rulers, 237
   Arabic substituted for, 11, 50

Romanisation, 149, 324

Romans of classical times, 244

Royalty, 13, 162, 237

Rulers, 13, 162, 237

Running time *see* Duration

Russian, items printed in, 324

S.I., use of, 304

Sacred scriptures
   uniform titles, 44, 45, 46, 145, 182, 250

Saints, 173

Sand paintings, 176

Scale (cartographic materials) *see under*
   Cartographic materials

Scale (technical drawings), 88

Schools, 139

Scope of item, notes on *see* Nature, scope
   or artistic form of item, notes on

Scores (music), 4, 75, 100, 109, 144, 265

Scottish ordinary lords of session, 212

Scriptures *see* Sacred scriptures

Sculpture, 357

Secondary entries *see* Added entries

"See" and "See also" references *see under*
   References

Selections, 281
   uniform titles
      Bible, 44
      music, 37, 38, 130, 144
      printed monographs, 102, 146, 286
      see also Extracts; Parts of works

Self-teaching books, 156, 199

Seminars *see* Conferences

Serials, 11, 15, 16, 23, 28, 41, 55, 59, 101, 103,
   155, 166, 194, 195, 198, 210, 216, 222, 241,
   347
   analytical added entries, 28
   annuals, 23, 41, 198
   availability, terms of, notes on, 28, 55
   change of designation system, 241
   change of frequency, notes on, 241
   change of issuing body, notes on, 23
   change of publisher, notes on, 241
   change of size, 23, 222, 241
   change of title proper
      notes on, 23, 222
      separate main entry, 101, 194, 210
   completed serials, 11, 41, 101, 195, 210
   continuations, 23, 41, 59, 101, 166, 194,
      195, 210
   current serials, 15, 16, 23, 28, 55, 59, 103,
      155, 194, 198, 216, 222, 241, 347
   entry under corporate body, 55, 216,
      222, 347
   entry under personal author, 198
   entry under title, 11, 15, 16, 23, 28, 41,
      59, 101, 103, 155, 166, 210, 241
   extracts from, 36, 227
   first issue not available, 15
   frequency
      change of, notes on, 241
      given in title proper, 16
      notes on, 11, 155
   key-titles, 55
   library's holdings, notes on, 155
   non-printed, 16
   official communications from heads of state,
      347
   parallel titles, 216
   presence within a serial of another serial,
      notes on, 222
   relationships with other serials, notes on,

Serials: relationships with other serials, notes on *(continued)*

23, 41, 101, 194, 195
some issues part of a series, notes on, 23
sound recordings, 16
sources of information, 11, 15, 241
special issues, 80
specific material designation, 11, 16, 155, 194, 195
standard numbers, 155
supplements to, notes on, 23, 166
with a personal author, 198

Series
added entries *see under* Added entries
beginning with name of responsible body, 123, 126
common authorship of series and part of series, 168, 285
enclosed in parentheses, 29, 319, 322
from source other than item being catalogued, 94, 322
given in two forms, 378, 382
including separate letters or initials, 123, 126
more than one series, 78, 164, 177, 188, 244, 319, 328
number of item within series
date given as numbering, 78, 330
recorded in terms given in item and preceded by semi-colon, 18, 29, 168, 244, 328, 330
other title information, 196, 212, 319
parallel titles, 215
sources of information, 322
statements of responsibility, 123, 138, 177
subseries, 94, 150, 152, 236, 319
transcription, 123, 126, 168
variant series title given in note, 178

Shared authorship *see* Shared responsibility, works of

Shared pseudonyms, 253

Shared responsibility, works of
between persons and corporate body, 314, 353
principal responsibility indicated, 79, 249, 320
principal responsibility not indicated
more than three responsible persons or bodies, 22, 29, 110, 262

Shared responsibility, works of: principal responsibility not indicated *(continued)*

two or three responsible persons or bodies, 68, 80, 123, 132, 141, 191, 305, 314, 319
shared pseudonyms, 253
see also Mixed responsibility, works of

Sheets, 97, 146, 148, 157, 193, 313
containing panel designed to appear on outside when sheet is folded, 120, 367

Signatories (treaties), notes on, 328

Signatures (early printed monographs)
on copy being described, 50, 52

Silverware, 289

Sine loco, use of, 304

Singers *see* Performers

Sir added to personal names, 53, 70, 100, 280

Size *see* Dimensions; Gauge; Height; Width; and specific materials, e.g. Globes; Medals; Microscope slides; Realia; Three-dimensional artefacts; etc.

Sleeves (sound recordings), 276 (footnote)
as sources of information, 375

Slides
as accompanying material, 122, 163, 352
as part of multimedia item, 352

Slides, microscope, 107

Sobriquets *see* Given names, etc.; Words or phrases

Societies and Associations, 18, 22, 205, 250, 290, 365

Sonatas
uniform titles, 38

Songs
collections, 234

Soprano, abbreviation for, 130

Statement of responsibility *(continued)*

more than one, 178, 236
recorded in the order of their sequence in
the chief source of information, 48, 315
same person named twice, 141
not appearing prominently on item, 171
not in chief source of information, 5, 80, 84,
235, 285
notes on, 7, 23, 92, 101, 218, 241, 369
noun phrase occurring in conjunction with,
12, 45, 146
preceding title proper, 50
recorded in form in which it appears in item,
17, 22, 47, 79, 96, 224, 239, 249, 302, 377
related to a series, 123, 138, 177
related to an edition, 22, 104, 206, 226
single statement recorded as such, 79, 353
subsequent statements, 12, 42, 135, 280
transcription, 1, 5
use of . . . [et al.] , 22, 29, 290, 318

Statements (machine-readable data files), 8, 197

States, abbreviations for, 156, 179

Statutes *see* Laws, etc.

Stereographs, 213

Study prints, 72, 151, 164
definition, 72

Subordinate bodies
headings for
containing term implying administrative
subordination, 18, 33, 312
intervening element in hierarchy included,
99, 192
intervening element in hierarchy omitted,
69, 345
legislative bodies, 340, 341, 346
name of higher body not required for identification, 188, 233
name of higher body omitted from
subheading, 269, 352
name which has been, or is likely to be used
by another higher body for one of its
subordinate bodies, 29, 67
name which includes entire name of higher
body, 352, 355

Subsequent edition statements, 232

Subsequent statement of responsibility, 12, 42,
135, 280

Summaries, 327

Summary of content of item, in notes, 3, 205,
256, 353

Supplements
to serials, notes on, 23

Supplied titles, 3, 242

Surnames
entry under, 1
compound surnames, 181
hyphenated surnames, 330
with prefixes, 93, 105, 130, 131,
322, 356, 357
consisting only of surname, 283
element of name which functions as
surname, 293
married woman identified by husband's
surname, 200
middle name of married woman maiden
surname, 200
nature uncertain, 371
person without surname, 12, 161
see also Forenames; Given names, etc.; Initials;
Personal names; Pseudonyms; Titles of honour,
nobility, address, etc., Words or phrases

Symphonies, 207

Symposia *see* Conferences

Tape-slide presentations, 352

Tapes
sound cassettes, 302
as part of multimedia item, 352
sound tape reels, 240
see also Sound recordings

Teaching materials *see* Specific medium, e.g.;
Dioramas; Filmstrips; Flashcards; Flipcharts;
Folders; Games; Globes; Jackdaws; Lesson
cards; Overhead projector transparencies;
Picture cards; Portfolios; Study prints;
Wallcharts; Workbooks

Technical drawings, 88

Width *(continued)*

    printed monographs
      specified if greater than height, 150,
        232, 307
      specified if less than half the height,
        112, 113
    sheets, 146, 148
    tapes, 302
    transparencies, 382
    see also Dimensions, Gauge, Height; Size

Wills (manuscripts), 228

"With" notes, 52, 159, 203, 238, 320

Woodcuts (early printed monographs), 52

Words or phrases
    added to corporate bodies, 66
    added to personal names, 161, 173
      distinguishing identical names, 277
      names entered under surname, 283
    characteristics, etc., in entry under given name,
      161, 173
    denoting place of origin, etc. in entry under
      given name, 161
    entry under, 52, 124, 249, 254, 283
    indicating relationships, 181

Workbooks (teaching materials), 156

Works created after 1500 (uniform titles), 90,
    131, 184, 252

Works created before 1501 (uniform titles), 50,
    86, 244

Works in a single form (collective uniform
    titles), 280, 286

Workshops *see* Conferences

Writers
    added entries *see under* Added entries
    collaborations with artists, 72, 121, 125,
      129, 156, 246, 284, 326
    see also Personal authors; Personal names

Writing, date of (manuscripts), 3, 87

Writing, place of (manuscripts), 228

X-rays, 242

Year(s) *see* Date(s)

Yearbooks, 23, 41, 198

RULE INDEX

All references are to numbers in the main entry sequence of this volume.

Rules are indexed only when they are specifically mentioned in a particular example.

The rules from Part 1 of AACR 2 are arranged (except for Ch.13) according to the numbers of the rules in Ch.1 so that, for instance, 1.1B and its divisions precede 2.1B, 3.1B, 4.1B, 5.1B, etc. and their divisions which precede 1.1C and its divisions. Rules from chapters other than Ch.1 are indented. If, therefore, the user wishes to find an example illustrating rule 6.1F1, this will be found indexed in the indented sequence following the divisions of 1.1F. This pattern has been adopted because of the close relationship between the rules in Ch.1 and other chapters and because of the mnemonic structure of the rule numbering.

0.8	171, 282
0.28	5
1.0A1	285
2.0B1	1, 112
2.0B2	235, 322
3.0B2	2
4.0B1	3, 320
5.0B1	4
6.0B1	5, 302, 375
6.0B2	276, 285
7.0B1	6
8.0B1	7, 26
9.0B1	8
9.0B2	8
10.0B1	9, 49, 363
11.0B1	10
12.0B1	11, 241
1.0C	23, 76, 232, 367
1.0E	149, 324
1.0F	24
1.0H(4)	112, 157
3.0J	378
1.1A1	1, 12, 42, 280
1.1A2	80, 313
2.1A1	12, 135
1.1B1	1, 2, 3, 4, 5, 6, 7, 10, 22, 88, 146, 149, 153, 155, 168, 209, 220, 225, 227, 258, 324
1.1B2	120, 123, 235, 238
1.1B3	179
1.1B4	340
1.1B5	97
1.1B6	123, 126, 271
1.1B7	9, 242, 316
1.1B8	46
1.1B9	182, 364
2.1B1	1
2.1B2	235, 321, 331
3.1B1	2
4.1B1	3
4.1B2	3, 87, 228, 320
5.1B1	4
5.1B2	4, 57, 207
6.1B1	5
7.1B1	6
8.1B1	7, 88
8.1B2	242
11.1B1	10
12.1B1	11
1.1C3	316
1.1D1	105, 107, 208, 215
1.1D3	57
5.1D1	57, 105
12.1D1	216
1.1E1	12
1.1E2	61
1.1E3	170, 226, 232, 261
1.1E4	42
1.1E6	56, 158, 220
2.1E1	12
1.1F1	1, 5, 10, 22, 47, 54, 79, 80, 84, 88, 96, 141, 205, 224, 239, 249, 302, 363, 377
1.1F2	99, 171, 208, 231, 285
1.1F3	50, 262
1.1F4	17, 79
1.1F5	22, 29, 79, 290, 318
1.1F6	12, 48, 53, 178, 236, 280, 302, 315
1.1F7	1, 53, 232, 264, 283
1.1F8	221, 315, 373
1.1F9	149, 324
1.1F11	216
1.1F12	12, 45, 146
1.1F13	15, 42, 47, 161, 172, 226, 238, 280
1.1F15	44, 133, 328
2.1F1	1
2.1F3	373
6.1F1	5, 66, 70, 89, 159, 225, 249, 276, 302, 318
6.1F2	43
7.1F1	6, 239, 292, 353
8.1F1	88
10.1F1	107
10.1F2	107
11.1F1	10, 239
12.1F2	216
12.1F3	16, 241
1.1G1	66
1.1G2	31, 66, 84, 158, 160, 180, 199
6.1G1	43, 66, 159, 160, 180, 202

(1.1G2)

6.1G2	66, 160, 180
6.1G4	43, 159
1.2A1	206
1.2B1	22, 168, 192, 243, 306
1.2B4	52, 168
2.2B1	132
1.2C1	20, 22, 104, 206, 226
2.2D1	131, 232
3.3B1	2, 54, 120, 204, 350, 367
3.3B2	120, 378
12.3B1	11, 155, 194
3.3C1	359
12.3C1	11, 16, 28, 59, 155
12.3C3	216
12.3C4	11, 155, 194
1.3D2	215
3.3D1	359
12.3F	11, 41, 101, 195
12.3G	241
1.4A1	1
8.4A2	176, 360
1.4B2	363
1.4B5	215
1.4B6	309
1.4B8	74, 103, 330
4.4B1	228, 320
1.4C1	1, 2, 4, 6, 10, 24, 88, 383
1.4C3	114, 143, 156, 179, 296
1.4C5	20, 122, 162, 321, 356
1.4C6	34, 204, 249, 304
2.4C1	1
3.4C1	2
5.4C1	4
7.4C1	6
8.4C1	88
10.4C2	245
11.4C1	10
12.4C1	11
1.4D1	1, 2, 4, 10
1.4D2	25, 48, 54, 300, 321
1.4D3	103, 269, 298, 330
1.4D4	18, 378
1.4D5	68, 186, 226, 290
2.4D1	1, 25
3.4D1	2
5.4D1	4
6.4D3	285
7.4D1	292
10.4D2	245, 295
11.4D1	10
12.4D1	11

1.4E1	6, 89
6.4E1	89
7.4E1	6, 290
1.4F1	1, 2, 4, 10, 31, 88, 226
1.4F3	232
1.4F5	181
1.4F6	100, 146, 378
1.4F7	9, 38, 179, 204, 249
2.4F1	1
3.4F1	2
5.4F1	4
8.4F1	88
10.4F2	73, 220, 245, 289, 348
11.4F1	10
12.4F1	155, 194, 195
12.4F3	11, 41, 101, 195
1.4G1	9, 73, 289
10.4G1	9, 73, 179, 289
2.4G2	286
1.5A1	1, 13
1.5B1	2, 24
1.5B5	155, 219
2.5B2	1, 113, 139, 193, 226, 230, 295, 313
2.5B3	129, 221, 364
2.5B5	214, 254
2.5B6	189, 196
2.5B7	13, 71, 199, 307
2.5B8	214
2.5B9	35, 219
2.5B10	81, 175, 246, 272
2.5B11	99
2.5B13	199
2.5B15	112
2.5B17	58, 212, 219, 287
2.5B18	157, 196, 298
2.5B20	157, 219, 287
2.5B21	37, 58
2.5B23	149
3.5B1	2, 204
3.5B2	97
3.5B3	258
4.5B1	3, 230
4.5B2	87
5.5B1	4, 37, 100, 265
5.5B3	37, 38, 109
6.5B1	5
6.5B2	5, 159, 240, 318, 352
6.5B3	43, 159
7.5B1	6, 76
7.5B2	6, 257
8.5B1	7, 26, 88, 92, 115, 136, 154, 176, 190, 213, 349, 368

8.5B2	10, 211, 213
8.5B3	92
8.5B4	136, 151, 332
8.5B5	151
9.5B1	8, 197, 260, 304
9.5B2	8, 197, 260
9.5B4	304
10.5B1	9, 34, 49, 179, 186, 205, 208, 220, 245, 248, 348, 349, 357, 363
10.5B2	111, 205, 247, 255, 297, 372
11.5B1	10, 140, 192, 381
12.5B1	11, 16, 155, 194, 195
12.5B2	11, 101, 195
2.5C1	57
2.5C2	81, 170, 171, 226, 227
2.5C3	221
2.5C4	117, 257, 312
2.5C5	19, 125
2.5C6	13, 63, 150, 261
2.5C7	218
3.5C2	258
3.5C3	204
3.5C4	54
6.5C3	5, 302
6.5C6	240, 302, 352, 380
6.5C7	5
6.5C8	302
7.5C3	6, 76, 257
7.5C4	6, 76, 257
8.5C2	114
8.5C3	329
8.5C4	127, 211
8.5C6	92
8.5C9	26
8.5C10	115
8.5C13	213
8.5C16	136, 332, 382
8.5C17	7, 190
10.5C1	34, 49. 73, 107, 179, 220, 248, 348, 363
10.5C2	34, 73, 107, 179, 205, 248, 357
11.5C1	192, 239
1.5D1	1
2.5D1	1, 44, 150
2.5D2	112, 113, 150, 178, 232, 248, 307
2.5D3	196, 222, 241, 277, 298
2.5D4	148, 157, 193
2.5D5	134

3.5D1	2, 120, 367
3.5D4	238
4.5D1	3
4.5D2	87
5.5D1	4
6.5D2	5
6.5D5	302, 352, 380
6.5D6	240
7.5D2	6, 257, 358
8.5D1	26, 92, 115, 213, 382
8.5D2	211
8.5D4	136, 332
8.5D5	7, 122, 352
8.5D6	7, 88, 190
9.5D2	260, 304
10.5D1	9, 34, 49, 73, 179, 205, 208, 220, 245, 297, 308, 357, 363, 372
10.5D2	34, 111, 186, 202, 203, 247, 248, 297, 348, 357
11.5D3	10, 192
11.5D4	381
12.5D1	11, 222
1.5E1	49, 64, 110, 122, 134, 164, 260, 285, 304, 315, 325, 365
2.5E1	64, 110, 122, 298, 315
2.5E2	64, 110, 122
6.5E1	285
8.5E1	369
10.5E1	49
1.6A1	29, 131, 138, 150, 168
1.6A2	94, 322
1.6B1	123, 126, 168
1.6B2	378, 382
2.6B1	168, 328
12.6B1	41
1.6C1	215
1.6D1	196, 212, 319
1.6E1	138, 168, 177
1.6G1	29, 78, 244, 328, 330
1.6H1	94, 152, 236, 319
1.6J1	164, 177, 319, 328
1.7A1	94
1.7A3	13, 26, 49, 156, 183
1.7A4	307
1.7A5	289
1.7B1	92, 190, 246
1.7B2	46, 112, 243
1.7B3	9
1.7B4	23, 46, 276
1.7B5	226, 232, 240

1.7B6	23, 41, 92, 99, 171, 208, 285
1.7B7	94, 140, 149, 219, 227, 260, 285
1.7B9	22, 219, 236
1.7B10	23, 46, 90, 112, 156, 287
1.7B11	64, 134, 285
1.7B12	23
1.7B13	381
1.7B14	150
1.7B16	187, 303
1.7B17	3
1.7B18	79, 219, 229, 323
1.7B19	215
1.7B20	155
1.7B21	238
2.7B1	135, 246, 313
2.7B2	46, 78, 112, 157, 173, 244, 260
2.7B3	67, 112, 313
2.7B4	23, 112, 157, 218, 315, 328
2.7B5	254
2.7B6	23, 29, 41, 218, 231
2.7B7	36, 149, 157, 173, 219, 227
2.7B9	22, 219, 236, 290
2.7B10	21, 46, 90, 112, 129, 156, 214, 218, 246, 259, 287, 354
2.7B11	63, 64, 110, 122, 325
2.7B12	23
2.7B13	381
2.7B14	150
2.7B18	79, 175, 219, 235, 331
2.7B19	215
2.7B20	155
3.7B7	359
3.7B18	204, 367
3.7B21	238
4.7B1	3, 87, 228, 230
4.7B3	3, 87
4.7B10	87
4.7B11	87
4.7B14	3, 257
4.7B17	3
4.7B18	87
5.7B1	100, 105, 130, 361
5.7B2	57
5.7B7	75
5.7B10	144, 361
5.7B18	24
5.7B19	38, 57, 109, 207
6.7B3	375
6.7B4	276
6.7B6	66, 70, 89, 159, 240, 276, 285, 302, 319
6.7B7	285

(1.7B21)	
6.7B10	202, 203, 352
6.7B11	285
6.7B16	187
6.7B18	375
6.7B19	5
6.7B21	43, 159
7.7B6	285, 292
7.7B10	6
7.7B16	358
7.7B18	6
8.7B1	92, 176, 190, 329, 360
8.7B3	242
8.7B6	7, 92, 369
8.7B7	369
8.7B8	185, 370
8.7B10	88, 114, 134, 136, 176, 211, 332, 352, 354
8.7B17	353
8.7B18	229, 354
8.7B19	7, 369
9.7B1	260
9.7B2	260
9.7B7	260
9.7B10	8, 260
9.7B14	8
10.7B1	49, 208, 348
10.7B3	9, 245, 289
10.7B6	208
10.7B7	247
10.7B10	34, 111, 255, 297, 348, 372
10.7B17	205, 247
10.7B19	372
11.7B	10
11.7B10	10, 94, 140, 381
11.7B13	381
11.7B19	10
12.7B1	11, 16, 155, 241
12.7B4	23
12.7B6	16, 23, 41, 101, 241
12.7B7	23, 41, 59, 101, 166, 194, 195
12.7B9	222, 241
12.7B12	23
12.7B18	222
12.7B20	155
1.8B1	1, 155
1.8B2	163
2.8B1	1
12.8B1	155
12.8C1	55
1.8D1	28, 55, 92, 312
8.8D1	92

PART 2. HEADINGS, UNIFORM TITLES AND REFERENCES

Chapter 21. Choice of access points

Chapter 22.   Headings for persons

Chapter 23.   Geographic names

Chapter 24.   Headings for corporate bodies

Chapter 25.   Uniform titles

GENERAL MATERIAL DESIGNATIONS

An optional inclusion, following the title proper, is a 'general material designation'. This consists of a term chosen from a supplied list enclosed within square brackets. AACR 2 includes (rule 1.1C1) two lists of designations, one for the use of British agencies (List 1) and the other for the use of North American agencies (List 2).

List 1	List 2
cartographic material	map
	globe
	art original
	chart
	filmstrip
graphic	flash card
	picture
	slide
	technical drawing
	transparency
machine-readable data file	machine-readable data file
manuscript	manuscript
microform	microform
motion picture	motion picture
multimedia	kit
music	music
	diorama
	game
object	microscope slide
	model
	realia
sound recording	sound recording
text	text
videorecording	videorecording

As explained in the introduction to this work, general material designations, being optional, are excluded from the examples presented here.

However, the following selection of headings and title statements from this sampler, together with their appropriate general material designations, illustrate the way in which entries would appear if such designations were desired. 'UK' indicates British usage and 'NA' North American usage.

ABRAHAMS, Gerald
  Trade unions and the law [text]

ACCRINGTON town centre [cartographic material]   UK

ACCRINGTON town centre [map]   NA

ADAMS, Samuel
  [Letter] 1829 Dec.8, Londonderry
Gaol [manuscript]

ADLER, Samuel
  Canto VII, tuba solo [music]

AGEE, James
  James Agee [sound recording] :
a portrait

AIDS for teaching the mentally retarded
  [motion picture]

AIR bearings [graphic] : some
  applications   UK

AIR bearings [chart] : some
  applications   NA

ALANSON, Eric
  A printed catalogue from punched
cards [machine-readable data file]

[ALARM clock] [object]   UK

[ALARM clock] [realia]   NA

ALBECK, Chanoch
  Untersuchungen über die halakischen
Midraschim [microform]

The ALBUM [text]

ALL England quarterly law cassettes
    [sound recording]

FALLA, Manuel de
    El sombrero de tres picos [music] = Le
tricorne = The three cornered hat : ballet

ROSSINI, Gioacchino
    [Il barbiere di Siviglia. Vocal score.
English & Italian] [music]
    The barber of Seville

UNIVERSITY OF SOUTHAMPTON. Library
    MARC at Southampton [multimedia]
                                        UK

UNIVERSITY OF SOUTHAMPTON. Library
    MARC at Southampton [kit]   NA

MAIN ENTRY SEQUENCE

†   against a tracing indicates that examples of added entries are included in Appendix 1 (p.169).

*   against a tracing or an annotation indicates that a relevant reference is illustrated in Appendix 2 (p.177).

The opening examples 1-11, which are arranged in the order of Chapters 2-12 of AACR 2, are representative and illustrate entries for the various media dealt with in these chapters. For further examples illustrating similar or related materials, the alphabetical index should be consulted.

Trade Unions
&
The Law

by

GERALD ABRAHAMS, M.A.

Sometime Scholar of
Wadham College, Oxford:
Of Gray's Inn
and the Northern Circuit,
Barrister-at-law

The opening eleven examples illustrate basic layouts for a variety of media, arranged in the order of Chapters 2-12 of Part I of AACR 2.

This initial example, no. 1, gives a complete statement of every rule which has been involved in producing the entry. For further information, see p vii in the Introduction.

CASSELL · LONDON

ABRAHAMS, Gerald
　　Trade unions & the law / by Gerald Abrahams. — London : Cassell, 1968.
　　xix, 254 p. ; 22 cm.
　　ISBN 0-304-91599-8.

1.　Title

Description of books, i.e. printed monographs — Ch.1 and Ch.2. Title transcribed from chief source of information (i.e. the title page — 2.0B1) exactly as to order, wording and spelling, but not necessarily as to punctuation — 1.1B1 and 2.1B1. First word only of title capitalised — A.4A. Title statement followed by statement of responsibility — 1.1F1 and 2.1F1 and statement of responsibility preceded by diagonal slash — 1.1A1. Academic degrees omitted — 1.1F7. Publication area contains: place of publication — 1.4C1 and 2.4C1; name of publisher — 1.4D1 and 2.4D1; and date of publication which, as there is no edition statement, is the date of the first edition — 1.4F1 and 2.4F1. Publisher is preceded by a colon and date by a comma — 1.4A1. Pagination of each sequence recorded — 2.5B2. Dimensions given — 1.5D1; for books this is the height in centimetres to the next whole centimetre up — 2.5D1. Dimensions preceded by a semi-colon — 1.5A1. ISBN recorded — 1.8B1 and 2.8B1.

Entry under heading for personal author, i.e. the writer of the book — 21.1A1, 21.1A2 and 21.4A. Name by which person is commonly known chosen as basis for the heading — 22.1A. Entry element selected is that part of the name under which the person would normally be listed in authoritative alphabetic lists in his or her language or country — 22.4A. Name containing surname entered under surname — 22.5A. If the entry element is not the first element of the name-, it is transposed and the entry element is followed by a comma — 22.4B3.

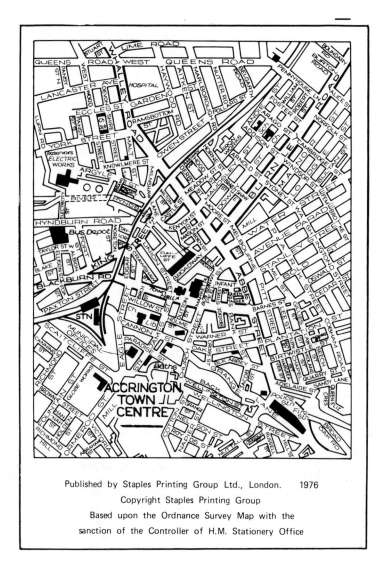

ACCRINGTON town centre. — Scale ca.
   1:10, 560. — London : Staples, 1976.
   1 map ; 17 x 14 cm.
   "Based upon the Ordnance Survey".

Description of cartographic materials (in this
case, a map) — Ch.1 and Ch.3. Title transcribed
as it appears in chief source of information — 1.1B1
and 3.1B1. (Chief source of information for a
cartographic material is the item itself — 3.0B2(a).)
Scale recorded as a representative fraction; if no
statement of scale is found on the item, its
container or accompanying material, it is computed (e.g. by comparison with map of known
scale) and preceded by 'ca.' — 3.3B1. Publication
details given — 1.4C1, 3.4C1, 1.4D1, 3.4D1,
1.4F1 and 3.4F1. Number of physical units and
an appropriate term from a supplied list given as
the specific material designation — 1.5B1 and
3.5B1. Dimensions of face of map (height and
width) given in centimetres to the next whole
centimetre up, measured between the 'neat lines',
i.e. the inner border of the map — 3.5D1.
Note on edition and history — 3.7B7.

Work of unknown authorship is entered under
title — 21.1C(1).

Sir,

    I have received your kind letter of the 26th ulto with the second and third parts of Mr Roscoe's work for which you have my best thanks. On a perusal I find them admirably adapted to the penitentiary system and have no doubt if properly induced to practice would be found much better adapted to the Reform of Criminals than any system yet tried, but in my opinion everything depends on a fair trial - it appears from the American and Milbank Penitentiarys that so long as they were properly conducted they were more than able to support themselves as well as reforming the Convicts, and I am satisfied that if such institutions (even on a smaller scale) were established either in large Towns or County Gaols remote from manufacturing districts they would be found to pay the County that would take the trouble of trying them and I conceive it one of the greatest misfortunes in Society that such is not the case. A great deal has been done of late years both in England and Ireland and Scotland but much has been done in error particularly in Ireland and I freely admit my conviction of the very bad tendency of both Tread Wheel and other species of what is called hard labour, and Solitary Confinement, the Tread Wheel I would utterly abolish as it is neither fit to correct body or mind and very little Hard Labour and Solitary Confinement would be quite enough in a Penitentiary. Solitary Confinement is a Brutal punishment a few days or weeks is enough for any human being, if a man must be kept alone give him exercise with the use of a yard it is necessary he should have both if you do not wish to immolate him. No penitentiary system yet tried has been found to answer the end sought for and I am satisfied that the buildings have as much tended to the obstruction of this end as the system pursued has. I enclose you with this a hasty ground sketch of the plan of a Prison I some time since struck out. It will be found simple easy wrought giving every man a sleeping cell to himself, with a yard to every man sentenced to Solitary Confinement with perfect classification which is the first consideration. Should you find it convenient any further communication will be most grateful to me.

               I am Sir
               your faithful & obedt servt

                   Sam: Adams

J McCreery Esq.
Liverpool

ADAMS, Samuel
   [Letter] 1829 December 8, Londonderry Gaol [to] J. McCreery, Liverpool / Sam: Adams.
   [1] leaf ; 25 cm.
   Holograph (transcript, typewritten), original ([3] p. on 2 leaves) in Liverpool City Libraries, available to researchers under library restrictions.
   Title supplied by cataloguer.
   Summary: Reaction to William Roscoe's Observations on penal jurisprudence, the second and third parts of which Adams had just received.

Description of manuscripts — Ch.1 and Ch.4. The chief source of information for a manuscript is the manuscript itself — 4.0B1. If a manuscript lacks a title or lacks some of the prescribed title data, this is supplied and enclosed in square brackets — 4.1B2. (The title for a single letter is 'Letter' and this is followed by the date of writing (expressed as year, month, day), the place of writing, the name of the addressee and the place to which addressed). The number of pages or leaves is recorded, whether numbered in the item or not — 4.5B1. (Optionally, the number of leaves may be added if this is different to the number of pages, as shown in the note relating to the original). Height given in centimetres to next whole centimetre up — 4.5D1. A manuscript handwritten by the author is recorded in note as 'Holograph' and, if the item being described is a copy, appropriate terms are added to indicate this — 4.7B1. Location of original recorded — 4.7B1 (see also 8.7B8). Source of title, if other than the chief source of information, is given in a note — 4.7B3. Note on access (in this case combined with the location of original note) — 4.7B14.

Entry under heading for personal author, i.e. the writer of the letter — 21.1A1 and 21.1A2. No added entry under addressee, as it is a single letter: an added entry would be made for a collection of letters — 21.30F. No added entry for a title that has been composed by the cataloguer — 21.30J(2).

4

SAMUEL ADLER

CANTO VII

Tuba Solo

$2.00

BOOSEY & HAWKES
New York

ADLER, Samuel
   Canto VII, tuba solo / Samuel Adler. —
New York : Boosey & Hawkes, c1974.
   11 p. of music ; 30 cm.

1.   Title

Description of music — Ch.1 and Ch.5. 'Tuba solo'
included as part of title proper (and so preceded by
comma) rather than as other title information
(preceded by colon), because title appears to
consist of generic term — 5.1B2. (See also example
no.207). Place of publication (1.4C1 and 5.4C1),
name of publisher (1.4D1 and 5.4D1) and date of
publication (1.4F1 and 5.4F1) recorded. Date
of publication rarely appears on music publications,
but there is usually a copyright date. If this is
found only on the first page of music, rather than
the title page (which, in most cases, is the chief
source of information for music — 5.0B1) it is not
enclosed in square brackets. Extent of item
recorded — 5.5B1. If none of terms listed as
specific material designations is appropriate, the
pagination is given, followed by 'of music'. The
term 'score' is not applicable, as the definition
(see Appendix D) implies that two or more parts
are aligned. Height in centimetres given to next
whole centimetre up — 5.5D1.

Entry under heading for personal author, i.e.
composer — 21.1A1 and 21.1A2.

for Harvey Phillips
CANTO VII
for Tuba Solo

I   SAMUEL ADLER

Quite fast ♩ : 120

CAEDMON

JAMES AGEE: A PORTRAIT

James Agee reading

TC 2042 A

Side 1
13:02

1. James Agee, Theme with Variations
2. James Agee, *White Mane*
3. A. E. Housman, Mercenary Soldiers
4. Shakespeare, from *King Lear*
5. The Lord's Prayer

LONGPLAYING · 33⅓ RPM · MICROGROOVE

WARNING: It is expressly forbidden to copy or reproduce this recording or any portion thereof in any manner or form; whether for profit, amateur, institutional, or educational use. Permission for broadcast, telecast or public performance use must be obtained in advance in writing. Caedmon Records, Inc. 505 Eighth Avenue, New York, N.Y. 10018.

MADE IN U.S.A.

CAEDMON
A 2 RECORD ALBUM TC 2042

JAMES AGEE: A PORTRAIT

James Agee reads from his work
Father Flye reads from Agee's work and reminisces about the author

CAEDMON TC 2042   JAMES AGEE: A PORTRAIT

SIDE 1	TIMING
James Agee reading	
1. James Agee, Theme with Variations	4:14
2. James Agee, White Mane (Agee's English translation of the French film, *Crin Blanc*)	6:58
3. A. E. Housman, Mercenary Soldiers	:27
4. Shakespeare, from *King Lear*	:26
5. The Lord's Prayer	:32

SIDE 2	TIMING
James Agee reading	
1. Letter to a friend (dictated)	17:58

SIDE 3	TIMING
Father Flye reading from James Agee's works	
1. *A Death in the Family*	
p. 11 ff. "We are talking now of summer evenings . . ."	
p. 13 ff. "Now is the night one blue dew . . ."	5:55
2. *The Morning Watch*	
p. 126 ff. "The ferment of the hogpen . . ."	7:40
3. *Let Us Now Praise Famous Men*	
p. 87 ff. "By now it is full glass light . . ."	
p. 91 "and the breakfasts ended . . ."	7:19
4. *Collected Short Prose*	
p. 125 ff. "Now as Awareness . . ."	5:21
Poems	
5. Delinquent	:54
6. A Lullaby	1:03
7. Rapid Transit	:41
8. Sonnet, "Now on the world and on my life as well"	1:01

SIDE 4	TIMING
Father Flye reminisces about his friendship with James Agee	
1. Early days at St. Andrews • travels • visits and correspondence	5:36
2. Agee's three marriages • Days on Fortune • Of the writing of Let Us Now Praise Famous Men, The Morning Watch and Death in the Family	11:42
3. Misfortunes and final hours	4:37
4. A summing up • Agee's insight, compassion and unfailing humor	5:00

CAEDMON TC 2042   JAMES AGEE: A PORTRAIT

5

AGEE, James
    James Agee : a portrait / James Agee
reading [from his work ; Father Flye reads
from Agee's work and reminisces about
the author]. — New York : Caedmon, 1971.
    2 sound discs (ca. 90 min.) : 33⅓ rpm,
stereo. ; 12 in.
    Contents: Side 1. James Agee reading:
Theme with variations (4 min., 14 sec.).
White mane (7 min.). A.E. Housman,
Mercenary soldiers (27 sec.). Shakespeare,
from King Lear (26 sec.). The Lord's
prayer (32 sec.) — Side 2. James Agee
reading: Letter to a friend (dictated)
(18 min.) — Side 3. Father Flye reading
from Agee's work: A death in the family
(6 min.). The morning watch (8 min.).
Let us now praise famous men (8 min.).
Collected short prose (6 min.). Poems
(3 min., 39 sec.) — Side 4. Father Flye
reminisces about his friendship with James
Agee: Early days at St. Andrews (6 min.).
Agee's three marriages (12 min.). Mis-
fortunes and final hours (4 min., 37 sec.).
A summing up (5 min.).
    Caedmon: TC 2042.

1.   Flye, James Harold†
2.   Optionally, author and title
    analytical entries for any particular
    part

Description of sound recordings (in this case a
sound disc) — Ch.1 and Ch.6. Title transcribed
as it appears in the chief source of information
(i.e. the label — 6.0B1) — 1.1B1 and 6.1B1.
Statements of responsibility are recorded in the
form in which they appear on the item — 1.1F1.
That part of the statement that is not taken from
the prescribed chief source of information is
enclosed within square brackets — 1.1F1. The
participation of Flye goes beyond that of mere
performance and his name can therefore be
recorded in the statement of responsibility area —
6.1F1. The number of physical units and an
appropriate term from a supplied list given as the
specific material designation — 6.5B1. Approximate duration in minutes added if this can
readily be ascertained — 6.5B2. Other physical
details required are: speed in rpm — 6.5C3;
number of sound channels — 6.5C7; and diameter
of disc — 6.5D2. (The examples in the relevant
rules give the diameter in inches but rule 0.28
permits it to be recorded in metric if metric
measurement is considered the normal measurement). Contents note — 1.7B18 and 6.7B18.
Duration of individual pieces given — 6.7B18.
Note of publisher's alphabetic and/or numeric
symbol preceded by label name — 6.7B19.

Work by a single personal author, i.e. that person
responsible for the creation of the intellectual
or artistic content, entered under heading for
that person — 21.1A1, 21.1A2 and 21.4A. Also
applicable is rule for sound recording of works
by the same person — 21.23B. Added entry
under Flye as collaborator — 21.30B. Omission
of "Father" from heading — 22.15C. No added
title entry as title proper is essentially the same
as the main entry heading — 21.30J(1).

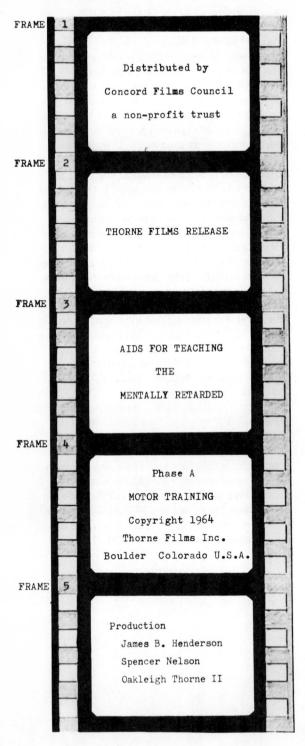

FRAME 1

Distributed by
Concord Films Council
a non-profit trust

FRAME 2

THORNE FILMS RELEASE

FRAME 3

AIDS FOR TEACHING
THE
MENTALLY RETARDED

FRAME 4

Phase A
MOTOR TRAINING
Copyright 1964
Thorne Films Inc.
Boulder Colorado U.S.A.

FRAME 5

Production
James B. Henderson
Spencer Nelson
Oakleigh Thorne II

CONCORD
FILMS COUNCIL
Nacton, Ipswich, Ipswich 76012

AIDS FOR TEACHING
THE MENTALLY RETARDED
PHASE A : MOTOR TRAINING

Please do NOT rewind
Please return films
promptly

6

AIDS for teaching the mentally retarded /
    production, James B. Henderson,
Spencer Nelson, Oakleigh Thorne II. —
Boulder, Colo. : Thorne Films ; Ipswich :
Concord Films [distributor], c1964.
    5 film reels (ca. 40 min.) : sd., col. ;
16 mm.
    One phase per reel.
    Contents: Phase A. Motor training —
Phase B. Initial perceptual training — Phase
C. Advanced perceptual training — Phase D.
Integrated motor perceptual training —
Phase E. Sheltered workshop.

1.   Henderson, James B.
2.   Nelson, Spencer
3.   Thorne, Oakleigh
4.   Optionally, analytical title entries
      for each part

Description of motion pictures — Ch.1 and Ch.7.
Title transcribed as it appears in chief source of
information — 1.1B1 and 7.1B1. (Chief source
of information for a motion picture is the film
itself — 7.0B1). Names of persons credited in
the chief source of information with the
production of a film are given in the statement
of responsibility area — 7.1F1. Places of
publication and distribution recorded in the form
in which they appear — 1.4C1 and 7.4C1.

7

Statement of function of distributor included optionally — 1.4E1 and 7.4E1. Number of physical units and an appropriate term from a supplied list given as the specific material designation — 7.5B1. Duration in minutes added (if no indication appears on the item, an approximation is made) — 7.5B2. Other physical details required are : sound characteristics (i.e. 'sd' or 'si') — 7.5C3 ; colour — 7.5C4 ; and gauge (i.e. width) of the film in millimetres — 7.5D2. Speed in frames per second is only given if this information is considered important — 7.5C5. Other physical details given in a note — 7.7B10(j). Individual works contained in motion picture listed in contents note — 7.7B18.

By definition (see Appendix D), the producers, although named in the statement of responsibility area, are not responsible for the intellectual or artistic content. This item is therefore treated as a work of which the personal authorship is unknown and cannot be determined, so entry is under title — 21.1C(1). Added entries would be made under the producers according to rule 21.30F, unless the cataloguing agency did not consider that they provided important access points.

See also example no. 292

AIR bearings : some applications. — Wakefield, Yorkshire : Educational Productions, c1973.
    1 wall chart : col. ; 51 x 76 cm.
    "Produced in collaboration with Frederick Mogul, Westwind Air Bearings Ltd."
    EP: C1180.

Description of wall charts as graphic materials — Ch.1 and Ch.8. Title transcribed as it appears in chief source of information (i.e. the item itself — 8.0B1) — 1.1B1 and 8.1B1. Number of physical units and an appropriate term from a supplied list given as the specific material designation — 8.5B1. Indication of colour given — 8.5C17. Dimensions (height x width) recorded — 8.5D6. Statement of responsibility not recorded in the statement of responsibility area given in a note — 8.7B6. Important number borne by the item given in a note — 8.7B19.

Work of unknown authorship entered under title — 21.1C(1) and 21.5A.

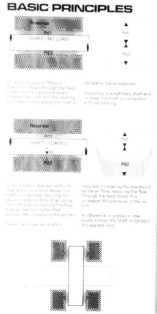

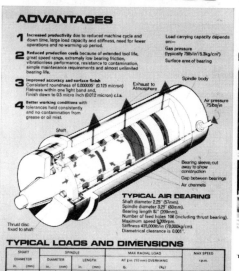

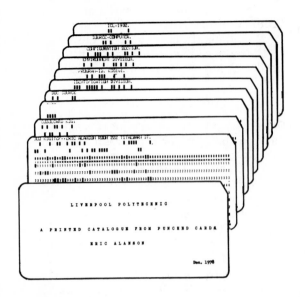

ALANSON, Eric
    A printed catalogue from punched
cards / Eric Alanson. — Liverpool :
Liverpool Polytechnic, 1978.
    1 program file (70 statements, COBOL).
    75 punched cards : 80 columns.
    Not generally available.

1.   Title

Description of machine readable data files — Ch.1
and Ch.9. Title and statement of responsibility
transcribed from chief source of information (i.e.
an adequate internal user label if there is one) and
from documentation — 9.0B1 and 9.0B2. Specific
material designation chosen from one of three
terms given in rule 9.5B1. For a program file,
number of statements and name of programming
language added in parentheses — 9.5B2. Note on
physical description of file if cataloguing agency
considers necessary — 9.7B10. Note on availability
— 9.5B2.

[ALARM clock]. — [197-] (Dumbarton :
    Columbia).
    1 clock ; 10 x 10 x 5 cm.
    Title supplied by cataloguer.

Description of three-dimensional artefacts and
realia — Ch.1 and Ch.10. Title devised for item
lacking one and enclosed in square brackets —
1.1B7. Exact date of publication, distribution,
etc. unknown, but decade known and enclosed in
square brackets — 1.4F7. Name of publisher not
applicable ; place and name of manufacturer
recorded — 1.4G1 and 10.4G1. None of listed
specific material designation terms is appropriate,
so specific name of item is given as concisely as
possible — 10.5B1. When multiple dimensions are
given, the order is height x width x depth — 10.5D1.
Source of title, if other than chief source of information, given in note — 1.7B3 and 10.7B3. (Chief
source of information is object itself together
with any accompanying material and container —
10.0B1).

Entry under title when personal authorship does
not apply and work does not emanate from
corporate body — 21.1C(1).

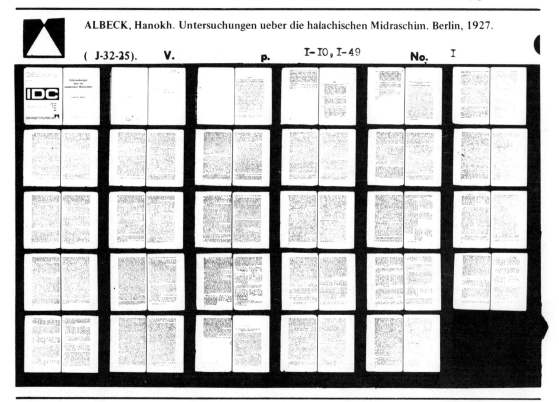

ALBECK, Hanokh. Untersuchungen ueber die halachischen Midraschim. Berlin, 1927.

(J-32-25).   V.   p.   I-IO, I-49   No.   I

ALBECK, Chanoch
    Untersuchungen über die halakischen
Midraschim / von Chanoch Albeck. — Zug,
Switzerland : Inter Documentation, 1976.
    3 microfiches (87 fr.) ; 11 x 15 cm.
J-32-25.
    Original published: Berlin : Akademie-
Verlag, 1927.

   1.   Title

Description of microforms (in this case a microfiche) — Ch.1 and Ch.11. Title recorded as it
appears in chief source of information — 1.1B1
and 11.1B1. (Chief source of information for
microfiche is title frame or frames; the eye-readable
data printed at the top of the fiche is used only if
the title frames provide insufficient information;
in this instance, therefore, the spelling on the title
frames has been followed — 11.0B1.) Statement
of responsibility recorded — 1.1F1 and 11.1F1.
Publication details of microfiche (not of original)
given in publication area — 1.4C1, 11.4C1, 1.4D1,

11.4D1, 1.4F1 and 11.4F1. Number of physical
units and an appropriate term from a supplied list
given as the specific material designation; number
of frames added in parentheses if this can be easily
ascertained — 11.5B1. In the example given for
this rule, the word 'frames' is spelled out in full.
However, the abbreviated form is used for filmstrips (see 8.5B2) and on p. 51 of AACR 2, this
form is also used for microfiches in example,
'Pre-Raphaelite drawings'. Appendix B gives 'fr'
as a prescribed abbreviation. Dimensions (height
x width) given in centimetres to the next whole
centimetre up — 11.5D3. No note on reduction
ratio, because it is within the standard 16x - 30x
range — 11.7B10. Important number borne by
item (other than ISBN or ISSN) given in note —
11.7B19. Description of original reproduced in
microform is given in notes following those relating
to microform — 11.7B.

Main entry under heading for personal author, i.e.
writer of original work — 21.1A1 and 21.1A2.

THE

A L B U M.

VOL. I.

APRIL—JULY

LONDON:

PRINTED FOR J. ANDREWS,

NEW BOND STREET.

————

MDCCCXXII.

C O N T E N T S

OF

T H E   A L B U M ,

No. I.,

APRIL, 1822.

————

ORIGINAL PAPERS.

The ALBUM. — Vol. 1, no. 1 (Apr. 1822)-
    v. 4, no. 8 (Apr. 1825). — London :
J. Andrews, 1822-1825.
    4 v. ; 21 cm.
    Two issues yearly.

Description of serials — Ch.1, Ch.12 and, for a printed serial, Ch.2. Title transcribed as it appears in chief source of information — 12.1B1. (Chief source of information for a printed serial is the title page of the first issue — 12.0B1). If the first word of the title of a work entered under its title proper is an article, the next word also is capitalised — A.4D. Numeric designation of first issue recorded — 12.3B1. Arabic numerals substituted for Roman in issue statement — C.1C. Chronological designation recorded, using standard abbreviations (B.15), and enclosed in brackets — 12.3C1 and 12.3C4. Source of information for numeric and chronological designation is title page, other preliminaries and colophon (in this instance, title page and contents page have been used) — 12.0B1.

For completed serial, designation of first issue is followed by that of last — 12.3F. (Note that, in this instance, both volumes and issues are numbered sequentially and the issues do not, as is more usual, form separate sequences within each volume.) Publication area includes: place of publication — 12.4C1; name of publisher — 12.4D1, and, for completed serial, date of publication of first and last issue, separated by hyphen — 12.4F3. Specific material designation for printed serial is 'v' — 12.5B1. Number of parts of completed serial given before specific material designation in Arabic numerals — 12.5B2. Dimensions of serial recorded — 12.5D1. Frequency recorded in note — 12.7B1.

Entry under title because personal authorship is diffuse — 21.1C(1).

This example illustrates the description of a completed serial; for the basic description of an incomplete serial see example no. 155.

ALCUIN 12
Son well-beloved : six poems / by
Alcuin ; translated by the Benedictines of
Stanbrook. — Worcester : Stanbrook Abbey
Press, 1967.
viii, 10 p. ; 21 cm.
Limited ed. of 260 copies.

1. Title

Noun phrase occurring in conjunction with statement of responsibility treated as other title
information if it is indicative of the nature of the
work — 1.1F12. (See also example no. 45). Other
title information preceded by colon — 1.1A1,
2.1A1, 1.1E1 and 2.1E1. Subsequent statement
of responsibility preceded by semi-colon — 1.1A1
and 1.1F6.

Entry for name that does not include surname —
22.8A. A case could be made for making an added
entry under the translators since the translation is
in verse — 21.30K1(a). However, it seems unlikely
that users would expect an entry under this heading,
and so it has been omitted in accordance with
general rule for added entries — 21.29B.

ALEXANDRA, Queen, consort of Edward 13
VII, King of the United Kingdom
Queen Alexandra's Christmas gift
book : photographs from my camera. —
London : Daily Telegraph, 1908.
[33] leaves : all ill. ; 30 cm.
"To be sold for charity".

1. Title

Unnumbered leaves — total ascertained and given
in square brackets — 2.5B7. Work consisting
wholly of illustrations — 2.5C6. Other physical
details, in this case a statement of the illustration
content, preceded by colon — 1.5A1. Note which
is quotation from item given in quotation marks.
Source of quotation is not included, as it is the
chief source of information, i.e. the title page —
1.7A3.

Entry under heading for person responsible for
the artistic content of the work — 21.1A1 and
21.4A. Royalty — entry under given name —
22.8A. Additions to name — 22.17A4.

ALICE through the looking glass . . . / 14
adapted from the story by Lewis
Carroll. — London : L. Miller, [19–].
20 p. : col. ill. ; 25 cm. — (A jolly
miller production).
"Alice meets Dum and Dee".

1. Carroll, Lewis   2. Series

Adaptation by unknown adapter entered under
title — 21.10. Uniform title could be made under
title proper of original edition (i.e. 'Through the
looking glass') if it were considered that 'Alice
through the looking glass' was not the best-known
title — 25.3A and 25.3B. Added entry is for
person whose works have appeared under a real
name (Charles Lutwidge Dodgson) and a pseudonym. Entry is under name by which person
has become predominantly identified in
reference sources — 22.2C2.

ALL-AMERICAN SOAP BOX DERBY 15
Top side : official newsletter of the
All-American Soap Box Derby. — Vol. 1,
no. 1 [(1974?)] -   . — Akron, Ohio :
A-ASPD, [1974?]-   .
v. : ill., ports. ; 28 cm.
Monthly.

1. Title

Description of printed serials — Ch.1, Ch.2 and
Ch.12. No statement of responsibility given, as
such a statement appears in other title information — 1.1F13. First issue not available to
cataloguing agency; chief source of information
becomes first issue that is available (i.e. Vol. 2,
no. 4). Item does not appear to be listed in guides
to periodicals; chronological designation is therefore estimated and followed by a question mark,
although there is no authority in the rules for this.
Month of issue does not appear on item, so year
only is given as chronological designation.

Work emanating from corporate body which is of
an administrative nature dealing with the procedures and operations of the body itself entered
under the heading for the body — 21.1B2(a).
Entry directly under name — 24.1.

16

ALL England quarterly law cassettes. —
   Oct. 1976-   . — London : Butterworth,
1976-   .
            sound cassettes : 1⁷/₈ ips, mono.
   "Edited and presented by Nigel Pascoe,
barrister".

Description of serials issued in the form of sound
recordings — Ch.1, Ch.6 and Ch.12. When chronological designation appears on first issue without
any accompanying numerical designation, date is
not enclosed in parentheses — 12.3C1. Relevant
specific material designation recorded, preceded by
three spaces — 12.5B1. Frequency is apparent
from the title and is not therefore recorded in a
note — 12.7B1. Statement relating to personal
editor of serial is not recorded in statement of
responsibility area, but is given in a note if it is
considered important — 12.1F3 and 12.7B6.

17

ALVES, Colin
   Religion and the secondary school : a
report / undertaken on behalf of the
Education Department of the British
Council of Churches by Colin Alves. —
London : S.C.M. Press, 1968.
   223 p. : ill., forms ; 23 cm.
   Bibliography: p. 220-223.

1.   Title
2.   British Council of Churches.
     Education Department†

Single statement of responsibility recorded as such
whether the two or more persons or bodies named
in it perform the same function or not — 1.1F4.

Foreword states that Alves is the author and that
this is not an official report of the British Council
of Churches; therefore treated as if no corporate
body were involved, i.e. single personal authorship
— 21.1A1, 21.1A2 and 21.4A. However, the
added entry is needed for the Council as a
prominently-named corporate body — 21.30E.

18

AMERICAN LIBRARY ASSOCIATION.
   Committee on Post-War Planning
   Post war standards for public libraries /
prepared by the Committee on Post-War
Planning of the American Library Association ; Carleton Bruns Joeckel, Chairman. —
Chicago : ALA., 1943.
   92 p. ; 23 cm. — (Planning for libraries ;
no. 1).

1.   Title   2.   Joeckel, Carleton
                     Bruns†
3.   Series

If name of publisher appears in recognisable form
in title or statement of responsibility area, it is
given in shortened form in publication area —
1.4D4.

Work emanating from corporate body and recording
its collective thought (in this case, the report of
a committee) is entered under heading for body —
21.1B2(c). Body is entered as a subheading of
the name of the body to which it is subordinate
because its name contains a word normally
implying administrative subordination (i.e.
Committee) — 24.13 (Type 2).

19

AMIS, Kingsley
   Colonel Sun : a James Bond adventure /
by Robert Markham. — London : Cape,
1968.
   255 p. : 2 maps ; 20 cm.
   Maps on lining papers.
   ISBN 0-330-02304-7.

1.   Title

Note of illustrations which appear on lining
papers — 2.5C5.

Pseudonyms — if person is known by more than
one name, the name by which he or she is most
commonly known and has come to be identified
predominantly in later editions of his or her works
is chosen — 22.2A and 22.2C2.* This can produce
somewhat unsatisfactory entries when, as in this
instance, the writer is using a pseudonym for a

particular genre and apparently does not wish such works to be collocated under the same heading as that for his or her other works.

20

ANDERSON, James
Shop theory. — 5th ed. / James Anderson, Earl E. Tatro. — New York ; London : McGraw Hill, 1968.
522 p. : ill. ; 24 cm.
Previous ed.: Henry Ford Trade School, Shop Theory Dept. New York : McGraw Hill, 1955.

1. Title   2.   Tatro, Earl E.
3. Henry Ford Trade School.
    Shop Theory Department.
    Shop Theory

Authors are responsible for edition, not for original work. Their names are therefore transcribed after the edition statement — 1.2C1. When several places of publication are named on the item, the first is always recorded, and if this is not in the same country as the cataloguing agency, it is followed by the first of any subsequent places that are — 1.4C5.

If wording of chief source of information indicates that body responsible for original is no longer considered responsible for work, entry is under heading for appropriate reviser — 21.12B. Name-title added entry is made under heading for original.

21

ANDRIYEVICH, V.
The fox, the hare and the rooster : a Russian folk tale / designed by V. Andriyevich ; translated by Tom Botting. — Moscow : Malysh Publishing, [197-].
[16] p. : chiefly col. ill. ; 23 cm.
Cover title.
Opens vertically and each double page 'pops up' to form 3-dimensional scene.

1.   Title

No specific rules for 'pop-up' books, so work has been treated as ordinary printed monograph and necessary details have been given as note on physical description — 2.7B10.

22

ANGLO-AMERICAN cataloguing rules / prepared by the American Library Association . . . [et al.]. — 2nd ed. / edited by Michael Gorman & Paul W. Winkler. — London : Library Association, 1978.
xvii, 620 p. ; 25 cm.
Published simultaneously: Chicago : A.L.A. ; Ottawa : Canadian Library Association.
ISBN 0-85365-681-9 (cased).
ISBN 0-85365-691-6 (pbk.).

1.   American Library Association†
2.   Library Association
3.   Gorman, Michael
4.   Winkler, Paul W.

Title transcribed exactly as to wording, order and spelling but not as to capitalisation — 1.1B1. Statement of responsibility recorded in the form in which it appears in item — 1.1F1. All but the first of more than three corporate bodies performing the same function omitted; omission indicated by (. . .) and 'et al.' added in square brackets — 1.1F5. Edition statement transcribed as it appears in item but standard abbreviations (Appendix B) used and numerals in place of words — 1.2B1. Statement of responsibility related to a particular edition follows the edition statement — 1.2C1. (It could be argued that all of the statement of responsibility should appear here as the responsible corporate bodies have changed. However, the first such body remains the same.) Note on publication — 1.7B9 and 2.7B9. Qualifications added to standard numbers — 1.8E1.

Entry under title when responsibility is shared between more than three corporate bodies and principal responsibility is not attributed — 21.6C2. Added entry for the first corporate body named — 21.6C2 and 21.30B. Added entry under Library Association (in the U.K.) as corporate body providing an important access point — 21.30F. Added entries under editors — 21.30D.

23

ANNUAL statement of the trade of the
United Kingdom with Commonwealth
countries and foreign countries. — 1853-   . —
London : H.M.S.O., 1853-   .
        v. ; 29-34 cm.
     Annual.
     Title varies slightly: 1853-1870, Annual
statement of the trade and navigation . . .
     Originally issued by Board of Trade;
subsequently by H.M. Customs and Excise.
     Continues figures previously published
in: Tables of the revenue . . .
     Shipping figures subsequently published
in: Annual statement of the navigation and
shipping . . .
     Annual supplement to v. 2 (1940-1958)
superseded by: Protective duties . . .
     Supplements to v. 4 published every 3
years (1948-1960) and in 1962; continued
annually as v. 5 from 1963.
     1900-1919 issued in 2 v. each year, with
annual supplementary v. 1904-1913.
1920-1962 issued in 4 v. each year. 1963-
issued in 5 v. each year.
     1853-1920 published as Command
papers and also available bound up in
sessional set.

1.   United Kingdom. Board of Trade
2.   United Kingdom. Customs and
         Excise

Variation in title too slight to warrant new entry —
21.2A. Change recorded in note area — 21.2A,
1.7B4, 2.7B4 and 12.7B4. Note on statement of
responsibility — 1.7B6, 2.7B6 and 12.7B6. Notes
on relationship with other serials — 12.7B7. When
an element ends with the mark of omission and
the subsequent punctuation begins with a full
stop, the full stop is omitted — 1.0C. Note on
supplements — 12.7B7(k). Note on physical
description — 12.7B10. Note that some issues
are part of a series — 1.7B12, 2.7B12 and 12.7B12.

Work emanates from a corporate body but does
not fall within any of the categories listed in 21.1B2
and is therefore entered under title — 21.1C(3).
Added entries under the corporate bodies — 21.30E.

24

ANTHOLOGY of music : a collection of
complete musical examples illustrating
the history of music / edited by
K.G. Fellerer. — Köln : Arno Volk.

     Vol. 1: Four hundred years of European
ceyboard [sic] music / [edited with an
introduction] by Walter Georgii. — 1959.
     140 p. of music ; 31 cm.
     Partial contents: Praeludium in E-flat
major / Johann Sebastian Bach — Capriccio
in G minor / Georg Friedrich Händel —
Adagio in B minor, K.540 / Wolfgang
Amadeus Mozart — Small piece for piano,
op. 19, no. 2 / Arnold Schönberg.

1.   Fellerer, K.G.
2.   Four hundred years of European
         ceyboard [sic] music
3.   Georgii, Walter
4.   Optionally, author and title
         analytical entries for each part

Description of music — Ch.1 and Ch.5. Multilevel
description for identification of both part and
comprehensive whole — 13.6. Inaccuracy or
mis-spelled word transcribed as it appears, followed
by [sic] or [i.e. keyboard] — 1.0F. Place of
publication recorded in the form in which it
appears (i.e. 'Köln' not 'Cologne') — 1.4C1.
None of listed terms is appropriate as specific
material designation, so number of 'pages of music'
is recorded — 1.5B1. Partial contents listed —
5.7B18.

Work produced under editorial direction entered
directly under collective title — 21.7A and 21.7B.

25

[ARABIAN nights. Selections]
     Tales from the Arabian nights / illu-
strated by Brian Wildsmith. — 2nd ed. —
London : Oxford University Press, 1961.
     281 p. : col. ill. ; 22 cm. — (Oxford
illustrated classics).

1.   Wildsmith, Brian   2.   Series

Shorter form of publisher's name might be used in
accordance with 1.4D2, but name is given in full
in example at 2.4D1.

Uniform title for work appearing in various manifestations under different titles — 25.1. * Uniform title for selections — 25.9. Optionally, a uniform title used as a main entry heading may be recorded without the square brackets — 25.2A.

26

The ARCADE, Cleveland, Ohio. —
    Cleveland : W. Evans, [197-?].
    1 postcard : col. ; 9 x 14 cm.
    "The largest of its type in the world . . .
a street under an arched glass roof".

Description of postcards as graphic materials — Ch.1 and Ch.8. Specific material designation selected from list and preceded by number of parts — 8.5B1. Indication of colour — 8.5C9. Dimensions (height and width) recorded — 8.5D1. Note which is quotation from item given in quotation marks. Source of quotation is not included, as it is the chief source of information — 1.7A3. (Chief source of information for graphic material is the item itself — 8.0B1).

Work of unknown authorship entered under title — 21.1C(1) and 21.5A.

27

ARISTOTLE
    [Ethics. English]
    The Nicomachean ethics of Aristotle /
translated, with notes, original and selected ;
an analytical introduction ; and questions
for the use of students / by R.W. Browne. —
London : Bohn, 1850.
    lxxxi, 347 p. ; 18 cm. — (Bohn's
classical library).

    1.   Title   2.   The Nichomachean
                            ethics of Aristotle
    3.   Series

Entry under well-established English form of name — 22.3B3. Well-established English title as uniform title for work originally written in classical Greek — 25.4B. Name of language of item added to uniform title if different from that of original — 25.5D.

28

ARTS alive Merseyside. — No. 1 (Sept.
    1969)-   . — Liverpool : Merseyside
Arts Association, 1969-   .
        v. : ill. ; 30 cm.
    Monthly.
    Free.

    1.   Merseyside Arts Association†

Description of printed serials — Ch.1, Ch.2 and Ch.12. Month in chronological designation abbreviated — 12.3C1 and B.15. Optional note on terms of availability — 1.8D1 and 12.8D1.

An analytical entry for an article from this serial is illustrated in Appendix 1.

The Communication Research Centre
University College London

Aspects of TRANSLATION

STUDIES IN COMMUNICATION 2

A. D. Booth

Leonard Forster

D. J. Furley

R. Glémet

Joseph Needham

C. Rabin

L. W. Tancock

with a Preface by

A. H. Smith

London
1958 | SECKER AND WARBURG

ASPECTS of translation / A.D. Booth . . .
[et al.]. — London : Secker and
Warburg, 1958.
viii, 145 p. ; 22 cm. — (Studies in
communication ; 2).
At head of title: The Communications
Research Centre. University College London.

1. Booth, A.D.
2. University College London.
   Communication Research Centre
3. Series

Statement of responsibility refers to more than
three persons or bodies; therefore all but the first
of these are omitted. Omission is indicated by
three dots and 'et al' added in square brackets —
1.1F5. Series statement enclosed in parentheses —
1.6A1. Number of the item within a series
recorded in the terms given in the item — 1.6G1.
Name appearing in chief source of information
but not used in main entry and with indeterminate
responsibility for work given as 'At head of
title' note — 2.7B6.

Work emanates from a corporate body but it does
not fall within any of the categories listed in
21.1B2. Personal authorship is also involved but
as there are more than three responsible persons,
none of whom is indicated as being the principal
author, entry is under title — 21.6C2. Heading
for added entry under corporate body — 24.13(3).

AUSTEN, Jane
Northanger Abbey ; and, Persuasion / by
Jane Austen ; with an introduction by
Austin Dobson ; illustrated by Hugh Thom-
son. — London : Macmillan, 1933.
xvi, 444 p. : 49 ill. ; 18 cm.
Both works first published: 1818.

1. Title
2. Austen, Jane   3. Persuasion
   Persuasion

For item lacking collective title and consisting of
individually titled works by the same person,
titles are recorded in order in which they appear
in chief source of information (if no one part
predominates) and separated by a semi-colon —
1.1G2. (Lines 2 and 8 have been transposed on
p.27 of AACR 2.) Rule 1.4F1 instructs that when
there is no edition statement the date of the first
edition is to be given. This is interpreted as the
date of the first edition of the particular version.
The date of the original first edition is here given
in a note.

Rules instruct that item consisting of two works
and entered under personal or corporate heading
should be given uniform title — 25.7. However,
each of the examples given for this rule has a
collective title which does not reveal the
individual title. A uniform title which merely
duplicates the title proper would seem super-
fluous.

ATTERBURY, Jasmine
Heidi / J. Spyri ; adapted by Jasmine
Atterbury ; illustrated by Marianne Clouzot. —
London : Golden Pleasure Books, 1964.
60 p. : ill. (some col.) ; 23 cm.

1. Title   2. Spyri, Johanna

Adaptation under the heading for the adapter
as it has substantially changed the content of the
original work — 21.9 and 21.10. Added entry for
illustrator not considered necessary under provisions
of 21.30K2.

AUSTRALIA
[Treaties, etc. New Zealand, 1965
Aug. 31]
New Zealand — Australia Free Trade
Agreement : with exchange of letters. —
Wellington : Govt. Printer, 1965.
95 p. ; 25 cm. — (A.17).

1. Title   2. New Zealand

Capitalisation in title for treaties — A20.

Treaties entered under heading for appropriate
corporate body — 21.1B2(b). For treaties
between two national governments, entry is under

first in alphabetical order, with added entry for the other — 21.35A1. Uniform title for single treaties — 25.16B1.

recorded. Dimensions of container recorded — 10.5D2. Important physical details not recorded in physical description area are given in note — 10.7B10.

35

AVERY, Karen
    Puss in boots / [illustrated by Karen Avery]. — London : Chatto & Windus, 1975.
    1 v. : col. ill. ; 18 cm. — (A peepshow book).
    Cover title.
    Five apertured scenes which open up and tie together to form one display.
    ISBN 0-7011-2142-6.

    1.   Title   2.   Series

Peepshow books not mentioned specifically in AACR 2, but are here treated as printed monographs. Pagination inappropriate, so 'lv.' used, by analogy with 2.5B9, and further physical details given in a note.

33

AUSTRALIAN WATER RESOURCES
    COUNCIL. Advisory Panel on
    Desalination
    A survey of water desalination methods and their relevance to Australia / prepared by the Advisory Panel on Desalination, Australia Water Resources Council. — Canberra : Dept. of Natural Development, 1966.
    45 p. : ill., maps ; 27 cm. — (Hydrological series ; no.1).

    1.   Title   2.   Series

Work emanating from corporate body and recording its collective thought is entered under heading for body — 21.1B2(c). Subordinate body contains term (i.e. 'Panel') implying administrative subordination and so is entered as subheading of higher body — 24.13 (Type 2).

36

B.B.C.
    Talking points, third series : B.B.C. comments on questions that viewers and listeners ask. — London : B.B.C., 1969.
    18 p. ; 22 cm.
    Reprinted from Radio times.
    ISBN 0-563-07444-2.

    1.   Title   2.   Radio times†

Note on bibliographic history of work — 2.7B7.

Work of administrative nature emanating from corporate body and dealing with its internal policies is entered under heading for body — 21.1B2(a). When the name of a corporate body contains initials, full stops are omitted or included according to the predominant usage of the body — 24.1.*

34

An AUTHENTIC replica of the Liberty
    Bell. — [United States] : Historical Souvenir Co., 1975.
    1 bell : metal, bronze col. ; 7 cm. high in box, 7 x 6 x 6 cm.
    Brief history and other facts on box.

Description of three-dimensional artefacts — Ch.1 and Ch.10. If the first word of the title of a work entered under its title proper is an article, the next word is capitalised — A.4D. Exact place of distribution cannot readily be established, so name of country is given — 1.4C6. Abbreviation (i.e. U.S.) not used because it is not an addition to name — B14. None of specific material designation terms listed at 10.5B1 is appropriate, so specific name of item given as concisely as possible. Material (10.5C1), colour (10.5C2) and dimensions (10.5D1)

See also example no. 81.

37

BACH, Johann Sebastian
  [Chorale preludes. Selections ; arr.]
  Organ choral preludes / J.S. Bach ;
arranged for pianoforte by William
Murdoch. — London : Schott, 1928.
    4 v. of music (14, 17, 18, 19 p.) ; 30 cm.
    Titles of individual pieces in German
and English.
    Four scores bound together.
    Partial contents: Liebster Jesu, wir sind
hier — Herzlich thut mich verlangen — Jesus
Christus, unser Heiland — Ein feste Burg ist
unser Gott.

1.   Title   2.   Organ choral
                      preludes
3.   Murdoch, William
4.   Optionally, analytical title entries
        for each part

Description of music — Ch.1 and Ch.5. No specific
material designation is applicable, so number of
volumes of music is given — 5.5B1. Pagination
added, in accordance with rules for printed monographs — 5.5B3. If volumes in multi-volume set
are individually paged, pagination of each volume
may optionally be given in parentheses after the
number of volumes — 2.5B21.

Arrangement of one or more works of one composer entered under heading for composer, with
added entry under heading for arranger — 21.18B.

Basis of uniform title is composer's original title
in language in which it was formulated — 25.27A.
When this consists solely of the name of one type
of composition, the accepted English form of name
is used — 25.27B. Medium of performance is
implied by title and so is omitted from uniform
title — 25.29A2. If uniform title for collection
containing works of one type is for collection
that is incomplete, 'Selections' is added — 25.36B
and 25.36C. If work described as arrangement is
entered under heading for original composer, 'arr'
is added to uniform title — 25.31B2.

38

BACH, Johann Sebastian
  [Sonatas, violin, harpsichord, BWV
1014-1019]
  Sechs Sonaten für Klavier und Violine /
Joh. Seb. Bach ; herausgegeben von Ferd.
David. — Leipzig : Peters, [ca. 1889].
    1 score (2 v.) + 1 part (2 v.) ; 31 cm.
    Contents: BWV 1014-1019.
    Pl. no.: 7281-7282.

1.   Title   2.   Sechs Sonaten für
                      Klavier und
                      Violine
3.   David, Ferdinand

Description of music — Ch.1 and Ch.5. Approximate date, estimated from plate number, given —
1.4F7. Pagination or number of volumes added
to statement of extent — 5.5B3. Plate number
recorded in note in preference to publisher's
number — 5.7B19.

Uniform title is name of work exclusive of medium
of performance and numerals — 25.26A. Accepted
English form of name used — 25.27B. Statement
of medium of performance added if not implied
by title — 25.29A1, 25.29A2, and 25.29A3. (The
use of the word 'Klavier' on the title page should
not be interpreted as 'piano' for music before
ca. 1775. Although rule 25.3B instructs that the
basis of the uniform title should be the title proper
of the original edition, it can be assumed that
this should be interpreted as 'original work' in the
case of the medium statement of new editions of
older music.) Thematic index numbers added in
the absence of serial and/or opus numbers and
preceded by generally accepted abbreviation —
25.31A4. Bach composed other sonatas for
harpsichord and violin not included in this
publication. However, as the selections form a
consecutively numbered group, the inclusive
numbering is used instead of 'Selections' — 25.36C.

39

BAILLIE, John
  A diary of private prayer / by John
Baillie. — London : Oxford University
Press, 1936.
    135 p. ; 17 cm.

1.   Title

Although a book of prayers, item is not a liturgical work as defined at 21.39A1, but a book intended for private devotion — 21.39A3. Entry is therefore under heading for personal author — 21.4A.

40

BARRATT, Michael
  Golf with Tony Jacklin : step by step, a great professional shows an enthusiastic amateur how to play every stroke of the game / Michael Barratt ; photographs by Mike Busselle and Behram Kapadia. — London : A. Barker, 1978.
    136 p. : ill. ; 26 cm.
    ISBN 0-213-16684-4.

    1.   Title   2.   Jacklin, Tony
    3.   Busselle, Mike
    4.   Kapadia, Behram

Reports of interviews or exchanges; this work is presented in the form of a conversation. The greater proportion of the words are Jacklin's. However, they are not 'confined' to Jacklin (21.25A), but are 'to a considerable extent' those of Barratt and entry is therefore under the heading for the latter — 21.25B. The added entry for Jacklin is under the form of name by which he is commonly known and a reference would be required. Added entries are necessary for the illustrators because the illustrations are an 'important feature' — 21.30K2(c).

41

BAUTATIGKEIT im Jahre. — 1952-1955. —
    Stuttgart : Kohlhammer, 1952-1955.
    4 v. ; 30 cm.
    Annual.
    Compiled by the German Federal Republic Statistisches Bundesamt.
    Issued as: Bd. 93, 111, 140 and 160 of Statistik der Bundesrepublik Deutschland.
    Continued by: Bauwirtschaft, Bautätigkeit, Wohnungen ; Reihe 3.

    1.   Germany. (Federal Republic).
         Statistisches Bundesamt

Serial that has ceased publication; designations and dates given for first and last issues — 12.3F and 12.4F3. Note on statement of responsibility — 1.7B6, 2.7B6 and 12.7B6. Serial is part of a larger serial but rules are not clear as to treatment. The particular situation is not specifically covered in the rule for relationships with other serials, although this rule does state that a note should be made about a relationship with any simultaneously published serial — 12.7B7. An alternative solution would be to record the larger serial in the series area — 12.6B1.

Work emanating from corporate body but not falling within any of the categories listed at 21.1B2 is entered under title — 21.1C(3). The form of heading for the added entry is chosen in accordance with rules 23.2A, 24.6A and 24.6C.

42

BEDFORD, Mary Russell, Duchess of
  The flying duchess : the diaries and letters of Mary, Duchess of Bedford / edited, with an introduction, by John, Duke of Bedford. — London : Macdonald, 1968.
    216 p., 31 p. of plates : ill., ports. ; 22 cm.

    1.   Title   2.   Bedford, John
                           Russell, Duke of

Statement of responsibility is integral part of other title information and is transcribed as such — 1.1E4. No further statement relating to this name made — 1.1F13. Subsequent statement of responsibility is normally preceded by semicolon — 1.1A1. However, if first statement of responsibility is omitted from statement of responsibility area, it can be assumed that the second statement is treated as the first and preceded by diagonal slash.

Entry under proper name in title of nobility if person is commonly known by that title, proper name is followed by part of title denoting rank — 22.4B4 and 22.6A. *

67

BEE GEES
43
How deep is your love / Bee Gees. — [London] : RSO Records, 1977.
on 1 side of 1 sound disc (ca. 3 min., 10 sec.) : 45 rpm, stereo. ; 7 in.
"From the Paramount/Robert Stigwood motion picture: Saturday night fever".
RSO: 2090 259.
With: Night fever.

1. Title 2. Saturday night fever

Separate description for separately titled work on sound recording lacking a collective title — 6.1G1, 6.1G4, 6.5B3 and 6.7B21. The members of the group (B., R., and M. Gibb) are also named in the chief source of information (the label) but they can be omitted from the statement of responsibility area — 6.1F2. They could be given in a note if considered important enough.

Sound recording resulting from the collective activity of a performing group as a whole is entered under the heading for the group where the responsibility of the group goes beyond that of mere performance, execution, etc. — 21.1B2(e). The Bee Gees fall into this category since they write and produce their own music.

44
[BIBLE. English. Authorised. Selections. 1968]
A little treasury of Christmas / selected from the words of the Holy Bible by Kenneth Seeman Giniger. — London : Collins, 1968.
62 p. : ill. ; 96 mm. — (Dolphin booklets).

1. A little treasury of Christmas
2. Giniger, Kenneth Seeman

Statements of responsibility may include words or phrases which are neither names nor linking words — 1.1F15. Height of volume under 10 centimetres given in millimetres — 2.5D1.

No added entry under series because items in series related to each other only by common

physical characteristics — 21.30L. Selections from the Bible entered under the uniform title 'Bible' — 25.18A1. Language added to heading — 25.18A10. Version added to heading — 25.18A11. 'Selections' added to heading — 25.18A9. Year of publication added to heading — 25.18A13.

45
[BIBLE. N.T. Gospels. English. Rieu. 1952]
The four Gospels / a new translation from the Greek by E.V. Rieu. — Harmondsworth : Penguin, 1952.
xxxiii, 245 p. ; 18 cm. — (Penguin classics ; L32).

1. The four Gospels
2. Rieu, E.V.
3. Series

Noun phrase which occurs in conjunction with statement of responsibility and indicates role of person named rather than nature of work is treated as part of the statement of responsibility — 1.1F12. (See also example no. 12).

Work that is accepted as sacred scripture by a religious group is entered under title — 21.1C(4) and 21.37A. Group of books from the Bible entered under the uniform title 'Bible' — 25.18A1. 'N.T.' added to heading — 25.18A2. 'Gospels' added to heading — 25.18A4. Language added to heading — 25.18A11. Translator as version — 25.18A11. Year of publication added to heading — 25.18A13.

46
[BIBLE. N.T. Welsh.]
Testament Newydd ein Harglwydd a'n Hiachawdwr Iesu Grist = The New Testament of our Lord and Saviour Jesus Christ. — Denbigh : Clwydian Press, 1824.
548 p. ; 17 cm.
At head of title: Y Testament Newydd dwyieithawg = The duoglott New Testament.
Text printed in parallel columns in Welsh and English.

1. [Bible. N.T. English.]

Title appears in two languages; Welsh is considered to be the main language in this instance and is also the first in order — 1.1B8. Note on variation of title — 1.7B4. Note on language of item and important physical details not included in physical description area — 1.7B2, 1.7B10, 2.7B2 and 2.7B10.

Uniform title for Bible — 25.18A1.* 'N.T.' added to heading — 25.18A2. Language added to heading — 25.18A10. Version not applicable — 25.18A11 (and see footnote to p. 463). Added entry with name of second language — 25.18A10.

Statements of responsibility recorded in the order of their sequence on the chief source of information (i.e. the title page) — 1.1F6. Name of publisher given in shortest form in which it can be understood internationally — 1.4D2. Therefore, initial has been omitted, as there is no other well-known publisher with this name.

Version in different literary form, i.e. not a libretto but written in story form — also an adaptation for children — entry in either case is under the heading for the adapter — 21.10.

47

BISHOP, Bernard W.
    Bishop's concise garden encyclopedia / by Bernard W. Bishop ; drawings by W.E. Davies and Susan Baillie (as initialled). — Kingswood, Surrey : Right Way Books, 1958.
    190 p., [16] p. of plates : ill., port. ; 20 cm.

    1.   Title

Name associated with responsibility transcribed as part of title proper and repeated in statement of responsibility area, because separate statement of responsibility appears in chief source of information — 1.1F13. Statements of responsibility recorded in the form in which they appear in item — 1.1F1.

Single personal authorship — 21.1A1, 21.1A2 and 21.4A.

48

BLASHFIELD, Jean
    The pirates of Penzance / W.S. Gilbert and Arthur Sullivan ; told by Jean Blashfield ; with drawings by Anne and Janet Grahame Johnstone. — [London] : Nelson, [1965].
    [28] p. : col. ill. ; 20 x 21 cm. — (Mikado books).
    Music and words of Song of Ruth and Song of the major-general on lining papers.

    1.   Title   2.   Gilbert, W.S.
    3.   Sullivan, Sir Arthur
    4.   Johnstone, Anne
    5.   Johnstone, Janet Grahame
    6.   Series

49

BODY exerciser : the portable fitness gym / American Consumer. — Philadelphia : American Consumer, [197-].
    1 exerciser : nylon rope and plastic + 1 pamphlet (15 p.).
    "Designed to permit almost everyone of any age to exercise effectively at a time and place convenient"—Introduction to pamphlet.

    1.   American Consumer

Description of three-dimensional artefacts and realia — Ch.1 and Ch.10. Chief source of information is the item itself together with any accompanying textual material — 10.0B1. Specific name used as material designation as none of terms listed is appropriate — 10.5B1. Material of which item is made recorded — 10.5C1. Dimensions not recorded as not appropriate in this instance — 10.5D1. Accompanying material given in physical description area — 1.5E1(d) and 10.5E1. Note on nature of item — 10.7B1 ; given as a quotation — 1.7A3.

Anicius Manlius Severinus BOETIUS,

OF THE

CONSOLATION

OF

PHILOSOPHY.

In Five BOOKS.

Made *Englifh* and Illuftrated with NOTES,
By the Right Honourable
RICHARD *Lord Vifcount* PRESTON.

The SECOND EDITION Corrected.

LONDON:

Printed for *J. Tonfon* in the *Strand*, and *J. Round*
in *Exchange-Ally*. MDCCXII.

50

BOETHIUS
[De consolatione philosophiae. English]
Of the consolation of philosophy /
Anicius Manlius Severinus Boetius ; made
English and illustrated with notes by
Richard Preston. — 2nd ed. corr. — London :
Printed for J. Tonson in the Strand and
J. Round in Exchange-Ally, 1712.
xlv, 273 p., [1] leaf of plates : port. ;
17 cm. (12mo.).
"In five books".
Calfskin binding, slightly rubbed and
worn.
Bookplate and signature of Alex Leslie,
Aberdeen.

   1.   Title   2.   Of the consolation
                                of philosophy

Description of early printed monographs — Ch.1
and Ch.2 (rule 12 onwards). An 'early printed
monograph' is defined as one published before
1821 in countries following European conventions
in bookmaking — 2.12. Chief source of information is title page if one exists — 2.13. Statement
of responsibility precedes title proper in chief
source of information. These are transposed to
the required positions as case endings are not
affected by transposition — 1.1F3. Statement
on title page which is separate from title proper
omitted — 2.14C. Edition statement recorded
as it appears on item, using standard abbreviations — 2.15A. Place of publication given as it
appears in item — 2.16B. If the full address or
sign of the publisher appears in the source of
information, this is added to aid identification —
2.16C. Words indicating the role of the publisher included — 2.16F. Date of publication
given as it appears in item, with Roman numerals
changed to Arabic — 2.16H. Pagination recorded
— 2.17A. Illustrations described — 2.17B.
Dimensions recorded, with format in abbreviated
form added in parentheses — 2.17C. Notes made
as for ordinary monographs — 2.18A. Addition
note on special features of copy — 2.18F.

English form of name chosen for Roman of
classical times whose name has become well
established in an English form — 22.3B3. For
work created before 1501, uniform title is
title in original language by which work is
identified in modern reference sources — 25.4A.
Name of language added to uniform title — 25.5D.

51

BOREL, Jacques
[L'adoration. English]
The bond / by Jacques Borel ; translated
by Norman Denny. — London : Collins,
1968.
479 p. ; 22 cm.
Previously published: Paris : Gallinard,
1965.

   1.   Title†   2.   The bond†

Uniform title for translation given as original title,
followed by language of translation — 25.5D. If
a work is entered under a personal or corporate
heading and a uniform title is used, a name-title
reference is made from variants of the title, and
an added entry under the title proper — 25.2D2.*

BRATHWAITE, R.
    Drunken Barnaby's four journeys to
the north of England. — [2nd ed.]. —
London, under Searle's Gate, Lincolns-
Inn New Square : Printed for S. Illidge,
1716.
    151 p., [2] leaves of plates : 2 ill.
(woodcuts) ; 14 cm. (8vo).
    "In Latin and English verse".
    Attributed to: R. Brathwaite.
    With: Bessy Bell / Corymbaeus.
    Calfskin binding.
    Signed: Geo. Whitmore.

1.   Title   2.   Barnaby, <u>Drunken</u>
3.   Optionally, author and title
        analyticals for Bessy Bell

Description of early printed monographs — 2.12-
2.18F. Chief source of information is title page
if one exists — 2.13. Additions to title omitted
from title proper — 2.14D. Optionally, edition
statement supplied and enclosed in square
brackets — 1.2B4. Place of publication given
as it appears in the item — 2.16B. If the full
address or sign of the publisher appears in the
source of information, this is added to aid
identification — 2.16C. Words indicating the
role of the publisher included — 2.16F. Date
of publication given as found in the item —
2.16H. Pagination recorded — 2.17A. Illustrations described, with type optionally added in
parentheses — 2.17B. Dimensions recorded with
format of volume in abbreviated form added in
parentheses — 2.17C. Notes made as for
ordinary monographs — 2.18A. Additional
note on special features of copy — 2.18F.

Authoritative reference sources indicate that
this work is by R. Brathwaite, so entry is made
under the heading for him as author — 21.1A1.
If responsibility is erroneously or fictitiously
attributed to a person (i.e. 'Drunken Barnaby'),
entry is made under the heading for the actual
personal author — 21.4C1. An added entry is
made under the heading for the person to whom
authorship is attributed, unless he or she is not a
real person. As the writer of the preface
concludes that the work was written by Barnaby
Harrington, an added entry is made under the
heading for him. The basis for this heading is
the form of name by which he is most commonly

known, i.e. 'Drunken Barnaby' 22.1A. For
a phrase consisting of forename with another
word, entry is under forename, with a reference
from the name in direct order — 22.11B.*
A further reference would be needed from
other name, i.e. 'Harrington, Barnaby' — 26.2A1.

BRITAIN'S GLORIOUS NAVY

Edited by
ADMIRAL SIR REGINALD H. S. BACON
K.C.B., K.C.V.O., D.S.O.

With a Foreword by
ADMIRAL SIR EDWARD R. G. R. EVANS
K.C.B., D.S.O., LL.D.

ODHAMS PRESS LIMITED, LONG ACRE, LONDON, W.C.2

BRITAIN's glorious navy / edited by
    Sir Reginald H.S. Bacon ; with a fore-
word by Sir Edward R.G.R. Evans. —
London : Odhams Press, [1943].
    320 p. : ill., ports. ; 23 cm.

1.   Bacon, <u>Sir</u> Reginald H.S.

Omission of decorations and title from statement
of responsibility — 1.1F7. Writer of foreword
recorded in second statement of responsibility —
1.1F6.

Work produced under editorial direction entered under title — 21.7A and 21.7B. Omission of 'Admiral' from heading for added entry — 22.15C. 'Sir' included but italicised — 22.12B.

Work emanating from corporate body which is of an administrative nature dealing with the operations and procedures of the body entered under the heading for the body — 21.1B2(a).

BRITISH Isles / made by L & A Relief Map
    Constructions Ltd. — Scale ca.
1:274,000. — London : L & A, [197-].
    1 relief model : col., vacuum moulded in VCP. ; 39 x 28 cm.

    1.   L & A Relief Map Constructions

Description of relief models — Ch.1 and Ch.3. Scale estimated — 3.3B1. Material included as part of physical description — 3.5C4.

Work emanating from corporate body but not falling within any of the categories listed at 21.1B2 is entered under title — 21.1C(3). 'Ltd' is not needed in added entry to make clear that name is that of corporate body and so is omitted — 24.5C1. (This applies also to publication area, in which name is given in shortest form in which it can be understood (1.4D2), but not to statement of responsibility, where name is given in form that it appears on item — 1.1F1.)

BRITISH MUSEUM
    Handlist of Persian manuscripts : [acquired by the British Museum] 1895-1966 / by G.M. Meredith-Owens. — London : The Museum, 1968.
    x, 126 p. ; 26 cm.
    ISBN 0-7141-0630-5.

    1.   Title   2.   Meredith-Owens, G.M.

Title proper needs explanation, so brief addition is made as other title information — 1.1E6.

Work of an administrative nature emanating from corporate body and dealing with the resources of the body itself is entered under heading for the body — 21.1B2(a). The phrase 'of an administrative nature' is a little ambiguous. It could be argued that a catalogue can be of an administrative nature only if it is an inventory for the use solely of the staff of the body and not a published work for general use. However, the above item would be of use to both the general public and members of staff, and so it is treated as falling within the compass of the rule. The examples: 'National Gallery'; 'First National Bank of Chicago', and 'Royal Ontario Museum'; included in rule 21.4B appear to corroborate this interpretation. Added entry under prominently named writer of a work when main entry has not been made under that heading — 21.30C.

BRITISH LIBRARY. Bibliographic Services Division
    The British Library Bibliographic Services Division newsletter. — No. 1 (May 1976)-   . — London : BLBSD, 1976-   .
    v. ; 30 cm.
    Four issues yearly.
    ISSN 0308-230X = British Library Bibliographic Services Division newsletter.
    Free to subscribers to BSD publications.

Description of serials — Ch.1, Ch.12 and, for printed serials, Ch.2. Key-title recorded if found on the item or otherwise readily available even if it is identical with title proper — 12.8C1. Optional note on terms of availability — 1.8D1 and 12.8D1.

57

BRITTEN, Benjamin
Children's crusade = Kinderkreuzzug : op. 82 : a ballad for children's voices and orchestra / Benjamin Britten ; words by Bertolt Brecht ; English translation by Hans Keller. — London : Faber Music, 1972.
1 vocal score (x, 105 p.) ; 31 cm.
English and German words.
"Written for the members of Wandsworth School Boys' Choir (musical director Russell Burgess) to perform on the 50th Anniversary of the Save the Children Fund at St. Paul's Cathedral, May 19th 1969".
Pl. no.: F0330.

1.   Title   2.   Kinderkreuzzug
3.   Brecht, Bertolt

Description of music — Ch.1 and Ch.5. Original title recorded as parallel title because item contains text in original language — 5.1D1 and 1.1D3. Opus number treated as other title information because title proper does not consist of generic term — 5.1B2. Two diagrams appear in the introduction to this work, but minor illustrations are disregarded — 2.5C1. Language of textual content needed if not clear from rest of description — 5.7B2. Plate number recorded in note — 5.7B19. Composer was created life peer but title is omitted as he is not commonly known by it — 22.6A.

58

BROWN, Josiah
Reports of cases upon appeals and writs of error in the High Court of Parliament : from the year 1701 to the year 1779 / by Josiah Brown. — Dublin, No. 6 Skinner Row and in the Four Courts : Printed by E. Lynch, 1784.
7 v. (x, 555; 602; 586; 618; 610; 624; 558 p.) ; 22 cm. (fol.)
Rebound: 1969.

1.   Title
2.   United Kingdom. High Court of Parliament

Description of early printed monographs — Ch.2.12 to 2.18. No publisher statement, so details of printer are recorded — 2.16A. Number of volumes in multi-volume set recorded — 2.5B17. If volumes are individually paged, pagination of each volume may optionally be recorded — 2.5B21.

Reports of one court which are ascribed to a reporter are entered under the heading for the court or the reporter according to whichever is used as the basis for accepted legal citation practice in the country where the court is located — 21.36A1. The example 'Common bench reports', included with this rule, appears to indicate that in the U.K. this would be the heading for the reporter. This is reflected in the above entry, although the legal experts whom the authors consulted seemed to be unsure whether there was such an accepted practice. However, when the practice is unknown, or cannot be determined, the entry for this item would still be under the heading for the reporter according to the same rule. An added entry is made for the court, entered as a subheading of the heading for the government — 24.18(6).

59

BULLETIN of labour statistics. — 1st quarter 1965-   . — Geneva : International Labour Office, 1965-   .
v. ; 27 cm.
Quarterly. Kept up to date by a supplement issued in intervening months.
Continues: International labour review statistical supplement.

1.   International Labour Office.

Chronological designation recorded in terms used in item — 12.3C1. When serial is continuation of one previously published, name of latter given in note — 12.7B7(b).

Work emanating from corporate body but not falling within any of the categories listed at 21.1B2 is entered under title — 21.1C(3).

60

BURLIN, Robert B.

The old English advent : a typographical commentary / by Robert B. Burlin. — New Haven ; London : Yale University Press, 1968.

xv, 202 p. ; 24 cm. — (Yale studies in English ; 168).

A study of the Advent poem in the Exeter book, attributed to Cynewulf.

Bibliography: p. 185-189.

1. Title   2. Series

Entry under commentator, as chief source of information presents item as commentary — 21.13B.

61

CAERNARVONSHIRE COUNTY RECORD OFFICE

Caernarvonshire records : the Caernarvonshire Record Office, twenty-one years, 1947-1968 : a catalogue of an exhibition held at Caernarvon, 19-26 October 1968. — Caernarvon : County Record Office, 1968.

71 p. : ill., facsim., map ; 22 cm.

ISBN 0-901337-005.

1. Title

Other title information recorded in order indicated by sequence on chief source of information — 1.1E2.

Work of administrative nature emanating from corporate body and dealing with its resources is entered under heading for body — 21.1B2(a). See also example on p.289 of AACR 2 : 'Rembrandt in the National Gallery of Art' — 21.4B.

62

CAMPBELL, Patrick

All ways on Sundays / by Patrick Campbell. — London : Sphere Books, 1967.

190 p. ; 19 cm.

Originally published: London : Blond, 1966.

1. Title

Author has title of nobility — 'Baron Glenavy'.* However, this is not recorded, as he is not commonly known by it and does not use it in his works — 22.6A and 22.12A.

63

CARPENTER, Anne-Mary

Human histology : a colour atlas / by Anne-Mary Carpenter. — New York ; Maidenhead : Blakiston Division of McGraw-Hill, 1968.

96 p. : chiefly col. ill. ; 26 cm.

Accompanied by: Text for "Human histology . . ." (93 p.) in pocket.

1. Title

Work consisting chiefly of illustrations — 2.5C6. Accompanying material recorded in note — 2.7B11.

Hyphen retained in given name — 22.1D2.

64

CARTER, Craig J.M.

Ships of the Mersey / Craig J.M. Carter. — London : Record Books, 1966.

79 p., 1 leaf of plates : ill. ; 20 cm. + 2 sound discs (33⅓ rpm, mono. ; 7 in.). — (Sound picture series).

Discs, which are recordings of ships' sounds, in pocket.

1. Title   2. Series

Sound recording accompanying textual material — 1.5E and 2.5E. Name and optionally the physical description of the accompanying material recorded at the end of the physical description — 1.5E1d, 2.5E1 and 6.5. Location of accompanying material given in note — 2.5E2, 1.7B11 and 2.7B11.

65

CATHOLIC CHURCH
    [Ritual]
    Pocket ritual / [compiled by the
Liturgical Commission of the Archdiocese
of Glasgow] . — [New ed.] . — Glasgow :
J.S. Burns, [1971].
        66 p. ; 13 cm.
        ISBN 0-900243-20-1.

        1.   Title   2.   Pocket ritual
        3.   Catholic Church. Archdiocese of
              Glasgow. Liturgical Commission

Liturgical work entered under the heading for
the church to which it pertains — 21.39A1.*
Well-established English title used as uniform
title — 25.19. In added entry, English form of
name used for a diocese, etc. of the Catholic
Church — 24.27C3.

66

CHICAGO (Musical group)
    If you leave me now / P. Cetera.
Together again / L. Loughnane. —
[London] : CBS, 1976.
    1 sound disc (8 min.) : 45 rpm, stereo. ;
7 in.
        "Taken from the LP Chicago".
        Performed by Chicago.
        CBS: S CBS 4603.

        1.   Title   2.   Cetera, P.
        3.   Together again
        4.   Loughnane, L.
              Together again

Sound recording without a collective title described
as a unit — 6.1G1. Neither of the constituent
titles predominates so both are recorded — 6.1G2
and 1.1G2. (An alternative interpretation would
be to take the title on the 'A' side as the predominant part and record the title on the 'B' side in
a note — 1.1G1.) Statements of responsibility
for item lacking a collective title — 1.1G2. Where
a sound recording is concerned, if the participation
of persons found in a statement in a chief source
of information is confined to performance,
execution or interpretation, such a statement is
given in a note — 6.1F1 and 6.7B6.

Entry is under the principal performer for a sound
recording containing musical works by different
persons — 21.23C. A suitable designation is added
to the heading if name alone does not convey
the idea of a corporate body — 24.4B. Note that
if there were no principal performer, rule 21.7C
would apply as indicated in 21.23D. A sound
recording could, for example, contain Elgar's
Enigma variations and Beethoven's Symphony
no. 6; the former being performed by the London
Symphony Orchestra and the latter by the Royal
Philharmonic Orchestra, neither being presented
as principal performer. Entry would, according
to 21.7C, be under the heading appropriate to the
first work, i.e. either Elgar or Beethoven.

It could perhaps be argued in the context of rule
6.1F1, that since the participation of a performing group such as Chicago is of prime
importance, it goes beyond that of mere performance. This interpretation would enable the group
to be named in the statement of responsibility
area. Some cataloguing agencies might even wish
to omit the composers, or give them only in a
note, as they are not of prime significance and
are not named prominently on the item. This
would give the clearer entry layout:

    CHICAGO (Musical group)
        If you leave me now ; Together again /
    Chicago. — London : CBS, 1976 . . .

67

CHRYSLER UNITED KINGDOM. Dealer
    Development Department
    Authorised dealers in the United
Kingdom and Eire / issued by Dealer
Development Department, Chrysler United
Kingdom Limited. — 7th ed. — Coventry :
Chrysler, 1977.
        48 p. ; 22 cm.
        Cover title.

        1.   Title

Source of title given if it is other than chief source
of information — 2.7B3.

Work of administrative nature emanating from
corporate body and dealing with body itself is
entered under heading for body — 21.1B2(a).
Chrysler U.K. has now been re-named Talbot
and a reference would be required for this change.

CONVERSATIONS
between
The Church of England
and
The Methodist Church

AN INTERIM STATEMENT

LONDON

S · P · C · K

and

THE EPWORTH PRESS

1958

Work emanating from corporate body and recording its collective thought is entered under heading for body — 21.1B2(c). Work emanates from two corporate bodies (21.6A(4)) and principal responsibility is not attributed to either; entry is therefore under heading for one named first — 21.6C1. Body entered directly under the name by which it is predominantly identified — 24.1.

69

CHURCH OF ENGLAND. Liturgical Commission
The calendar and lessons for the Church's year : a report submitted by the Church of England Liturgical Commission to the Archbishops of Canterbury and York, November, 1968. — London : S.P.C.K., 1969.
x, 95 p. ; 22 cm.
ISBN 0-281-02323-9.

1.   Title

Work emanating from corporate body and recording its collective thought is entered under heading for body — 21.1B2(c). (See also example on p. 290 of AACR 2 : 'Capital and equality : report of a Labour Party study group' — 21.4B.) Councils, etc. of single religious body entered as subheading of heading for religious body — 24.27A1. Full name of body is : 'Church of England. National Assembly. Liturgical Commission'. Intervening elements in hierarchy omitted unless needed to distinguish subordinate body — 24.14.

68

CHURCH OF ENGLAND
Conversations between the Church of England and the Methodist Church : an interim statement. — London : S.P.C.K., 1958.
vii, 49 p. ; 22 cm.

1.   Title   2.   Methodist Church†

Second publisher omitted because not given prominence by typography — 1.4D5.

70

CHURCHILL, Sir Winston Spencer
I can hear it now : speeches / Sir Winston Churchill ; edited by E.R. Murrow and F.W. Friendly. — [Croydon] : Philips, [195-].
1 sound disc (ca. 40 min.) : 33⅓ rpm, mono. ; 12 in.
Narration by Edward R. Murrow.
Philips: SPL 100.

1.   Title   2.   Murrow, Ed
3.   Friendly, F.W.

When the participation of a person found in a statement in the chief source of information is confined to performance, such a statement is given in a note — 6.1F1 and 6.7B6.

Entry under the heading for the person responsible for the intellectual content — 21.1A1, 21.1A2 and 21.4A. Entry under the name by which person is commonly known — 22.1A. British title of honour "Sir" commonly appears with the name and is therefore added to the heading — 22.13B. Added entry for Murrow is made under the form of name by which he is commonly known — 22.2A.

J. COCKERILL

Beatrix Potter's House
Hilltop, Sawrey, Near Hawkshead

This was Beatrix Potter's first home in the Lake District. She moved here from London in 1904. Here she produced some of her best loved works.

The house was built in 1602 and is little changed from the days when Beatrix Potter lived here. It is now cared for by the National Trust. In the cottage are items such as the Welsh dresser, familiar from the illustrations in her books. At the age of 47 Beatrix Potter married William Heelis and moved to Castle Cottage. She continued to work at Hilltop. In later years Beatrix Potter bought substantial amounts of property with preservation in mind. She left some 4,000 acres to the National Trust.

Beatrix Potter died in 1943 at the age of 77. The cottage was opened to the public three years later.

LOCAL HISTORY CARDS   No. 508   C Gatehouse Prints

71

CICRIS
    Cicris directory and guide to resources / compiled and edited by James W. Thirsk. — London : Cicris, 1968.
    [55] p. ; 21 cm.

    1.   Thirsk, J.W.

Volume printed without pagination, so number enclosed in square brackets — 2.5B7.

Work of administrative nature emanating from corporate body and dealing with its resources is entered under heading for body — 21.1B2(a). Corporate body entered under name by which it is commonly identified; full stops omitted from initialism in accordance with predominant usage of body — 24.1. Variant forms of name found in items issued by body, so name as it appears in chief sources of information is used — 24.2B.

72

COCKERILL, J.
    Beatrix Potter's house : Hilltop, Sawrey, near Hawkshead / [illustration by] J. Cockerill. — [Robin Hood's Bay, Yorkshire] : Gatehouse Prints, [197-?].
    1 study print : b&w ; 15 x 11 cm. — (Local history cards ; no. 508).

    1.   Title

Description of study prints as graphic materials — Ch.1 and Ch.8. (A study print is not defined in AACR 2. It may be defined as: a picture with accompanying text which makes the print significant for study purposes).

Item is work of collaboration between artist and writer. Normally, entry is under heading for one named first, unless other is given greater prominence. In this instance, only one is named — 21.24.

COLDSTREAM Guards drummer, 1832. —
[19—?] (Potschappell : C. Thieme).
1 figure : porcelain, col. ; 28 cm. high.
Manufacturer deduced from factory
mark on base.

Description of three-dimensional artefacts — Ch.1
and Ch.10. Artefact not intended primarily for
communication has date as first element of publication, etc. area — 10.4F2 — followed, as name of
publisher is not applicable, by place and name of
manufacturer in parentheses — 1.4G1 and 10.4G1.
Material and colour added to designation — 10.5C1
and 10.5C2. Word added to measurement to
indicate which dimension is being given — 10.5D1.

74

COMENIUS, John Amos
Orbis sensualium pictus / by John Amos
Comenius ; with an introduction by James
Bowen. — 3rd ed. — Sydney : Sydney
University Press ; London : Methuen, 1967.
x, 43, 320 p. : ill., maps, port. ; 19 cm.
Facsim. of: 3rd ed. London : S. Mearne,
1672.

1.   Title

Details of second publisher given, as it is in country
of cataloguing agency — 1.4B8. Details of original
of facsimile given in note — 1.11F.

Person's name which appears in different language
forms (original name of author was Jan Amos
Komensky) is given in form corresponding, to
language of most of works — 22.3B1. (A reference
would be required.)*

75

A COMPILATION of the litanies, vespers,
hymns and anthems as sung in the
Catholic Church / by John Aitken ; reissued
in facsimile with a new introduction by
J.C. Selner, Jules Baisnée, Albert Hyma. —
Philadelphia : Musical Americana, 1956.
1 vocal score (8, 136 p.) ; 26 cm.
"Adapted to the voice or organ".
Facsim. reprint. Originally published:
Philadelphia, 1787.

1.   Aitken, John
2.   Catholic Church

Description of music — Ch.1 and Ch.5. Note
relating to bibliographic history of work — 5.7B7.

Liturgical music treated as general liturgical work —
21.22. Liturgical work is normally entered under
heading for church or denomination to which it
pertains — 21.39A1. However, although the
Catholic Church is named on the title page, this
work appears to be a miscellany of Catholic and
Protestant music, with no strict liturgical structure.
It is therefore considered to fall into one of the
categories listed at 21.39A3 and is entered in
accordance with the general rules, i.e. under collective title — 21.7B.

76

COMPUTER programming. — Hull : University of Hull, AVC, [197-] .
1 videocassette (Philips VCR) (20 min.) :
sd., b&w. — (Where do we go from here? ;
10).
University of Hull production.

1.   University of Hull. <u>AVC</u>
2.   Series

Description of videorecordings — Ch.1 and Ch.7.
Appropriate term chosen as specific material designation (i.e. 'videocartridge', 'videocassette',
'videodisc' or 'videoreel'). Trade name added if
use of item is conditional upon this information
and if it is available only in this particular form —
7.5B1. Sound and colour characteristics indicated
— 7.5C3 and 7.5C4. No dimensions given for
videocassette. Prescribed punctuation retained
after question mark — 1.0C.

CONFERENCE OF BRITISH TEACHERS
   OF MARKETING AT ADVANCED
   LEVEL (3rd : 1968 : Harrogate)
   Third Conference of British Teachers
of Marketing at Advanced Level, Harrogate,
June 1968 : conference proceedings. —
Lancaster : University of Lancaster, Dept.
of Marketing, [1969].
   51 leaves ; 30 cm.
   ISBN 0-901272-00-0.

   1.   University of Lancaster.
        Department of Marketing

Conference as corporate body — 21.1B1. Words
denoting number omitted from heading for
conference — 24.7A. Number, place and date
added to heading — 24.7B1.

[CONVENTION ON INTERNATIONAL
   CIVIL AVIATION (1944) Protocols,
   etc., 1968 Sept. 24]
   Protocol on the authentic trilingual
text of the Convention on International
Civil Aviation (Chicago, 1944), Buenos
Aires, 24 September 1968. — London :
H.M.S.O., 1969.
   87 p. ; 25 cm. — (Treaty series ;
no. 115, 1969) (Cmnd. ; 4198).
   Text in English, French and Spanish.
   ISBN 0-10-141980-5.

   1.   Title   2.   Series

Date recorded as numbering within series — 1.6G1.
Note on language of item — 2.7B2.

Separately published protocol entered under
heading for basic agreement — 21.35E. Uniform
title consists of uniform title for original work,
followed by 'Protocols, etc.' and the date of
signing — 25.16B3.

CAMBRIDGE STUDIES IN INDUSTRY

EFFECTS OF MERGERS
Six Studies

P. LESLEY COOK

WITH THE COLLABORATION OF

RUTH COHEN

University of Cambridge

Ruskin House

GEORGE ALLEN & UNWIN LTD

MUSEUM STREET LONDON

COOK, P. Lesley
   Effects of mergers : six studies /
P. Lesley Cook with the collaboration of
Ruth Cohen. — London : Allen & Unwin,
1958.
   458 p. ; 22 cm. — (Cambridge studies
in industry).
   Contents: The cement industry /
P. Lesley Cook — The calico printing
industry / P. Lesley Cook — The soap
industry / Ruth Cohen — The flat-glass
industry / P. Lesley Cook — The motor
industry / George Maxcy — The brewing
industry / John Vaizey.

   1.   Title   2.   Cohen, Ruth
   3.   Series
   4.   Optionally, author and title
        analytical entries for each part†

Statement of responsibility recorded in form in which it appears in the item — 1.1F1. No semi-colon separating principal from secondary author because both are named in single statement — 1.1F4. (See also example 'A short-title catalogue . . . ' at 1.1F5.) Contents note — 1.7B18 and 2.7B18.

Entry under the principal author indicated by both wording and layout — 21.6B1 (also supported by information given in preface).

80

COTTON, G.B.
    Libraries in the North West / [G.B. Cotton, D.H. Varley, G.R. Cliffe]. — Manchester : Library Association, North Western Branch, 1971.
    39 p. : ill. ; 23 cm.
    Special issue of: North Western newsletter. No. 116.
    "Published on the occasion of the Council Meeting of the International Federation of Library Associations in Liverpool, 27th August to 4th September, 1971".
    Contents: Public libraries in the North West / G.B. Cotton — Academic libraries in the North West / D.H. Varley — Industrial libraries in the North West / G.R. Cliffe.

    1.   Title   2.   Varley, D.H.
    3.   Cliffe, G.R.
    4.   North Western newsletter
    5.   Library Association. North
            Western Branch
    6.   Optionally, author and title
            analytical entries for each part

Statement of responsibility appears prominently in item, but not in chief source of information (i.e. on contents page, not title page). It is therefore recorded in statement of responsibility area but enclosed in square brackets — 1.1A2 and 1.1F1.

Responsibility shared between three persons; principal responsibility not attributed to any. Main entry under first named, with added entries for others — 21.6C1. Special number of serial is related work — 21.28A. Entry is under its own heading with added entry for work to

which it is related — 21.28B. Added entry for prominently named publisher whose responsibility extends beyond merely publishing work — 21.30E.

81

COUNTRY magazine : book of the B.B.C. programme / compiled and edited by Francis Dillon. — London : Odhams Press, [1950?].
    256 p., [17] p. of plates : ill., music, ports. ; 22 cm.

    1.   Dillon, Francis

Number of pages of plates recorded — 2.5B10. Music as illustrative matter — 2.5C2.

Related work under its own heading — 21.28B. See 'Over the garden wall' example on p. 320. Work produced under editorial direction entered under title — 21.7A and 21.7B. It is merely coincidence that the title of the book is the same as that of the radio programme.

See also example no. 36.

82

CROSBY CENTRAL LIBRARY
    Local maps & documents in the Local History Library / Crosby Central Library. — 2nd ed. — Crosby : The Library, 1972.
    72 p. ; 21 cm.

    1.   Title

Work of administrative nature emanating from corporate body and dealing with its resources is entered under heading for body — 21.1B2(a). Body entered directly under the name by which it is predominantly identified — 24.1.

The Municipal Borough of Crosby became part of the Metropolitan District of Sefton in the local government reorganisation of 1974. Explanatory references would therefore be needed to link each of the two headings :
    Sefton Libraries and Arts Services and
    Crosby Central Library — 26.3C1.*

See also next example.

CROSBY in the past : a photographic
      record of the history of Crosby and
district / Sefton Libraries and Arts
Services. — Sefton : Libraries and Arts
Services, 1977.
      30 p. : chiefly ill., maps ; 21 cm.

1.   Sefton Libraries and Arts Services

Work emanating from corporate body but not
falling within any of the categories listed at
21.1B2 is entered under title — 21.1C(3).

See also previous example.

CUNDALL, Arthur E.
      Judges / [Arthur E. Cundall]. Ruth /
[Leon Morris]. — London : Tyndale Press,
1968.
      318 p. : maps, plans ; 19 cm. —
(Tyndale Old Testament commentaries).
      Bibliography: p. 49.
      ISBN 0-85111-622-1.

1.   Title   2.   Morris, Leon
                        Ruth
3.   Ruth†   4.   Series

For item lacking collective title and consisting
of individually-titled works by different persons,
the parts are recorded in order in which they
appear in chief source of information (if no one
part predominates), with a full-stop followed by
two spaces to separate them — 1.1G2. Statements
of responsibility taken from source other
than chief source of information enclosed in
square brackets — 1.1F1.

Work lacking collective title entered under heading appropriate to first work named in chief source
of information — 21.7C. Added entry (name-title)
needed for other work.

DAILY Mail children's pictorial encyclo-
      paedia. — London : Associated
Newspapers, [196-].
      [76] p. : chiefly col. ill. ; 34 cm.

Work of unknown authorship entered under
title — 21.1C(1) and 21.5A.

DANTE ALIGHIERI
      [De monarchia. English]
      On world government = De monar-
chia / Dante Alighieri ; translated by
Herbert W. Schneider ; with an introduction
by Dino Bigongiari. — 2nd rev. ed. — New
York : Bobbs-Merrill, 1957.
      80 p. ; 19 cm.

1.   Title   2.   On world
                        government
3.   Schneider, Herbert W.

Translation entered under heading appropriate
to the original — 21.14A. For works created
before 1501, title in original language is used as
uniform title — 25.4A. Language added if
different from original — 25.5D. Added entry
under heading for translator, because work has
been translated into same language more than
once — 21.30K1(e).

DAVIES, Harry
      [Letters] / Harry Davies. — 1916-19.
      10 items : ill., plans, port. ; 26 x 21 cm.
or smaller.
      Conscientious objector. Letters to
friend, Edith, mainly relating to prison
conditions he was experiencing at various
centres. Includes detailed account of
Wormwood Scrubs (30 p.).
      Title supplied by cataloguer.
      Some pages of letters missing.
      Accompanied by hand-drawn plans of
Scrubs, Wakefield Centre and Dartmoor
and self-portrait.
      Also contains official regulations from
Scrubs concerning communications between
prisoners and visitors.

Description of manuscripts — Ch.1 and Ch.4.
Collection of letters by individual given title
'[Letters]' — 4.1B2. Number of items recorded —
4.5B2. When size of items is not uniform, size
of largest is recorded optionally — 4.5D2. Information to identify writer recorded, followed by
summary — 4.7B1. Source of title — 4.7B3.
Additional physical description given — 4.7B10.
Accompanying material — 4.7B11. Further
contents recorded — 4.7B18.

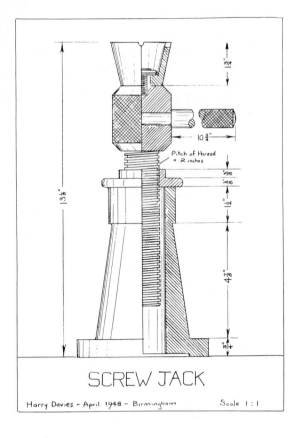

SCREW JACK

Harry Davies - April 1948 - Birmingham   Scale 1:1

Entry under heading for personal author, i.e. the person responsible for the intellectual and artistic content of the drawing — 21.1A1. Name is identical to that in previous example. However, neither dates nor distinguishing terms are available, so same heading is used for both persons — 22.20.

89

DAVRATH, Netania
    Songs of the Auvergne / arr., Joseph Canteloube. — New York : Vanguard ; London : RCA [distributor] , 1972.
    2 sound discs (ca. 80 min.) : 33⅓ rpm, stereo. ; 12 in. — (Vanguard recordings for the connoisseur).
    "Sung in the original dialect — Full translation inside"—Container.
    Netania Davrath, soprano ; Pierre de la Roche, conductor.
    Vanguard: VSD 713/714.

1.   Title   2.   Canteloube, Joseph
3.   Series

Optionally, statement of function of distributor may be added — 6.4E1 and 1.4E1. Where a sound recording is concerned, if the participation of persons found in a statement in a chief source of information is confined to performance, execution or interpretation, such a statement is given in a note — 6.1F1 and 6.7B6. (But see also example no. 66).

Entry is under the heading for the principal performer for a sound recording containing musical works by different persons — 21.23C.

88

DAVIES, Harry
    Screw jack / Harry Davies. — Birmingham, 1948.
    1 technical drawing ; 43 x 30 cm.
    Scale 1:1.

1.   Title

Description of technical drawings as graphic materials — Ch.1 and Ch.8. Title transcribed exactly as it appears on item — 1.1B1 and 8.1B1. Title statement followed by statement of responsibility — 1.1F1 and 8.1F1. Publication area contains place (1.4C1 and 8.4C1) and date (1.4F1 and 8.4F1); there is no publisher as such in this instance. Specific material designation recorded, preceded by number of items — 8.5B1. Dimensions (height x width) given — 8.5D6. Scale given as note — 8.7B10. (For cartographic materials, the scale is given in the mathematical data area, but no such area exists for graphic materials.)

90

DICKENS, Charles
    [David Copperfield]
    The story of David Copperfield / by Charles Dickens ; abridged by W. Jewesbury. — London : Pan, 1970.
    128 p. : ill. (some col.) ; 20 cm.
    Includes photographs from the 20th Century-Fox film.
    ISBN 0-330-02502-3.

1.   Title   2.   The story of David Copperfield
3.   Jewesbury, W.

Note on physical description — 1.7B10 and
2.7B10.

Abridgment under heading for the original work —
21.12A. (Person responsible for original is named
in a statement of responsibility and it also states
in the item that it is told in Dickens' own words.)
Uniform title — 25.3A.*

Compare with example no. 321.

91

DIOCLES
   The home medical encyclopedia / by
Diocles. — 4th large ed. — Kingswood,
Surrey : Right Way Books, 1956.
      254 p. : ill. ; 20 cm.
   "Including guide to the Health and
Insurance Service"—Dustjacket.

   1.   Title

Entry under single personal author — 21.1A1,
21.1A2 and 21.4A. Basis of heading is name
by which person is commonly known — 22.1A
— determined from the chief source of information of works by that person in his or her
language — 22.1B. Entry under pseudonym with
reference from the real name if known — 22.2C1.

92

DISPLAY. — [Liverpool, 1977].
   1 flip chart (22 sheets) : some col. ;
90 x 58 cm.
   Examples of posters, other publicity
materials, lettering, etc.
   Prepared by Eric J. Hunter.
   Not generally available.

   1.   Hunter, Eric J.

Description of flip charts as graphic materials —
Ch.1 and Ch.8. Physical description — 8.5B1,
8.5B3, 8.5C6 and 8.5D1. Note on the nature and
scope of the item — 1.7B1 and 8.7B1. Note on
statement of responsibility — 1.7B6 and 8.7B6.
Note on availability (optional) — 1.8D1 and
8.8D1.

Item treated as a collection of works by independent persons or bodies and entered under title —
21.7A and 21.7B.

93

DOS PASSOS, John
   The best times : an informal memoir /
by John Dos Passos. — London : Deutsch,
1968.
      ix, 229 p. : ill. ; 22 cm.
   Originally published: New York : New
American Library, 1966.

   1.   Title

Entry under prefix for names in English language —
22.5D1. *

94

DRAPER, A.S.
   American education / A.S. Draper. —
Chicago : Library Resources, 1970.
      1 microfiche (399 fr.) ; 8 x 13 cm. —
(Microbook [library series. Library of
American civilisation, beginnings to 1914] ;
LAC 10589).
   Microreproduction of original
published: Boston : Houghton Mifflin,
1909. x, 383 p.
   Very high reduction.

   1.   Title   2.   Series
   3.   Library of American civilisation

Description of microforms — Ch.1 and Ch.11.
Series statement as it appears in chief source of
information is: 'Microbook LAC 10589'.
Additional series statement found in publicity
material and so enclosed in square brackets
within the parentheses enclosing the series
statement — 1.6A2. Name of subseries follows
that of series — 1.6H1. Publication details of
original given in note — 1.7B7. Reduction is
90x. 'Very high reduction' is term used — 11.7B10.
Introductory wording of note separated from
main content by colon and space — 1.7A1.

DREXEL UNIVERSITY FACULTY CLUB
    Handbook / Drexel University Faculty
Club, Inc. — Philadelphia : The University,
[1973?].
    12 p. ; 23 x 11 cm.
    Cover title.

    1.   Title

Work of administrative nature emanting from
corporate body and dealing with its policies is
entered under heading for body — 21.1B2(a).
Body entered directly under name — 24.1. Term
indicating incorporation omitted as it is not an
integral part of the name nor is it needed to make
clear that name is that of a corporate body —
24.5C1.

DUFFERIN AND AVA, Frederick Temple
    Hamilton-Temple Blackwood, <u>Marquess</u>
    Letters from high latitudes / Lord
Dufferin. — London : Dent, 1910.
    xv, 252 p. : ill. ; 18 cm. — (Everyman's
library).

    1.   Title

Statement of responsibility recorded in the form
in which it appears in item — 1.1F1.

Entry under the proper name in the title of
nobility for a person who uses his title in his
works or is listed under his title in reference
sources — 22.6A. A reference would be required
from the surname — 26.2A3. No added entry
under heading for series, as items in series are
related to each other only by common physical
characteristics — 21.30L(1).

Château Dundurn Castle, *Hamilton Ontario*

1. Entrance Hall Hall d'entrée	7. Butler's Pantry Office
2. Drawing Room Salon	8. Sitting Room Petit salon
3. Library Bibliothèque	9. Bedroom Chambre
4. Estate Office Bureau de propriété	10. Ablution Room Salle de bain
5. Dining Room Salle à manger	11. MacNab Arms Restaurant Restaurant "MacNab Arms"
6. Butler's Bedroom Chambre du maître d'hôtel	12. Assembly Hall Salle de réunion

GROUND FLOOR

The magnificent entrance hall (1) with its curved staircase and authentic period wallpaper leads you to the superbly restored drawing room (2). Sir Allan entertained in baronial splendour in the dining room (5). His sister-in-law Sophia had a private sitting room (8) with adjoining bedroom (9). Be sure to visit the MacNab Arms Restaurant (11) for an appetizing snack or luncheon.

REZ-DE-CHAUSSÉE

Le magnifique hall d'entrée (1), avec son grand escalier et son papier peint d'époque, donne accès au somptueux salon remarquablement restauré (2). Sir Allan recevait avec sa magnificence coutumière dans la salle à manger (5). Sa belle-soeur, Sophie, disposait d'un petit salon privé (8) avec une chambre attenante (9). Ne manquez pas de visiter le restaurant "MacNab Arms" (11) où vous pouvez prendre un repas léger ou un repas complet.

1. Nursery Chambre d'enfants	8. Sick Room Salle de malade
2. Bedrooms of MacNab daughters Chambre des filles MacNab	9. Lady MacNab's Boudoir Boudoir de Lady MacNab
3. School Room Salle d'étude	10. Sir Allan's Bedroom Chambre de Sir Allan
4. Pent-up Green Room Salle verte	11. Dressing Room Salle d'habillage
5-6-7. Dundurn Museum Musée Dundurn	12. Upper Hall Hall supérieur

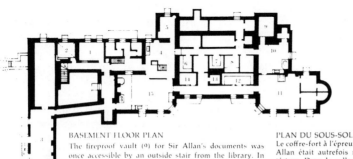

SECOND FLOOR PLAN

When the MacNab girls grew to womanhood the nursery (1) became their private sitting room. Private tutors instructed them in the school room (3). Today's museum (5, 6, 7) was originally three guest bedrooms. MacNab died in the sick room (8). Lady MacNab's boudoir (9) is tastefully furnished in the style of the 1830's and early 1840's. The wallpaper in Sir Allan's bedroom (10) is a replica of the original design. The hand-painted imitation marble in the upper hall (12) was found under several layers of paint at the time of restoration.

PREMIER ÉTAGE

Lorsque les filles MacNab grandirent, elles utilisèrent la chambre d'enfants (1) comme petit salon privé. L'enseignement leur était dispensé par un précepteur dans la salle d'étude (3). Le musée d'aujourd'hui (5, 6, 7) formait autrefois des chambres d'invités. MacNab mourut dans la salle de malade (8). Le boudoir de Lady MacNab (9) est décoré dans le style des années 1830 et du début de 1840. Le papier peint de la chambre de Sir Allan (10) est une réplique exacte de l'original. Le simili-marbre peint à la main dans le hall supérieur (12) a été découvert sous plusieurs couches de peinture au moment de la restauration.

1. Dairy Laiterie	9. Vault Coffre-fort
2. Ice Pit Fosse à glace	10. Well Room Salle du puits
3. Wash House Lavoir	11. Servant's Hall Hall des serviteurs
4. Scullery Arrière-cuisine	12. Dry Larder Garde-manger (denrées sèches)
5. Brew House Brasserie	13. Furnace or Plenum Chamber Salle de chauffage
6. Wine Cellar Cave à vin	14. Cook's Bedroom Chambre du cuisinier
7. Wet Larder Garde-manger	15. Kitchen Cuisine
8. Box Room Débarras	

BASEMENT FLOOR PLAN

The fireproof vault (9) for Sir Allan's documents was once accessible by an outside stair from the library. In the well room (10) with its cistern can be seen evidence of the original home on this site built by Richard Beasley. The furnace (13) is a large box stove that heated the air in a brick-lined chamber. The warm air rose in wooden flues. The spacious kitchen (15) has been fully restored. Cooking demonstrations can be seen here.

PLAN DU SOUS-SOL

Le coffre-fort à l'épreuve du feu (9) contenant les documents de Sir Allan était autrefois relié à la bibliothèque par un escalier extérieur. Dans la salle du puits (10) avec sa citerne on peut distinguer l'emplacement de la maison construite à l'origine par Richard Beasley. La chaudière (13) est un énorme poêle carré qui réchauffait l'air contenu dans une chambre garnie de brique. L'air chaud circulait par des tuyaux en bois. La spacieuse cuisine (15) a été entièrement restaurée. On peut y assister à des démonstrations d'art culinaire.

DUNDURN CASTLE

Château Dundurn = Dundurn Castle, Hamilton, Ontario. — Scale ca. 1:400. — Hamilton : The Castle, [197-?].

3 plans on 1 sheet ; 28 x 21 cm. folded to 10 x 22 cm.

Includes text in English and French.

On verso: Brief biography of Allan Napier McNab, the builder, a list of castle facilities and 2 ill., one a port.

Description of plans as cartographic materials — Ch.1 and Ch.3. Title as it appears on chief source of information is: Château Dundurn Castle. If a word appears only once but design of chief source of information makes it clear that it is intended to be read more than once, the word is repeated without the use of square brackets — 1.1B5. If there is more than one map, plan, etc. on a sheet, the number is specified — 3.5B2.

Work emanates from a corporate body and is considered to be of an administrative nature as it is intended to assist visitors when touring the building. It therefore appears to fall within the scope of 21.1B2(a) and is entered under the heading for the body. Name appears in two languages, both of which are official, so entry is under the English form — 24.3A.* No title added entry because title is essentially the same as main entry heading and could be covered by a reference.

E.R.P.B.

Nursery rhymes of Gloucestershire / by E.R.P.B. — Gloucester : British Publishing Co., [1967].

36 p. ; 19 cm.

1.	Title

Name consisting of initials entered under initials in direct order. Name-title reference from inverted form beginning with last letter — 22.10. *

ELECTRONICS. — London : H.M.S.O., 1967.

72 p., 2 folded leaves of plates : ill., forms ; 25 cm. — (Manpower studies ; no. 5).

Prepared by: Ministry of Labour. Manpower Research Unit.

1.	United Kingdom. <u>Ministry of Labour</u>. <u>Manpower Research Unit</u>

Statement of responsibility given in note — 1.1F2 and 1.7B6. Folded leaves described as such — 2.5B11.

Work emanating from corporate body but not falling into any of the categories listed at 21.1B2 is entered under title — 21.1C(3). Intervening element in hierarchy included in added entry heading as name of subordinate body might be used by another body entered under heading for same higher body — 24.14.

ELGAR, <u>Sir</u> Edward

Pomp and circumstance : military march no. 1, op. 39 / Edward Elgar. — London : Boosey and Hawkes, c1929.

1 miniature score (26 p.) ; 19 cm. — (Hawkes pocket scores).

For orchestra.

1.	Title†

Description of music — Ch.1 and Ch.5. Copyright date given as date of publication is unknown — 1.4F6. Term 'miniature score' used as specific material designation for score reduced in size and not primarily intended for performance — 5.5B1. Medium given in note because absent in description — 5.7B1.

Title of nobility or honour commonly appearing in association with name included — 22.1C.

101

EMPLOYMENT and productivity gazette. —
Vol. 76, no. 6 (Jun. 1968)-v. 78,
no. 12 (Dec. 1970). — London : H.M.S.O.,
1968-1970.
2-3 v. ; 28 cm.
Monthly.
Produced by the Department of
Employment and Productivity.
Continues: Ministry of Labour Gazette.
Continued by: Department of
Employment Gazette.

1.   United Kingdom. <u>Department of
Employment and Productivity</u>

Designation for completed serials — 12.3F. Date of
first issue and last issue given in publication area —
12.4F3. Specific material designation preceded by
number of parts — 12.5B2. Note on statement of
responsibility — 12.7B6. Note on relationship
with other serials — 12.7B7(c).

Work emanating from corporate body but not
falling within any of the categories listed at
21.1B2 is entered under title — 21.1C(3).
Separate main entry made if the title proper of
a serial changes — 21.2C.

See also example no. 210.

102

[ENCYCLOPAEDIA Britannica. Selections]
An anthology of pieces from early
editions of Encyclopaedia Britannica. —
London : Encyclopaedia Britannica, 1963.
64 p. : ill. ; 26 cm.
Extracts from the 1st ed., 1768-1771,
to the 8th ed., 1853-1860.

1.   An anthology of pieces from early
editions of Encyclopaedia
Britannica

Collection of extracts from a work entered under
the uniform title for the whole work followed by
'Selections' — 25.6B3. Optionally, a uniform
title used as a main entry heading may be
recorded without the square brackets — 25.2A.

103

ENROUTE / Air Canada. — Vol. 1, no. 1
(Jan. 1973)-   . — Weston, Ont. :
Southam Murray for Air Canada, 1973-   .
v. : ill. (some col.) ; 28 cm.
Ten times a year.
Inflight magazine.
In English and French.

1.   Air Canada

Description of printed serials — Ch.1, Ch.2 and
Ch.12. Two bodies named in publication area;
both are included in accordance with rule
authorising addition of words indicating
function of publisher — 1.4D3. (See also last
example in rule 1.4B8).

Work emanating from corporate body which
does not fall within any of the categories
listed in rule 21.1B2 and is therefore entered
under title — 21.1C(3). Added entry directly
under name of body — 24.1.

104

FAIRLESS, Michael
The roadmender and other writings / by
Michael Fairless ; with a biographical note
by M.E. Dowson ; an introduction by
Frederick Brereton ; and wood engravings
by Lennox Patterson. — New ed. / edited
by G.F. Maine. — London : Collins, 1950.
256 p. : ill. ; 25 cm.

1.   Title   2.   Maine, G.F.

Statement of responsibility relating to edition
recorded — 1.2C1.

Entry under pseudonym if person is predominantly
identified by that pseudonym — 22.2C1. (Reference
needed from real name: Barber, Margaret Fairless.)*
Added entry for prominently-named editor —
21.30D.

105

FALLA, Manuel de
    El sombrero de tres picos = Le tricorne =
The three-cornered hat : ballet / by Martinez
Sierra ; after a story by Alarcon ; [music by]
Manuel de Falla. — London : Chester, c1921.
    1 miniature score (xiv, 254 p.) ; 19 cm.
    Synopsis in English and French.
    Duration: 30 min.

1.   Title†   2.   Le tricorne
3.   The three-cornered hat†*
4.   Sierra, Martinez

Description of music — Ch.1 and Ch.5. Parallel
titles recorded in the order indicated on chief
source of information — 1.1D1 and 5.1D1. Work
is for orchestra, so no note is made on medium
of performance — 5.7B1.

Musical setting for ballet entered under heading
for composer — 21.20. Spanish name entered
under part following the prefix unless the prefix
consists of an article only — 22.5D1.

106

FARQUHAR, George
    The recruiting officer / by George
Farquhar ; edited by Michael Shugrue. —
London : Arnold, 1966.
    xxi, 137 p. ; 21 cm. — (Regents
Restoration drama series).

1.   Title   2.   Shugrue, Michael†
3.   Series

Not a work produced under editorial direction
but single personal authorship — 21.1A2 and 21.4A.

107

FASCIOLA hepatica = The liver fluke /
    [mounted by] Liverpool School of
Tropical Medicine. — Liverpool, 1975.
    1 microscope slide : glass, stained ;
3 x 8 cm.

1.   The liver fluke

Description of microscope slides — Ch.1 and Ch.10.
Parallel titles recorded in order indicated by chief

source of information — 1.1D1. Body responsible
for display of item recorded — 10.1F1. Words
added to statement of responsibility to indicate
relationship to title — 10.1F2. Material of which
object is made is given — 10.5C1. If a microscope
slide is stained (i.e. chemically treated so that the
specimen turns a reddish brown colour and it
becomes possible to see an outline of its interior
structure), this is stated — 10.5C2.

Entry under title because item does not fall into
one of the categories listed at 21.1B2 — 21.1C(3).

108

FILM guide for marketing executives / Sales
    and Marketing Executive-International ;
edited by William Wachs. — New York :
SME, 1966.
    xiii, 71 p. ; 28 cm. — (Research report).

1.   Sales and Marketing Executives-
        International

Foreword states that this item is the result of
staff research and enquiries made to a random
selection of SME members. It consists, however,
of a list of films and cannot be said to record
the collective thought of the corporate body
(see 21.1B2(c)). It is therefore entered under
title — 21.1C(3). If treated as a work produced
under editorial direction (21.7A(3)), entry
would still be under title. Added entry is under
the form of name which predominates in the
chief source of information. A reference would
be required from the alternative brief form of
name (SME).

109

FINZI, Gerald
    By footpath and stile : for baritone
solo with accompaniment of string
quartet / poems by Thomas Hardy ; music
by Gerald Finzi. — London : Curwen,
c1925.
    1 score (37 p.) + 4 parts ; 30 cm.
    Publisher's no.: 902902.

1.   Title   2.   Hardy, Thomas

Description of music — Ch.1 and Ch.5. Pagination and number of parts added to statement of extent — 5.5B3. Publisher's number recorded in note — 5.7B19.

110

FIRST over Everest : the Houston-Mount
    Everest Expedition, 1933 / by
P.F.M. Fellowes . . . [et al.] ; with a
foreword by John Buchan ; and an account
of the filming of the flight by Geoffrey
Barkas. — London : John Lane, the
Bodley Head, 1933.
    xix, 279 p., [50] leaves of plates
(some folded) : ill., maps, ports. ; 24 cm.
+ 1 pair spectacles.
    Spectacles, for viewing anaglyph in
stereoscopic relief, in pocket.

    1.   Fellowes, P.F.M.
    2.   Houston-Mount Everest Expedition
          (1933)

Accompanying material recorded in physical
description — 1.5E1(d) and 2.5E1. Additional
details of accompanying material and its location
given in a note — 2.5E2 and 2.7B11.

Work reporting the collective activity of an
expedition is entered under heading for expedition as corporate body provided that the work
emanates from body — 21.1B2(d). However,
although all of the four authors named on the
title page were members of the expedition, they
were writing in a personal, not an official,
capacity. Work is therefore treated as if no
corporate body were involved, and, since it is
by more than three personal authors, none of
whom has principal responsibility, entry is under
title — 21.6C2. An added entry may be made
under the heading for the expedition as a
prominently-named corporate body — 21.30E.

111

FLAX : from flax to linen. — Dundee : Flax
    Spinners' and Manufacturers'
Association, [196-?].
    1 display unit (various pieces) ; in box,
22 x 29 x 2 cm.
    Contents include various types of flax,
drawing of plant from which linen is made,
2 pamphlets and map on lid.

Description of three-dimensional artefacts — Ch.1
and Ch.10. If pieces of item cannot be named
concisely, the term 'various pieces' is used —
10.5B2. Details may then optionally be given in
a note — 10.7B10. Container named and its
dimensions given — 10.5D2.

112

FORT George National Historic Park,
    Ontario. — Ottawa : Parks Canada
under the authority of the Minister of
Indian Affairs and Northern Development,
1973.
    13, 13 p. : ill., plan, ports. ; 21 x 9 cm. —
(IAND publication ; no. QS-2073-000-
BB-A3).
    Text in English and French.
    Cover title.
    Pages numbered in opposite directions.

    1.   Series

Description of 'tête-bêche' work, that is one printed
in opposite directions. Chief sources of information
in more than one language — 1.0H(4). 1.0H(4)(a)
not applicable. Not known which is original
language of work — 1.0H(4)(c) therefore applies
and source in English used as it is the language
that occurs first in the list included in this rule.
Pages numbered in opposite directions — 2.5B15.
Width less than half the height — 2.5D2. Note
on source of title when there is no title page
as such — 2.0B1 and 2.7B3. Note on variation
of title — 2.7B4. Note on language of item and
physical description — 1.7B2, 2.7B2, 1.7B10
and 2.7B10.

113

FOSS, Sam Walter
    Song of the library staff / Sam Walter
Foss. — Detroit : Gale Research, [19—].
    5 broadsides.
    Five stanzas originally read by the
author (Librarian of Somerville, Mass.)
at the 1906 Annual Meeting of the
American Library Association and now
republished by Gale.

    Stanza 1: The cataloguer.
    1 broadside : ill. ; 56 x 22 cm.

    1.   Title   2.   The cataloguer

Multilevel description — 1.9B and 13.6. Choice of term 'broadside' — 2.5B2. Numeral which is the first word of a note that has not been quoted directly is spelled out — Appendix C.3. Width recorded, as it is less than half the height — 2.5D2.

Entry under person responsible for intellectual content — 21.1A1 and 21.1A2.

114

FOSTER, C.R.
    1907 Napier [from] National Motor Museum, Beaulieu / C.R. Foster. — Alresford, Hants. : Etchmaster Originals, [197-?].
    1 art print : copper engraving ; 21 x 28 cm.
    Size when framed: 25 x 32 cm.

    1.   Title

Description of art prints — Ch.1 and Ch.8. Word added to title enclosed in square brackets — 1.1A2. Name of county added to place of publication if considered necessary for identification — 1.4C3. (If 'Hants' had not appeared on item, it would have been enclosed in square brackets and spelled out in full as no abbreviations are prescribed for counties in United Kingdom — B.14). Printing process recorded — 8.5C2. Size when framed given as note — 8.7B10.

115

FREDDIE Mercury (Queen) / by London
    Features International. — London : Big O Posters, c1977.
    1 poster : col. ; 85 x 61 cm.
    B205.

    1.   London Features International

Description of posters as graphic materials — Ch.1 and Ch.8. Copyright date given — 1.4F6. Physical description — 8.5B1, 8.5C10 and 8.5D1.

Work emanating from corporate body which does not fall within categories listed at 21.1B2 and is therefore entered under title — 21.1C(3).

116

FREEMAN, William
    Dictionary of fictional characters / by William Freeman. — London : Dent, 1963.
    ix, 458 p. ; 20 cm.
    "4500 references to over 2000 works of fiction from 500 British and American authors"—Dustjacket.

    Dictionary of fictional characters : author and title indexes / J.M.F. Leaper. — 1965.
    p. 461-532 ; 20 cm.

    1.   Title   2.   Leaper, J.M.F.

Supplementary item catalogued as a dependent work using a multilevel description — 1.9B(3) and 13.6.

Alternatively, a supplementary item could be described independently as a separate item. The author and title indexes to Freeman's work could be catalogued in this way as illustrated in example no. 189.

117

FREEMASONS. Grand Lodge (Sussex)
    The ritual of Craft Masonry as practised in the province of Sussex complete with the ceremony of installation / published with the authority of the Grand Lodge of Sussex. — 2nd ed. — London : A. Lewis, 1968.
    vii, 183 p. : 3 ill. ; 14 cm.
    ISBN 0-85318-000-8.

    1.   Title

Number of illustrations specified if it can be easily ascertained — 2.5C4.

Work of administrative nature emanating from corporate body and dealing with its operations is entered under heading for body — 21.1B2(a). Name of body of ancient origin or that is international in character and that has become firmly established in English form is given in English — 24.3C2. Branch that carries out activities of corporate body in particular locality has name of locality added to it — 24.9.

FREUD, Sigmund
A psycho-analytic dialogue : the letters
of Sigmund Freud and Karl Abraham
1907-1926 / edited by Hilda C. Abraham
and Ernst L. Freud ; translated by Bernard
Marsh and Hilda C. Abraham. — London :
Hogarth Press, 1965.
xvii, 406 p., [2] leaves of plates : ports. ;
23 cm. — (The international psycho-
analytical library / edited by John D.
Sutherland ; no. 68).

1. Title   2. Abraham, Karl
3. Abraham, Hilda C.
4. Freud, Ernst L.   5. Series

Work consisting of exchange between two persons
is treated as work of shared responsibility —
21.6A(3). Principal responsibility not indicated
by wording or layout, so entry is under heading
for first named — 21.6C1.

119

The FUTURE role of business in society : a
special report of conference proceedings
from The Conference Board / edited by
Lillian W. Kay. — New York : The Board,
1977.
v, 57 p. ; 23 cm. — (Conference Board
report ; no. 710).
ISBN 0-8237-0143-3.

1. Kay, Lillian W.   2. Series

Conference without name (see definition — 21.1B1)
entered under title — 21.5A. 'The future role of
business in society' appears to be a general subject
description rather than a specific appellation.

120

GALL and Inglis' map of the Cumberland
and Westmorland Lake District. —
Scale [1:126,720]. ½ in. to 1 mile. —
Edinburgh : Gall and Inglis, [19—?].
1 map : col. ; 80 x 51 cm. folded to
22 x 8 cm.

Description of maps — Ch.1 and Ch.3. Title
proper includes statement of responsibility —

1.1B2. Verbal scale statement reads: 'Half an
inch to a mile.' Verbal scale is recorded as representative fraction in square brackets — 3.3B1.
Optionally, additional scale information found
on the item may be given — 3.3B2. Dimensions
of map given, measured between the 'neat lines',
i.e. the inner border of the map — 3.5D1. Map
contains section designed to appear on outside
when sheet is folded, so sheet size in folded form
is recorded — 3.5D1.

Work emanating from corporate body but not
falling within any of the categories listed at
21.1B2 is entered under title — 21.1C(3).

See also example no. 378.

121

GALLICO, Paul
The snow goose / by Paul Gallico ;
illustrations by Peter Scott. — [New]
illustrated ed. — London : M. Joseph, 1946.
55 p., [4] leaves of plates : ill. (some
col.) ; 26 cm.
First published: 1941.

1. Title   2. Scott, Peter†

Work which consists of text for which artist has
provided illustrations entered under the heading
appropriate to the text — 21.11A. Added entry
under illustrator as illustrations are considered an
important feature of work — 21.30K2(c).

122

GALLOWAY, John
Origins of modern art, 1905-1914 / by
John Galloway. — New York ; London :
McGraw-Hill, 1965.
47 p. : ill. ; 20 cm. + 24 slides : col.
Slides in pockets.

1. Title

If more than one place of publication is named
in the item, the first named place is always
recorded and the first of any subsequently
named places that are in the home country of
the cataloguing agency. 'London' would therefore be omitted if the item were being catalogued
in the United States — 1.4C5. (It is assumed,

though this is not made explicit in the rules, that when both the first-named place and a subsequently-named place are in the home country of the cataloguing agency, the latter is omitted, unless it is given prominence by the layout of the source of information.) Slides accompanying textual material — 1.5E1(d) and 2.5E1. Slides are standard 5 x 5 cm. size, so no dimensions are recorded — 8.5D5. Location of accompanying material given in note — 2.5E2 and 2.7B11.

Description of early printed monographs — Ch.2.12 - 2.18.

If name of personal author is unknown, and the only indication of authorship is the appearance in the chief source of information of a characterising word or phrase, entry is under the phrase in direct order, with the initial article omitted — 21.5C and 22.11D.

123

GARRETT, John
    Management by objectives in the civil service / John Garrett and S.D. Walker. — London : H.M.S.O., 1969.
    16 p. ; 25 cm. — (CAS occasional paper ; no. 10).
        ISBN 0-11-630014-0.

1. Title   2. Walker, S.D.
3. Series

Title proper of series is recorded in accordance with rules for title proper — 1.6B1. If title proper includes statement of responsibility as an integral part of it, it is transcribed as such — 1.1B2. If title proper includes separate letters or initials without full stops, these are recorded without spaces between them — 1.1B6. *

Work of shared responsibility in which principal responsibility is not indicated is entered under heading for the person or body named first — 21.6C1.

124

GENTLEMAN
    The lion and fawn : a legend / by a gentleman. — London : Printed for the author, [1797?].
    13 p. : coat of arms ; 23 cm. (4to).
    "Presented on their marriage to the Right Honourable the Earl and Countess of Derby".
    From the subject matter of the legend, it may be inferred that it refers to the marriage of the 12th Earl of Derby and Elizabeth Farren, the actress, on May 1, 1797.

1. Title

125

GEOGRAPHIC encyclopaedia for children / picture maps and illustrations by Wilhelm Eigener and August Eigener. — Rev. ed. — London : Hamlyn, 1967.
    257 p. : col. ill., maps ; 35 cm.
    One map on lining paper.

1. Eigener, Wilhelm
2. Eigener, August

Map on lining paper recorded in note — 2.5C5.

Work for which artist has provided illustrations entered under heading appropriate for text — 21.11A. Work of unknown authorship entered under title — 21.5A. Added entry under heading for illustrator if illustrations are considered important feature of work — 21.30K2(c).

126

GEORGE FRY & ASSOCIATES
    Study of circulation control systems : public libraries, college and university libraries, special libraries / George Fry & Associates, Incorporated. — Chicago : Library Technology Project of the American Library Association, 1961.
    vii, 138 p. ; 28 cm. — (LTP publications ; no. 1).
    Published jointly with the Council on Library Resources.
    Partially thumb indexed.

1. Title   2. Series
3. American Library Association.
        <u>Library Technology Project</u>
4. Council on Library Resources

Title proper of series recorded as instructed in 1.1B – 1.6B1. Title proper includes initials without full stops; the letters are recorded without spaces between them – 1.1B6.

Work emanating from corporate body which records the collective thought of the body entered under the heading for the body – 21.1B2(c). Entry directly under name – 24.1 Omission of 'Incorporated' – 24.5C1. Added entries under prominently named publishers when responsibility extends beyond that of merely publishing (the bodies named commissioned the work and assisted in the study) – 21.30E.

127

GERING, Robert L.
    Introduction to the water cycle / Robert L. Gering ; developed by Information Applications. — New York : Ward, 1970.
    1 filmstrip (99 fr., 4 title fr.) : sd., col. ; 35 mm. — (Ward's solo-learn system).
    Filmstrip and sound cassette contained in Bell & Howell Autoload Synchronous Cartridge for use in Bell & Howell Film-sound. Program selector should be set for 1,000 Hz.

    1.   Title   2.   Information
                                 Applications
    3.   Series

Description of filmstrips – Ch.1 and Ch.8. Sound noted as it is integral to item – 8.5C4.

128

GILBERT, Stuart
    James Joyce's Ulysses : a study / by Stuart Gilbert. — London : Faber, 1930.
    407 p. ; 22 cm.

    1.   Title   2.   Joyce, James†
                                 Ulysses

Texts published with commentary – 21.13. Chief source of information ambiguous, but entry is under heading for commentator because work is described as commentary in preface and only

selected passages from 'Ulysses' are included – 21.13D(1) and 21.13D(3). Rule 21.15A might also be relevant: text published with critical work and presented as critical work is entered under heading for critic – 21.15A.

129

GLAUERT, R.H.
    Trinity College / [photographs by R.H. Glauert ; text by R. Robson]. — Cambridge : Trinity College, 1967.
    [47] p. : chiefly ill. (some col.), map, plan ; 26 cm.
    Col. ill. reproduced from Ackermann's History of the University of Cambridge, 1815, and the endpapers from Loggans Cantabrigia illustrata, 1690.

    1.   Title   2.   Robson, R.

Unnumbered sequence of pages constitutes the whole of the item and exact number is enclosed within square brackets – 2.5B3. Note on important physical description details – 2.7B10.

Item appears to be a work of collaboration between an artist, i.e. a photographer, and a writer. Neither is given greater prominence and entry is therefore under heading for one named first (although the names appear in the colophon, not the chief source of information) – 21.24. Item in fact emanates from a corporate body but it is not of an administrative nature and therefore falls outside the categories listed in rule 21.1B2.

130

GLUCK, Christoph Willibald von
    [Alceste. English. Selections ; arr.]
    Scenes from Alcestis / C.W. von Gluck ; edited and arranged by Philip L. Baylis. — London : Oxford University Press, 1957.
    1 vocal score (64 p.) ; 25 cm.
    For solo voices (SSMMMAAA), chorus and piano.
    "For stage or concert presentation by female choirs and schools".

    1.   Title   2.   Scenes from Alcestis
    3.   Baylis, Philip L.

Description of music — Ch.1 and Ch.5. Note on medium of performance includes parenthetical statement of component voice parts, using prescribed abbreviations (i.e. the work is for two sopranos, three mezzo-sopranos and three altos) — 5.7B1.

Arrangement of composer's work entered under heading for composer — 21.18B. German whose name contains prefix which is not article or contraction of article and preposition is entered under the part following the prefix — 22.5D1. Uniform title for musical work is composer's original title in language in which it was formulated — 25.27A. If text is a translation the name of language is added — 25.5D and 25.31B7. 'Selections' added — 25.6B3 and 25.32B1. 'arr' added — 25.31B2.

131

GOETHE, Johann Wolfgang von
    [Faust]
    Urfaust : Johann Wolfgang Goethe's Faust in its original version (1775) / edited by R.H. Samuel. — 1st ed. repr. — London : Macmillan, 1967.
    xxviii, 110 p. : 2 facsims. ; 20 cm.
    First ed. originally published: London : Allen and Unwin, 1951.
    Bibliography: p. 109-110.

1.   Title   2.   Urfaust
3.   Samuel, R.H.

Statement relating to reprinting of particular edition included because changes have resulted from reprinting — 2.2D1.

German name with prefix entered under part of name following prefix unless prefix consists of article or contraction of article — 22.5D1. Uniform title for work created after 1500 is title in original language by which work has become known — 25.3A.

132

GONZALES, Pancho
    How to play and win at tennis / by Pancho Gonzales & Dick Hawk ; edited by Gladys Heldman. — 1st British ed. — London : Souvenir Press, 1963.
    123 p. : 126 ill. ; 23 cm.
    Originally published: New York : Fleet Publishing, 1962.

1.   Title   2.   Hawk, Dick†
3.   Heldman, Gladys

Edition statement (in this instance, relating to first edition in one country) transcribed as it appears in item — 2.2B1.

Principal responsibility not indicated on chief source of information, so entry is under heading for first-named person — 21.6C1. Entry is under name by which person is commonly known (Gonzales' initials are 'R.A.') — 22.1A. *

133

GOOD Housekeeping's cookery book / compiled by Good Housekeeping Institute. — Completely rev. and reset ed. — London : Cookery Book Club, 1968.
    608 p., [24] p. of plates : ill. (some col.) ; 26 cm.

1.   Good Housekeeping Institute

In the chief source of information appears the statement 'Completely rewritten and with new colour plates and black and white photographs'. As this statement neither constitutes other title information nor forms part of the statement of responsibility, it is omitted — 1.1F15. There is no instruction to indicate this omission by the mark of omission, i.e. three dots.

Work emanating from corporate body but not falling within any of the categories listed at 21.1B2 entered under title — 21.1C(3).

134

GOYA, Francisco
   Goya. — London : Visual Publications, [1969].
      1 filmstrip (38 fr.) : col. ; 35 mm. — (History of western art. Master painters ; no. 15).
      Cine mode.
      With teachers' notes (28 p.).

   1.   Series   2.   Master painters

Description of filmstrips — Ch.1 and Ch.8. No rules for distinguishing between cine mode (i.e. read top to bottom) and comic mode (i.e. read left to right or right to left); details are therefore given in note on physical description — 8.7B10 (see also example no. 185). Details of accompanying material recorded in note — 1.5E1(c) and 1.7B11.

Work consisting of reproductions of the works of an artist without accompanying text is entered under heading for the artist — 21.17A.

135

GRAHAM, Colin
   A penny for a song : an opera in two acts / [music by] Richard Rodney Bennett ; libretto by Colin Graham ; adapted from the play by John Whitling. — London : Universal Edition, 1967.
      64 p. ; 21 cm.
      Libretto only.

   1.   Title   2.   Bennett, Richard
                        Rodney
   3.   Whitling, John

Other title information preceded by colon; each subsequent statement of responsibility preceded by semi-colon — 2.1A1. No specific material designation for librettos, so details given in note on artistic form — 2.7B1. (It would be evident to a cataloguer that this item were a libretto, since a score would always be recorded as such in the physical description area. This would not be clear, however, to most catalogue users. Where a uniform title is used, the word 'Libretto' would be added to the uniform title in accordance with rule 25.31B5.)

Libretto as related work under its own heading — 21.28A and 21.28B. An alternative rule (p. 318, footnote 7) permits entry under the heading appropriate to the musical work which is, in this case, the composer.

136

GRANT, Alexander
   The Union Jack / Alexander Grant. — [Liverpool, 1975].
      1 transparency (2 attached overlays) : col. ; 14 x 20 cm.
      Illustrates how the Union Jack is made up from the Crosses of St. George, St. Andrew and St. Patrick.
      Size when framed: 32 x 32 cm.

   1.   Title

Description of overhead transparencies as graphic materials — Ch.1 and Ch.8. Physical description — 8.5B1, 8.5B4, 8.5C16, 8.5D4. Note on nature of item — 8.7B1. Note on physical description — 8.7B10.

Entry under person responsible for artistic content — 21.1A1 and 21.1A2.

See also next example.

137

GRANT, Alexander, B. Com.
   Modern method book-keeping . . . / by Alexander Grant. — Glasgow : R. Gibson, c1934.
      152 p. ; 19 cm.
      "For day and evening classes".

   1.   Title

If dates are not available to distinguish between two identical names (see previous example) entered under surname, a term of address, title of position or office, initials of an academic degree, etc. are added — 22.19B.

GREATER LONDON COUNCIL
[Building acts]
London building acts 1930-1939 :
constructional bylaws. — London : Greater
London Council, 1968.
    100 p. ; 30 cm. — (Publications /
Greater London Council ; 156).

1.   Title   2.   London building
                              acts 1930-1939

Statement of responsibility relating to series
preceded by diagonal slash — 1.6A1 and 1.6E1.

Laws entered under heading for appropriate
corporate body — 21.1B2(b). Laws governing
one jurisdiction entered under heading for
jurisdiction governed by them — 21.31B1.
Uniform title for collection of laws is 'Laws, etc.'
unless they all deal with one subject, in which
case citation title is used — 25.15A1.

138

GREENBANK HIGH SCHOOL FOR GIRLS
    (Sefton)
    Parents' handbook / Greenbank High
School for Girls. — [Sefton : The School],
1978.
    11 leaves ; 26 cm.

1.   Title

Pagination recorded in terms of leaves — 2.5B2.

Work of administrative nature emanating from
corporate body and dealing with body itself is
entered under heading for body — 21.1B2(a).
Body entered directly under name — 24.1.
Addition of local place name in which body is
located if body could be confused with others of
the same or similar names — 24.4C3. References
would be required for change of name — 26.3C1.*
Until 1978, name of school was Southport High
School for Girls.

139

Greene, Robert — Friar Bacon & Friar Bungay.
London. 1594. 63p. complete on 1 card.

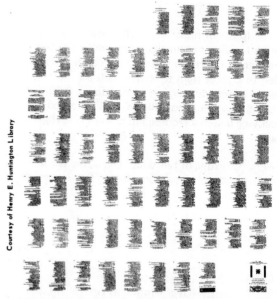

Courtesy of Henry E. Huntington Library

Three Centuries of Drama: English   1500 - 1641   Readex Microprint * New York 1965

140

GREENE, Robert
    Friar Bacon & Friar Bungay / Robert
Greene. — New York : Readex Microprint,
1965.
    1 microopaque (64 fr.). — (Three
centuries of drama. English, 1500-1641).
    Microreproduction of original published:
London, 1594. 63 p.

1.   Title   2.   Series

Description of microforms — Ch.1 and Ch.11. No
instructions given for recording the number of
frames on a microopaque but, as it seems useful
to include this information, the rules for microfiches have been followed — 11.5B1. Reduction
is between 16x and 30x, so this need not be
recorded — 11.7B10. Details of original given in
note — 1.7B7.

96

141

GROSSMITH, George
    The diary of a nobody / by George and Weedon Grossmith ; with the original illustrations by Weedon Grossmith. — London : Heinemann Educational, 1968.
    180 p. : ill. ; 20 cm. — (New windmill series ; 120).

  1.   Title   2.   Grossmith, Weedon
  3.   Series

Same person named twice in successive statements of responsibility but as such statements are to be recorded as given in the item — 1.1F1, both statements must be given and name repeated.

Responsibility shared between two persons; principal responsibility not attributed to either, so entry is under heading for one named first — 21.6C1.

142

GUIDE to inns of character in Lancashire / D.G. Jackson Advertising Service. — Halifax : Jackson, [1964?].
    63 p. : ill., maps ; 19 cm.

  1.   D.G. Jackson Advertising Service

Work emanating from corporate body but not falling within any of the categories listed at 21.1B2 is entered under title — 21.1C(3). No modification in added entry heading of name of corporate body containing initials — 24.1. *

143

A GUIDE to the better care of L.P. and stereo records : their mechanics and maintenance / Cecil E. Watts Limited. — 2nd ed. — Sunbury-on-Thames [Middlesex] : Watts, 1968.
    48 p. : ill. ; 22 cm.

  1.   Cecil E. Watts Ltd.

Name of county added to name of place of publication when considered necessary for identification — 1.4C3.

Work emanating from corporate body but not falling within any of the categories listed at 21.1B2 is entered under title — 21.1C(3). Term indicating incorporation included in added entry heading to make it clear that the name is that of corporate body — 24.5C1.

144

HANDEL, George Frederic
    [Messiah. Selections. Vocal score ; arr.]
    Unto us a child is born : music from Handel's Messiah / arranged as a Christmas cantata for two-part chorus with optional ripieno chorus by Watkins Shaw. — London : Novello, c1964.
    1 vocal score (40 p.) ; 16 cm.
    Duration: 20 min.

  1.   Title   2.   Unto us a child is
                            born
  3.   Shaw, Watkins

Duration of performance given if stated in the item of music being described — 5.7B10.

Uniform titles for music — for item consisting of extracts from a work, uniform title is title for whole work followed by 'Selections' — 25.32B1 and 25.6B3. 'Vocal score' added — 25.31B3. Addition of 'arr.' — 25.31B2.

145

HARRINGTON, Wilfred J.
    The Gospel according to St. Luke : a commentary / by Wilfred J. Harrington. — London : Chapman, 1968.
    vi, 297 p. ; 23 cm.
    Originally published: Westminster : Newman, 1967.
    Bibliography: p. 295-297.

  1.   Title
  2.   [Bible. <u>N.T. Luke. English.
          Revised Standard. 1946</u>]

Chief source of information presents item as commentary, and so it is entered as such, with added entry under heading appropriate to text — 21.13B. In added entry heading, individual book entered as subheading of appropriate testament of Bible — 25.18A3. *

Planning...

Pre-notification...

Preparation...

Processing...

Putting it on record...

Drawings by Tony Hart from the film "Meetings, Bloody Meetings"

© Copyright Video Arts Limited 1976

Video Arts Limited, 205 Wardour Street, London W1V 3FA

146

HART, Tony
    [Meetings, bloody meetings. Selections]
    Planning — pre-notification — prepara-
tion — processing — putting it on record — :
drawings / by Tony Hart. — London : Video
Arts, c1976.
    5 pictures on 1 sheet : b&w ; 30 x 22
cm.
    "From the film "Meetings, bloody
meetings". "

    1.   Title
    2.   Planning — pre-notification —
          preparation — processing —
          putting it on record

— replaces . . . when the latter punctuation mark
appears in title proper — 1.1B1. Noun occurring
in conjunction with a statement of responsibility
which is indicative of the nature of the work is
treated as other title information — 1.1F12.
Copyright date given — 1.4F6. This item, which
is considered to be a graphic, is difficult to describe
using Ch.8. 'Picture' seems to be the most relevant
specific material designation but
    1 picture : b&w ; 30 x 22 cm.
or   5 pictures : b&w ; 30 x 22 cm.
provide misleading information. The above
interpretation has therefore been formulated
by analogy with 3.5B2. An alternative interpretation would be to treat the item as a printed
sheet according to Ch.2, i.e.
    1 sheet : ill. ; 30 x 22 cm.

Entry is under the person responsible for the
artistic content — 21.1A1 and 21.4A. When an
item consists of a collection of extracts from a
work, the uniform title for the whole work is
used followed by 'Selections' — 25.6B3.

147

HAVELOK ; and, Sir Orfeo / translated
    into modern English by Robert
Montagu. — Leicester : Ward, 1954.
    118 p., 4 leaves of plates : 6 ill. ;
19 cm. — (The golden legend series).
    Includes as appendix: Orpheus and
Eurydice / Boethius ; translated by Alfred
the Great.

    1.   Sir Orfeo
    2.   [Havelok the Dane. English]
    3.   Montagu, Robert   4.   Series
    5.   Optionally, author and title
          analyticals for Orpheus and
          Eurydice

Collection of translations of works by different
authors entered as general collections — 21.14B.
Collection lacking collective title entered under
heading appropriate to first work, with added
entry under heading for other work — 21.7C.
Translation entered under heading appropriate
to original — 21.14A. Work of unknown
authorship entered under title — 21.5A. If
added entry is required for basic story found in
many versions, title that is established in
English-language reference sources is used as
uniform title; language of item is added — 25.12A.

HERRMANN, Reinhard
    The wedding at Cana /illustrated by
Reinhard Herrmann. — [English ed.]. —
London : Methuen Children's Books, 1972.
    1 folded sheet ([16] p.) : chiefly col.
ill. ; 95 mm. — (Zig zag books ; 15).
    "Based on John 2, I-XI".
    First published in West Germany: 1959.
    Brief text on verso.
    ISBN 0-416-75220-9.

    1.   Title

Sheet designed to be used only in folded form is
described as '1 folded sheet'. Number of imposed
pages and height of sheet when folded given --
2.5D4.

HILTON, John Buxton
    [Death of an alderman /John Buxton
Hilton]. — London : National Library for
the Blind, 1969.
    3 v. of braille ; 35 cm.
    Previously published: London : Cassell,
1968.

    1.   Title

Description of work in braille — Ch.1 and Ch.2.
Title proper is given in braille, i.e. in symbols
that cannot be reproduced by the typographic
facilities available, and it is therefore romanised
by the cataloguer and given in square brackets —
1.1B1 (see also 1.0E). The same applies to the
statement of responsibility — 1.1F9. Physical
description for braille or other raised types —
2.5B23. Note on history — 1.7B7 and 2.7B7.

Heading for name written in nonroman script
is romanised — 22.3C2.

See also example no. 324.

HIM, George
    Ann and Ben /artist George Him. —
London : Macmillan Educational, 1974.
    [12] p. : all col. ill. ; 97 mm. x
20 cm. — (The language project.
Language in action).
    "Core book at pre-literacy level,
devised to develop skill in left-to-right
orientation and ability to follow story
sequence".
    ISBN 0-333-16565-9.

    1.   Title   2.   Series

Book consisting solely of illustrations — 2.5C6.
Height less than 10 cm. given in mm. — 2.5D1.
Width given as it is greater than height — 2.5D2.
Note on intended audience — 1.7B14 and 2.7B14.

Entry under heading for person responsible for
creation of intellectual or artistic content of
work — 21.1A1.

HISTORICAL reconstructions of Pompeii. —
    Chicago : Encyclopaedia Britannica
Educational, 1965.
    4 study prints (1 attached overlay each) ;
33 x 46 cm. + 1 teacher's study guide
card. — (History series ; no. 5680).
    Each print shows part of ruins of
Pompeii. Addition of transparent overlay
depicts original building. Verso of each
print has historical details, photo., diagrams
and questions for students.
    "Suggested uses: World history, Latin,
art".
    Produced in collaboration with John
W. Eadie.
    In plastic wallet.

    1.   Series

Description of study prints as graphic materials —
Ch.1 and Ch.8. Overlays for study prints have
been recorded by analogy with rules for
transparencies — 8.5B4 and 8.5B5.

HODIN, J.P.
      Edvard Munch / J. P. Hodin. — London :
Thames and Hudson, 1972.
      216 p. : 168 ill. (some col.) ; 21 cm. —
(World of art library. Artists).
      Bibliography: p. 211.

      1.   Title   2.   Munch, Edvard

Series and subseries recorded — 1.6H1.

Work consisting of reproductions of the works
of an artist and text about the artist. Entry is
under the heading for the writer, as he is
represented as the author of the work in the
chief source of information — 21.17B. Added
entry under heading for artist.

Ministry of Public
Building and Works

THE CROWN JEWELS

at the
TOWER OF LONDON

BY MARTIN HOLMES, F.S.A.

LONDON
HER MAJESTY'S STATIONERY OFFICE
1968

HOLMES, Martin
      The crown jewels at the Tower of
London / by Martin Holmes. — 3rd ed. —
London : H.M.S.O., 1968.
      36 p. : ill. (some col.) ; 20 cm. —
(Ministry of Public Building and Works
official guide).
      At head of title: Ministry of Public
Building and Works.

      1.   Title   2.   Series
      3.   United Kingdom. Ministry of Public
           Building and Works

Title transcribed exactly as to wording, order and
spelling but not as to capitalisation — 1.1B1. Not
considered necessary to capitalise 'crown jewels'
but 'Tower of London' capitalised in accordance
with A.16. Her Majesty's Stationery Office
abbreviated — B.9.

Work emanates from a corporate body but does
not fall into any of the categories listed in rule
21.1B2 and is therefore entered under the personal
author — 21.1A2 and 21.4A.

Compare with example no. 325.

HOLOGRAPHIC portrait of Professor
      Gabor / produced by McDonnel
Douglas Electronics Company. — St Charles,
Mo. : The Co., [197-].
      1 hologram : col. ; on photographic
plate, 44 x 59 cm.
      "Taken with a 30 nanosecond, 10 Joules
pulsed laser of a coherent length of about
5 metres".

      1.   McDonnel Douglas Electronics
           Company

There are no specific rules in AACR 2 for describing
a hologram (a record of three-dimensional images
on a photographic plate). Although the image
projected from it is three-dimensional, the hologram itself is two-dimensional. It is therefore
treated here as a graphic, except that, as none of
the listed designations in rule 8.5B1 is appropriate,
the specific name is given by analogy with Ch.10.

HOME beer and winemaking. — Vol. 1, no. 1
   (Jan. 1970)-   . — Wirral : Foremost
Press, 1970-   .
      v. : ill. ; 28 cm.
   Monthly.
   Library has v.8, no.3 (Apr. 1977)-
   ISSN 0041-090X.

Description of printed serials — Ch.1, Ch.2 and
Ch.12. Transcription of title — 1.1B1. Volume
designation and dating — 12.3B1, 12.3C1 and
12.3C4. Publication details — 1.4 and 12.4. Date
followed by hyphen and four spaces — 12.4F1.
Specific material designation for a printed serial
is 'v'. For a serial that is still in progress, this is
preceded by three spaces — 1.5B5 and 12.5B1.
Physical description of a printed serial — 2.5
i.e. the chapter dealing with the type of material
to which this serial belongs. Note on frequency —
12.7B1. Note on library's holdings if required —
1.7B20, 2.7B20 and 12.7B20. ISSN — 1.8B1
and 12.8B1.

HORN, Gladys M.
   Adventures with language / by Gladys
M. Horn ; illustrated by Roberta Paflin. —
Racine, Wis. : Whitman Publishing, 1961.
   80 p. : col. ill. ; 31 cm. — (Help yourself
series).
   "Beginning workbook in English . . .
planned so that a child can work indepen-
dently"—Cover and inside cover.
   Pages are perforated to tear out.

   1.   Title   2.   Paflin, Roberta
   3.   Series

Name of state added to place of publication —
1.4C3, using abbreviation appearing in Appendix B.
Note which is a quotation given in quotation
marks and source indicated — 1.7A3. Note on
physical description — 1.7B10 and 2.7B10.

Work for which artist has provided illustrations
under the heading appropriate to the text —
21.11A. Added entry for illustrator because name
is given equal prominence in the chief source of
information — 21.30K2(a).

HOY, Peter
   Silence à minuit / par Peter Hoy ;
illustrations de Rigby Graham. — Wymond-
ham, Leics. : Brewhouse Press, 1967.
   1 portfolio (2 broadsides : ill. ;
54 x 39 cm. folded to 17 x 20 cm.).
   French and English text.
   Second title page in English: Silence
at midnight.
   Limited ed. of 200 copies.

   1.   Title   2.   Graham, Rigby

Chief sources of information in 2 languages, but
as translation is not the purpose of the publication, the source in original language is taken as
authority — 1.0H(4b). Choice of term 'portfolio' —
2.5B18. Specific instructions for describing the
contents of a portfolio are not included in rules.
Such contents could be described in a note, but,
if it is desired to include fuller details in the physical
description area, a format similar to the one
illustrated here — adopted by analogy with rule
for 'monographs contained in more than one
volume' (2.5B20) — could be used. Both height
and width of single sheets recorded, including
dimensions when folded if sheet is designed for
issue folded — 2.5D4. Language of item and
variation in title recorded in notes — 2.7B2 and
2.7B4. Note relating to edition — 2.7B7.

HOYLAKE AMATEUR OPERATIC AND
   DRAMATIC SOCIETY
   "A pair of silk stockings" and "The
man in the bowler hat" : [programme of
a production] / presented by The Hoylake
Amateur Operatic and Dramatic Society
[at the] Winter Gardens, Hoylake, March
15th to 19th 1927. — [Hoylake : Winter
Gardens] , 1927.
   [12] p. ; 23 cm.
   Chiefly advertisements.
   Cover title.

   1.   Title

Titles of individual parts of a work are separated
by a semi-colon — 1.1G2. However, in this
example, the two titles together constitute the

single title proper of the programme and so there is no semi-colon. First word of every title quoted is capitalised — A.4B. If title proper needs explanation, a brief addition is made as other title information — 1.1E6.

Work emanating from corporate body and recording collective activity of an event is entered under heading for body — 21.1B2(d). If considered necessary, a name-title added entry could be made for each of the works involved — 21.30G.

159

HUPFELD, Herman
    As time goes by / Herman Hupfeld. — London : United Artists, [1977].
    on 1 side of 1 sound disc (3 min., 10 sec.) : 45 rpm, mono. ; 7 in.
    Sung by Dooley Wilson ; with the voices of Humphrey Bogart and Ingrid Bergman.
    Edited from original soundtrack of the film : Casablanca, cWarner Bros., 1943.
    With : I'll string along with you / Harry Warren, Al Dubin ; sung by Dick Powell.
    United Artists : UP 36331A.

    1.   Title   2.   Wilson, Dooley

Separate description for separately titled work on sound recording lacking a collective title — 6.1G1, 6.1G4, 6.5B3 and 6.7B21. Duration less than five minutes given in minutes and seconds — 6.5B2. Performers named in note — 6.1F1 and 6.7B6.

When an item has been described separately, entry is made under the heading appropriate to that work — 21.23A, which, in this instance, is that of the composer of the music — 21.1A1, 21.1A2 and 21.4A.

An alternative method would be to describe the sound recording as a unit, as illustrated in next example.

The above example and the next example reflect a strict interpretation of the rules but example no. 66 should also be examined.

See also examples no. 202 and 203.

HUPFELD, Herman
    As time goes by / Herman Hupfeld. I'll string along with you / Harry Warren, Al Dubin. — London : United Artists, [1977].
    1 sound disc (8 min.) : 45 rpm, mono. ; 17 in.
    Sung by Dooley Wilson, with the voices of Humphrey Bogart and Ingrid Bergman, and Dick Powell.
    Edited from the original soundtracks of the films : Casablanca and 20 million sweethearts.
    United Artists : UP 36331.

    1.   Title
    2.   Warren, Harry
            I'll string along with you
    3.   Dubin, Al
            I'll string along with you
    4.   I'll string along with you
    5.   Wilson, Dooley
    6.   Powell, Dick

Sound recording without collective title described as a unit — 6.1G1, 6.1G2 and 1.1G2.

Collection of independent works by different persons — 21.7A — item without collective title is entered under the heading for the first work named in the chief source of information. If item lacks a collective chief source of information, as in this instance, it is entered under the heading for the first work — 21.7C. The 'first work' is taken to be that named on the 'A' side of the disc.

An alternative method would be to produce a separate description for each separately titled work, as illustrated in previous example.

The above example and the previous example reflect a strict interpretation of the rules but example no. 66 should also be examined.

IAMBLICHUS, of Chalcis
    Iamblichus on the mysteries of the
Egyptians, Chaldeans and Assyrians /
translated from the Greek by Thomas
Taylor. — 3rd ed. — London : Stuart and
Watkins, 1968.
    xxvi, 365 p. : port. ; 23 cm.
    ISBN 0-7224-0081-0.

Name associated with responsibility for item
transcribed as part of title proper, so no further
statement relating to name is made — 1.1F13.

Name that does not include surname entered
under part of name under which person is listed
in reference sources. Phrase commonly associated
with name and denoting place of origin is
included — 22.8A. No added entry under translator unless work falls within one of categories
listed at 21.30K1. No added entry under title
because it is essentially the same as main entry
heading — 21.30J.

[IMPERATORIS Iustiniani institutiones.
    English]
    The institutes of Justinian : text,
translation and commentary / J.A.C.
Thomas. — Amsterdam ; Oxford : North-
Holland Publishing, 1975.
    xviii, 355 p. ; 26 cm.
    Latin text, parallel English translation.
    ISBN 0-7204-8038-8.

1.   Title   2.   The institutes of
                              Justinian
3.   Thomas, J.A.C.
4.   Justinian, Emperor of Rome

When more than one place of publication is named
in the item, the first is always recorded, followed
by the first of any subsequent ones in the home
country of the cataloguing agency — 1.4C5.

Texts published with commentary — 21.13. Chief
source of information presents item as original
work, so entry is under heading for that, with an
added entry under the heading for the commentator — 21.13C. Laws of ancient jurisdiction are
entered under uniform title, which is established
in accordance with the general rules for uniform
titles for ancient works — 21.31C and 25.15B.
Uniform title for work created before 1501 is
the title in the original language — 25.4A. For
work entered under uniform title, added entry
is made under title proper — 25.2D1. Added
entry under heading for person having relationship to work if heading provides important
access point — 21.30F. English form of name
used for person entered under given name —
22.3B3. To the heading for a monarch is added a
phrase consisting of the title in English and the
name of the state governed — 22.17A1.

IN the beginning. — London : Scripture
    Union ; Loughborough : Ladybird,
1978.
    [28] p. : chiefly col. ill. ; 27 x 13 cm. —
(A Ladybird Bible book ; [1]).
    16 slides : col.
    Majority of slides correspond to scenes
from book.
    In transparent folder.
    ISBN 0-0-85421-724-X (Scripture
Union).
    ISBN 0-7214-0562-2 (Ladybird).

1.   Series

Description of items made up of more than one
material — 1.10. Separate physical descriptions
for each class of material recorded on separate
lines — 1.10C2(b). Description of printed
monographs — Ch.2. Description of slides — Ch.8.
If an item bears two ISBN's, both may optionally
be recorded, with appropriate qualifications —
1.8B2 and 1.8E1.

164

INSECTS harmful to man / produced by
    Encyclopaedia Britannica Films in
collaboration with John A. Wagner. —
Chicago : E.B. Films, 1966.
    8 study prints : col. ; 44 x 28 cm.
folded to 22 x 28 cm. + 1 introductory
card + 1 teacher's guide and answer card. —
(Basic life science program) (Study print
series ; no. 5650).
    Each card has holes at corners for
pinning to wall.
        Contents: Aphids — Boll weevils —
Earwigs — Cockroaches — Houseflies.

    1.   Encyclopaedia Britannica Films
    2.   Wagner, John A.   3.   Series

Description of study prints — Ch.1 and Ch.8.
Accompanying material recorded in physical
description area — 1.5E1(d). More than one
series statement — 1.6J1.

See also example no. 353.

165

INTERNATIONAL EXHIBITION OF WILD
    LIFE PHOTOGRAPHY (2nd : 1950 :
    Westminster)
    Wonders of wild life photography : being
a selection of photographs from the second
'Country Life' International Exhibition. —
London : Country Life, 1950.
    96 p. : all ill. ; 26 cm.

    1.   Title   2.   Country Life

Exhibition as corporate body — 21.1B1 and
21.1B2(d). * Entry directly under the name,
which is given in a publisher's note as The Second
International Exhibition of Wild Life Photography — 24.1. Omission of number — 24.8A.
Addition to heading of number, date and
place — 24.8B.

166

INTERNATIONAL labour review. — Vol. 1
    (1921)-   . — Geneva : International
Labour Office, 1921-
        v. ; 25 cm.
    Monthly.
    Vol. 66 (July-Dec. 1952)-v. 90 (July-
Dec. 1964) includes: Statistical supplement,
which is continued from 1965 by: Bulletin
of labour statistics.

    1.   International Labour Office
    2.   International labour review
            statistical supplement.

Note on supplement to serial — 12.7B7.

Work emanating from corporate body but not
falling within any of the categories listed at 21.1B2
is entered under title — 21.1C(3). The International
Labour Office would need to be linked by references to the related corporate heading International
Labour Organisation — 26.3B1. *

167

INTERNATIONAL SUNDAY SCHOOL
    CONVENTION. (11th : 1905 : Toronto)
    The development of the sunday-school,
1780-1905 : the official report of the
Eleventh International Sunday-School
Convention, Toronto, Canada, June 23-27,
1905. — Boston [Mass.] : International
Sunday-School Association, 1905.
    xx, 712 p. : ill., ports. ; 21 cm.

    1.   Title

Conference as corporate body — 21.1B1 and
21.1B2(d).

168

JACOB, Naomi
    Four generations / Naomi Jacob. —
[New ed.] . — London : Hutchinson, 1973.
    256 p. ; 20 cm. — (The Gollantz saga /
Naomi Jacob ; 4th).
    Originally published: 1934.
    ISBN 0-09-114900-2.

    1.   Title

Popes — a work which is not an official communication entered under personal heading — 21.4D2.
Designation *Pope* added to heading — 22.17B.

A work written by a Pope acting in an official
capacity would be entered as a subheading under
'Catholic Church' — 24.27B2. In the above example
an explanatory reference would be made from the
corporate heading to the personal heading — 21.4D2
and 26.3C1. *

Item contains 4 pages and 1 leaf of plates, so
number is recorded in terms of whichever is predominant — 2.5B10. Contents note for bibliography — 2.7B18.

The typography of the title page, and the use of
the indefinite article (see 21.1B1), indicate that this
is a conference which lacks a name and so is entered
under title — 21.5A.

John Dalton
& the progress
of science

*Papers presented
to a conference
of historians
of science
held in
Manchester
September 19-24
1966 to mark
the bicentenary
of Dalton's birth*

Edited by
D S L Cardwell

Manchester University Press

Barnes & Noble Inc, New York

175
JOHN Dalton and the progress of science :
    papers presented to a conference of
historians of science held in Manchester,
September 19-24, 1966, to mark the bi-
centenary of Dalton's birth / edited by
D.S.L. Cardwell. — Manchester : Manchester
University Press, 1968.
    xxii, 352 p., 5 p. of plates : ill., ports. ;
23 cm.
    Bibliography: p. 344.
    ISBN 0-7190-0301-6.

1.   Cardwell, D.S.L.

176
JOHNSON, Jeanette
    Mother Earth : in the bosom of Mother
Earth radiates the life energy of the sun /
Jeanette Johnson. — [19-].
    1 art original : sand on board, col. ;
33 x 18 cm.
    Indian sand painting originating from
New Mexico.
    Size when framed: 35 x 20 cm.

1.   Title

Description of art originals — Ch.1 and Ch.8. For
art originals, publication area includes date only —
8.4A2. No authority for using term 'sand painting'
as specific material designation (8.5B1), so this is
recorded as note on artistic form — 8.7B1. Size
when framed recorded as note — 8.7B10.

177
JOINT F.A.O./W.H.O. EXPERT
    COMMITTEE ON AFRICAN
    TRYPANOSOMIASIS
    African trypanosomiasis : report of a
Joint F.A.O./W.H.O. Expert Committee. —
Geneva : W.H.O., 1969.
    79 p. ; 24 cm. — (Technical report
series / World Health Organisation ; no. 434)
(Agricultural studies / Food and Agricultural
Organisation ; no. 81).

1.   Title   2.   Series
3.   Agricultural studies / Food and
        Agricultural Organisation

Statements of responsibility relating to series
included — 1.6E1. Two separate series statements
recorded — 1.6J1.

Work emanating from corporate body and recording its collective thought is entered under heading for body — 21.1B2(c). Body made up of representatives of two or more bodies entered under its own name — 24.15A. *

178

KFA

　Juelich Nuclear Research Center : facts and trends / edited and arranged by Helmuth F. Wust ; translated by Ralf Friese ; illustrations by Hans Schneider ; photographs by Karl Peters and Heinz Josef Ohling ; aerial photographs by Aerolux, Frankfurt ; plates by Walter Haarhaus, Cologne and Zerreiss & Co., Nuremberg. — Juelich : KFA, 1971.
　　102 p. : ill. ; 21 x 24 cm.

　1.　Wust, Helmuth F.

More than one statement of responsibility — 1.1F6. Width greater than height — 2.5D2.

Work is of an administrative nature in that it serves as an advertisement for the operations of the corporate body from which it emanates. It is therefore entered under the heading for the body — 21.1B2(a). Body entered directly under the name by which it is predominantly identified in items issued by that body in its language — 24.1 (The Juelich Nuclear Research Center is commonly called KFA for Kernforschungsanlage). References will be required from the alternative forms of name — 26.3A3. As title proper is essentially the same as a reference to the main entry heading, no added title entry is necessary — 21.30J(1).

179

KENT State University, Ohio, 1910. — [197-] (East Liverpool, Ohio : W.C. Bunting).
　　1 miniature souvenir tankard : pottery, black and gold ; 6 cm. high.

Description of three-dimensional artefacts and realia — Ch.1 and Ch.10. Title proper consists solely of the body responsible for the item — 1.1B3. Approximate date of manufacture — 1.4F7. Place and name of manufacture given — 10.4G1. Name of state added to place of manufacture if considered necessary — 1.4C3. Name of state is not abbreviated as it does not appear in list in B14. None of listed terms appropriate so specific name of item is given as concisely as possible — 10.5B1. Material recorded — 10.5C1, colours given — 10.5C2. Dimension given with word added to indicate which dimension — 10.5D1.

180

KHACHATURIAN, Aram

　The "Onedin Line" theme ; Sabre dance / Khachaturian. — London : Decca, 1971.
　　1 sound disc (ca. 8 min.) : 45 rpm, stereo. ; 7 in.
　　Vienna Philharmonic Orchestra, Aram Khachaturian, conductor.
　　First item consists of "Music from "Spartacus" as adapted for the BBC-TV series by Anthony Isaac".
　　Decca: F 13259.

　1.　Title　　2.　Sabre dance
　3.　Vienna Philharmonic Orchestra
　4.　Isaac, Anthony†

Sound recording without a collective title described as a unit — 6.1G1, 6.1G2 and 1.1G2.

Sound recording of two or more works all by the same person under the heading appropriate to those works — 21.23B.

181

KING, Martin Luther

　Stride toward freedom : the Montgomery story / by Martin Luther King ; with a foreword by Trevor Huddleston. — London : Gollancz, 1959, c1958.
　　216 p. ; 21 cm.

　1.　Title

Latest date of copyright may optionally be given after the date of publication if they are different — 1.4F5.

Name containing compound surname is entered in accordance with the preferred or established form if this is known — 22.5C2. Surname is frequently followed by 'Jr'. Words indicating relationship are omitted (except when they are needed to distinguish between two or more identical names), unless the surname is Portuguese — 22.5C8.

182

[KORAN. al-Súrah XXI-CXIV. English]
The Koran interpreted. Volume two : Suras XXI-CXIV / by Arthur J. Arberry. — London : Allen and Unwin, 1955.
    367 p. ; 22 cm.
    Second of 2 v.

1. The Koran interpreted
2. Arberry, J.

If title proper for an item that is a section of another item appears in two parts not grammatically linked, the title of the main work is recorded first, followed by a full stop and the title of the section — 1.1B9.

Uniform title for sacred scripture is title by which it is most commonly identified in English language reference sources — 25.17. Individual chapters of the Koran are entered by name as a subheading of the Koran in the form: KORAN. Surat al-Baqarah. A reference is then made from the sūrah number in the form: KORAN al-Súrah II — 25.18M1. There is no specific rule for recording a sequence of chapters identified only by numbers, but additions to uniform title may be made as instructed in 25.5 and 25.6, so the rule for items consisting of consecutive numbered parts has been followed — 25.6B1. Language added — 25.5D.

183

LADYBIRD flash cards. — Loughborough : Ladybird Books, 1977.
    2 sets.

    Set 2: 128 word cards for school and home use including spare blanks.
    128 flash cards : b&w ; 9 x 24 cm. in box, 24 x 18 x 2 cm.
    "For use with books 5a, 5b, 6a, 6b of the Ladybird key words reading scheme"— Box.
    ISBN 0-7214-3018-X.

Description of flash cards as graphic materials — Ch.1 and Ch.8. Rules in Ch.8 do not provide for including dimensions of container in physical description area but, as this is useful information, it is recorded by analogy with Ch.10. Note consisting of quotation given in quotation marks — 1.7A3. Multilevel description — 1.10D and 13.6.

184

LAMB, Charles
    [Tales from Shakespeare]
    Ten tales from Shakespeare / Charles and Mary Lamb ; pictures by Grabianski. — London : J.M. Dent, 1969.
    223 p. : ill. (some col.) ; 24 cm.
    ISBN 0-460-05103-2.

1. Title   2. Ten tales from
                    Shakespeare
3. Lamb, Mary
4. Grabianski, Janusz
5. Shakespeare, William

Version of an author's works presented in a different literary form entered under the heading for the adapter — 21.10. Title by which work created after 1500 has become known through use and in reference sources used as uniform title — 25.3A.

185

The LAMBETH apocalypse. — [Wakefield] : Micro Methods, 1963.
    1 filmstrip (ca. 100 fr.) : col. ; 35 mm. + teacher's notes (31 p.).
    Also known as: De Quincy apocalypse.
    Original: "Ms 209, Lambeth Palace Library late 13th century. Reproduced . . . by permission of His Grace the Lord Archbishop of Canterbury and the Trustees of the Lambeth Palace Library".
    Cine mode, with title fr. and 1st fr. in comic.

Description of filmstrips — Ch.1 and Ch.8. Location and other information about original given in note — 8.7B8. Re. note 'Cine mode' see also example no. 134. It is sometimes difficult to distinguish between a filmstrip and a microfilm (see definitions in Appendix D of AACR 2). If this item were treated as a microfilm, the physical description would read: 1 microfilm : col & ill. ; 35 mm.

LANGUAGE for learning. — Rev. and
    expanded ed. — London : Heinemann
Educational : Inner London Education
Authority, Media Resources Centre, 1976.
    5 units.
    Devised by Eve Boyd . . . [et al.] ;
editor: Sandy Mahon ; designer: Melvin
Raymond.
    First published: ILEA, Media Resources
Centre, 1973.

    Unit 1: Classification.
    124 lesson cards : col. ; 8 x 11 cm. in
box, 16 x 23 x 2 cm. + 1 teacher's guide
(19 p. ; 21 cm.).
    Picture cards for various activities
involving classifying into sets.
    ISBN 0-435-01920-1 (Heinemann).

    Unit 2: Story telling.
    74 lesson cards : col. ; 15 x 11 cm. in
box, 22 x 31 x 2 cm. + 1 board (col. ;
21 x 30 cm.) + 1 teacher's guide (23 p. ;
21 cm.).
    Picture cards for arranging into
sequences to make stories.
    ISBN 0-435-01921-X (Heinemann).

Description of graphic materials — Ch.1 and Ch.8. Multilevel description to identify both part and comprehensive whole in single record — 13.6. Second publishing agency included because it is given prominence by typography ; the two names are separated by a colon — 1.4D5. A third publishing agency, the Centre for Urban Educational Studies is, however, omitted. Specific name of item (i.e. 'lesson cards') given as specific material designation by analogy with rule 10.5B1. (See also example no. 368). Measurements of container given by analogy with 10.5D2. (See also example no. 183).

Item has no personal author and does not emanate from corporate body, so entry is under title — 21.1C(1).

LAST, James
    Love must be the reason / James Last
[and his orchestra] ; produced and arranged
by James Last. — [London] : Polydor,
1972.
    1 sound disc (ca. 40 min.) : 33⅓ rpm,
stereo. ; 12 in.
    Also available as stereo cassette and
8-track stereo cartridge.
    Partial contents: Wedding song /
Stookey -- Heart of gold / Young — I don't
know how to love him / Lloyd Webber --
Love must be the reason / Schuman.
    Polydor: 2371-281 (disc).
    Polydor: 3150-256 (cassette).
    Polydor: 3811-152 (cartridge).

1.   Title
2.   Optionally, author and title
            analyticals for each part

Same item available in different formats. Note on the other formats — 1.7B16 and 6.7B16. Brief qualifications added when item bears two or more numbers — by analogy with 1.8E1 as sound recording publisher's numbers are given in a note rather than in the standard number area.

Sound recording containing works by different persons entered under the person represented as principal performer — 21.23C. A reference would be necessary from Last's real name (Hans Last).

LAW COMMISSION
    Statute law revision : first report / the
Law Commission. — London : H.M.S.O.,
1969.
    42 p. ; 25 cm. — (Law Commission ;
no. 22) (Cmnd. ; 4052).
    "Draft Statute Law (Repeals) Bill
prepared under section 3(1)(i) of the
Law Commissions Act 1965.".

1.   Title

Work emanating from corporate body and recording its collective thought is entered under heading for body — 21.1B2(c). Name of body contains term normally implying administrative subordination (i.e. 'Commission'), but name of higher body is not required for identification — 24.13 (Type 2).* Body is therefore entered directly under its own name — 24.12.

189

LEAPER, J.M.F.
William Freeman['s] dictionary of fictional characters : author and title indexes / by J.M.F. Leaper. — London : Dent, 1965.
p. 461-532 ; 20 cm.

1. Title
2. Freeman, William
Dictionary of fictional characters

Supplementary item which is to be described independently catalogued as a separate item — 1.9A. If pages are numbered as part of larger sequence, first and last numbers of pages are given, preceded by appropriate abbreviation — 2.5B6.

Related work which is to be catalogued separately is entered under its own heading — 21.28B. Name-title added entry made under heading for work to which it is related — 21.30G.

An alternative solution is to catalogue a supplementary item as a dependent work. This would produce a more useful entry in this instance. Supplementary items may be described dependently in one of three ways (see rule 1.9B): 1. as accompanying material; 2. in a note; 3. using a multilevel description. The above item is shown catalogued using the last of these methods in example no. 116.

190

LETRASET UK
Letratone / Letraset UK Ltd. — London : Letraset, [197-].
1 wallchart : b&w ; 102 x 76 cm. folded to 34 x 38 cm.
Shows all 236 Letratone patterns (screens, grids, perspectives, etc.) with three reductions from full size (¾, ½, ¼) to illustrate which patterns reduce well.

1. Title

Description of wallcharts as graphic materials — Ch.1 and 8. Physical description — 8.5B1, 8.5C17 and 8.5D6. Note on nature of item — 1.7B1 and 8.7B1.

In the context of rule 21.1B2, this item most certainly emanates from a corporate body and it appears to fall within category (a) of that rule in that it deals with the body itself and illustrates its products. The question that is crucial, however, seems to be whether the item is, in the words of rule 21.1B2(a), 'of an administrative nature'. The examples included in rule 21.4B are not of any great assistance. The interpretation that the above entry is based upon is that the item *is* of an administrative nature because it serves as an advertisement for the company.

191

LIBRARY ADVISORY COUNCIL
(England)
A report on the supply and training of librarians / Library Advisory Council (England) [and] Library Advisory Council (Wales). — London : H.M.S.O., 1968.
viii, 64 p. ; 25 cm.
ISBN 0-11-270006-3.

1. Title   2. Library Advisory Council (Wales)

Work emanating from corporate bodies and recording their collective thought is entered under heading for appropriate body — 21.1B2(c). Work of shared responsibility emanating from two corporate bodies — 21.6A(4). Principal responsibility not indicated by wording or layout, so entry is under first-named, with added entry under the heading for the other — 21.6C1. Government agency that does not fall within any of the categories listed at 24.18 is entered under its own name — 24.17.* To distinguish between two bodies with the same name, the name of country is added — 24.4C2.

LIBRARY OF CONGRESS. <u>Subject</u>
   <u>Cataloguing Division. Processing</u>
   <u>Department</u>
   Library of Congress subject headings /
Subject Cataloguing Division, Processing
Department. — 8th ed. in microfiche. —
Washington : L.C., 1975.
   22 microfiches : negative ; 11 x 15 cm.
   ISBN 0-8444-0156-0.

   1.   Title

Description of microfiches — Ch.1 and Ch.11.
Edition statement transcribed as given on item —
1.2B1. Number of frames of microfiches added
to specific material designation only if it can be
easily ascertained — 11.5B1. Microfiche is
negative (i.e. white lettering on black), so this
is stated — 11.5C1. Dimensions (height x width)
recorded — 11.5D3.

Work emanating from corporate body which is
of an administrative nature and which deals with
the procedures and operations of the body is
entered under the heading for the body —
21.1B2(a). Intervening element in the hierarchy
of the heading is retained as the name of the
subordinate body could be used by another body
entered under the same higher body — 24.14.

LIVER SKETCHING CLUB EXHIBITION
   OF PAINTINGS (<u>1970 : Liverpool</u>)
   Liver Sketching Club . . . 1970
Exhibition of Paintings, November 2nd
to 14th . . . : catalogue. — Liverpool :
The Club, 1970.
   1 sheet ; 32 x 23 cm. folded to
23 x 11 cm.
   "During December at the Bootle Art
Gallery".

Single sheet described as 'sheet' — 2.5B2. Height
and width recorded, together with dimensions
when folded if sheet is designed for issue
folded — 2.5D4.

Exhibition as corporate body — 21.1B1. Work
emanating from corporate body and dealing with
its resources is entered under heading for body,

because function of work is considered to be
partly administrative — 21.1B2(a). (See also
example no. 56). Date and place added to name
of exhibition — 24.8B.

The Bulletin

| Liverpool Polytechnic | No. 75/1 | 10 January 1975 |

LIVERPOOL POLYTECHNIC
   The bulletin / Liverpool Polytechnic. —
No. 75/1 (10 Jan. 1975)-   . -- Liver-
pool : The Polytechnic, 1975-   .
   v. ; 30 cm.
   Weekly in term time.
   Continues: Liverpolybulletin.

   1.   Title

See annotation following next example.

Live**POLYBULL**etin

| 9th May 1974 | | Vol. 1 No. 1 |

LIVERPOOL POLYTECHNIC
   Liverpolybulletin. — Vol. 1, no. 1
(9 May 1974)-v. 1, no. 15 (18 Dec. 1974). —
Liverpool : The Polytechnic, 1974.
   1 v. ; 30 cm.
   Weekly in term time.
   Continued by: The bulletin / Liverpool
Polytechnic.

   1.   Title

Description of printed serials — Ch.1, Ch.2 and
Ch.12. Two items presented together to compare
entries for completed and current serials. For
current serial, hyphen and four spaces follow
numeric and chronological designation of first
issue — 12.3B1 and 12.3C4. For completed

serial, designation of last issue follows the hyphen — 12.3F. In publication area, year of publication of first issue of a current serial is recorded, followed by a hyphen and four spaces — 12.4F1. For a completed serial, the year of the last issue is recorded after the hyphen — 12.4F3. ('Liverpolybulletin' began and finished in the same year, so only one date has been given.) Specific material designation for printed serial (i.e. 'v') is preceded by three spaces if the serial is current — 12.5B1 ; if it is completed, it is preceded by the number of parts (this has been interpreted as one volume) — 12.5B2. Note on relationship with other serials — 12.7B7(b) and 12.7B7(c).

Work of administrative nature emanating from corporate body and dealing with body itself is entered under heading for body — 21.1B2(a). Separate main entry made if the title proper of a serial changes — 21.2C. The title is considered to have changed because there is a change in the first word — 21.2A(1).

LOUGHBOROUGH UNIVERSITY OF TECHNOLOGY. Library
Issues system : job control macro LBL404 / Loughborough University of Technology, Library. — Loughborough : The University, 1972.
1 program file (23 statements, PLAN).

1.   Title

Description of machine-readable data files — Ch.1 and Ch.9. Specific material designation chosen from one of three terms given in rule 9.5B1. For a program file, number of statements and name of programming language added in parentheses — 9.5B2.

Item emanating from corporate body which is of an administrative nature and deals with the procedures and operations of the body itself is entered under the heading for the body — 21.1B2(a).

LIVERPOOL transport. — Liverpool : Scouse Press, 1970.
58 pieces : ill., facsims., maps, plans (some col.) ; 57 x 78 mm.-46 x 31 cm. — (Liverpool packets : a pictorial history of Liverpool ; no. 1).
Descriptive notes by Fritz Spiegl.
Includes photos., postcards, byelaws, tickets, drawings, etc. concerning transport in Liverpool, principally 19th century.

1.   Series

Items of varying character assembled as collection designated as 'pieces' — 1.10C2(c) and 2.5B18. (Item is catalogued as printed material, although some components, if catalogued on their own, would be treated as cartographic or graphic material.) When items in multi-volume set differ in height by more than two centimetres, smallest and largest size are given, separated by hyphen — 2.5D3. Other title information of a series included if it provides valuable information identifying the series — 1.6D1. Statement of responsibility not recorded in title and statement of responsibility area is given as note — 2.5B6.

See also example no. 298.

McCORMACK, Mark H.
The world of professional golf / by Mark H. McCormack. — 1968-   . — London : Hodder and Stoughton, 1968-   .
v. : ill., ports. ; 28 cm.
Annual.
1969 and subsequent issues sub-titled Mark H. McCormack's golf annual.
Imprint and size vary.

1.   Title

Serial entered under the personal author — 21.1A2 and 21.4A.

McGARRY, K.J.
   Logic in the organisation of knowledge ; and, Semantics in the organisation of knowledge : a programmed text for students of information retrieval / K.J. McGarry & T.W. Burrell. — London : Bingley, 1972.
   [64, 64] p. ; 23 cm. — (Programmed texts in library and information science).
   Two separate but interrelated texts printed in reverse format so that each appears only on the right hand pages.
   Diagrams on lining papers.
   ISBN 0-85157-134-4.

1.   Title
2.   Semantics in the organisation of
         knowledge
3.   Burrell, T.W.   4.   Series

Description of 'tête-bêche' work, that is one printed in opposite directions. Item without collective title — 1.1G2. Usually, for volume printed without pagination, total number of pages is ascertained and given in square brackets — 2.5B7. However, as this item has pages running in opposite directions, pagination is recorded by analogy with 2.5B13.

MACKAY, David
   My sentence maker / David Mackay and Brian Thompson. — London : Longman for the Schools Council, 1970.
   1 folder, 155 cards. — (Breakthrough to literacy. Schools Council programme in linguistics and English teaching).
   Each card contains single word, part of word or punctuation mark, designed to be slotted into folder against same word, part of word or punctuation mark.
   "This sentence maker, together with 26 books and other materials for children and teachers, forms a self-contained scheme of work in initial reading and writing".
   ISBN 0-582-19061-4.

1.   Title   2.   Thompson, Brian
3.   Series

Description of item made up of more than one component — Ch.1. Extent of each part may be given successively as first element of physical description — 1.10C2(a). It is normal for the dimensions of a container to be given after the extent but, in this example, the folder is both a container and an integral part of the item.

McGRAW, Eloise Jarvis
   The golden goblet / by Eloise Jarvis McGraw ; illustrated by Owen Wood. — Harmondsworth : Penguin, 1968.
   208 p. : ill. ; 18 cm. — (Puffin books).
   Originally published: New York : Coward, McCann, 1961.

1.   Title

For married women whose surname consists of maiden name and husband's surname, entry is under husband's surname (unless the woman's language is Czech, French, Hungarian, Italian or Spanish) — 22.5C5.*

McKENZIE, Robert
   The modern election : a critical appraisal / Robert McKenzie and David Butler. — London : Audio Learning, 1971.
   on 1 track of 1 sound cassette (ca. 28 min.) : 1⅞ ips, mono. + 1 pamphlet (22 p. ; 21 cm.). — (Audio Learning discussion tapes. Politics ; POAOO3).
   In box 21 x 14 x 3 cm.
   Supplementary pamphlet by Maurice Willatt.
   With: The modern electoral system : the alternatives / Robert McKenzie and David Butler.

1.   Title   2.   Butler, David
3.   Series   4.   Willatt, Maurice

See annotation following next example.

McKENZIE, Robert
The modern election : a critical appraisal ; The modern electoral system : the alternatives / Robert McKenzie and David Butler. — London : Audio Learning, 1971.
1 sound cassette (ca. 56 min.) : 1⅞ ips, 2 track, mono. + 1 pamphlet (22 p. ; 21 cm.). — (Audio Learning discussion tapes. Politics ; POAOO3).
In box 21 x 14 x 3 cm.
Supplementary pamphlet by Maurice Willatt.

1. Title   2. The modern elect-
                 oral system
3. Butler, David
4. Series   5. Willatt, Maurice

Sound recording lacking a collective title described as a unit (203) *or* a separate description is made for each separately titled work (202).

Details of container are given as a note on additional physical description — 6.7B10. There is no rule in Ch.6 to authorise the recording of this information in the physical description area. However, this might be done by analogy with rule for 3-D materials — 10.5D2.

See also examples no. 159 and 160.

MAP of Westfield Village. — Scale indeterminable. — [Hamilton-Wentworth, Ontario, 196-?].
1 bird's eye view ; 20 x 29 cm.
Village is now named: Wentworth Pioneer Village.
On verso: ill., and descriptions of village buildings.

Description of maps — Ch.1 and Ch.3. If scale cannot be determined, this is stated — 3.3B1. No publication details are given, so probable place of publication and approximate date are

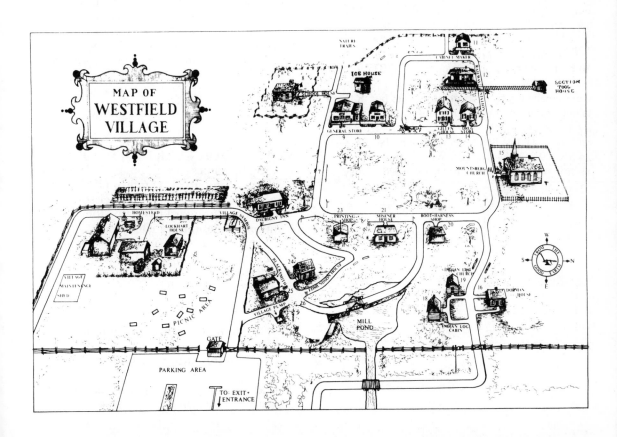

given in square brackets — 1.4C6 and 1.4F7.
Specific material designation — 3.5B1. Map
is black and white, so no colour statement is
recorded — 3.5C3. Note of contents on verso
of item — 3.7B18.

205

MAPS and man / The British Cartographic
Society and the Science Museum. —
London, [197-].
1 exhibit (2 stereographs, 9 photos.,
16 maps, microfilm map, Racal-zonal
calculus) : col. — (Making maps : the science
of cartography ; 8).
Air photos. of Big Bend, Swaziland
and the country around Stravrovouni
Monastery, Cypress.

1. British Cartographic Society
2. Science Museum

Description of exhibits as three-dimensional artefacts — Ch.1 and Ch.10. Specific material designation chosen from list of terms — 10.5B1. Number
and names of pieces added to designation —
10.5B2. Colour indicated — 10.5C2. Dimensions
not appropriate in this instance, so omitted —
10.5D1. Summary given in note — 10.7B17.

Work emanating from corporate bodies but not
falling within any of the categories listed at 21.1B2
is entered under title — 21.1C(3). Initial articles
omitted from heading for corporate bodies —
24.5A. (When given as statements of responsibility, however, the names are recorded as they
appear on the item — 1.1F1.)

MEE, Arthur
Worcestershire / by Arthur Mee. — New
ed. / fully revised and edited by Lord
Hampton and Richard Pakington ; illu-
strated with new photographs by
A.F. Kersting. — London : Hodder and
Stoughton, 1968.
194 p., 16 p. of plates : ill., map ;
21 cm. — (King's England).
ISBN 0-340-00108-9.

1. Title
2. Hampton, Humphrey Pakington,
Lord
3. Pakington, Richard
4. Series

Statement of responsibility relating to edition
follows edition statement, preceded by diagonal
slash; subsequent statement of responsibility
preceded by semi-colon — 1.2A1 and 1.2C1.

Work is a revision, but entry is under heading for
original author, as wording of chief source of
information indicates that he is still considered
responsible for work — 21.12A. 'Lord' added
to name in added entry heading if it commonly
appears with name in person's works — 22.12B.

207

MENDELSSOHN-BARTHOLDY, Felix
[Symphonies, no. 5, op. 107, D minor]
Symphony no. 5, D minor (Reforma-
tion), op. 107 / by Felix Mendelssohn-
Bartholdy ; foreword by Max Alberti. —
London : Eulenburg, [1960?].
1 miniature score (iv, 90 p.) ; 19 cm.
Foreword in English and German
dated 1960.
Pl. no.: E.E.6176.

1. Title
2. Symphony no. 5, D minor
(Reformation), op. 107
3. Reformation [symphony] †*

Title, exclusive of key and opus numbering,
consists of generic term. Therefore, key and

opus numbering included in title proper and not separated by colons — 5.1B2. (See also example no. 4). Plate number recorded in note — 5.7B19.

Uniform title for work consisting solely of one type of composition — 25.27B. Medium of performance is omitted from uniform title as it is implied by title — 25.29A2. Serial number, opus number and key added to uniform title — 25.31A1, 25.31A2, 25.31A3 and 25.31A5.

208

MILKWEED = Danaus plexippus,
    Linnaeus. — [Liverpool : City Museum,
19—].
    2 butterflies : col. ; 7 cm. wingspan.
    Prepared for display by the Museum.

    1.   Danaus plexippus, Linnaeus

Description of exhibits as three-dimensional arte-facts and realia — Ch.1 and Ch.10. Parallel titles recorded in order indicated on chief source of information — 1.1D1. No publisher or distributor. Specific name of item given as concisely as possible in physical description area — 10.5B1. Alterna-tively, the term 'exhibit' could be selected from the list of specific material designations and a more explicit description given in a note — 10.7B1. Word added to measurement to indicate what dimension is being given — 10.5D1. No statement of responsibility appears on item and so it is given in note — 1.1F2, 1.7B6 and 10.7B6.

Added entry under any title significantly different from title proper — 21.30J.

209

MILLIGAN, Spike
    A book of bits, or, A bit of a book / by
Spike Milligan. — London : Tandem, 1967.
    95 p. : chiefly ill. ; 18 cm.

    1.   Title   2.   A bit of a book *

Alternative title preceded by *or,* with commas, and first word of alternative title capitalised — 1.1B1.

Entry under name by which person is commonly known — 22.1A. A reference would be required from Milligan's real name (Terence Alan Milligan).

210

MINISTRY of Labour gazette. — Vol. 30,
    no. 6 (June 1922)-v. 76, no. 5 (May
1968). — London : H.M.S.O., 1922-1968.
    46 v. ; 34 cm.
    Monthly.
    Continues: The labour gazette.
    Continued by: Employment and
productivity gazette.

    1.   United Kingdom. <u>Ministry of
          Labour</u>

Title proper of serial has changed (there is an alteration in the first five words and an important proper name has been added — 21.2A); a separate main entry must therefore be made for the new title — 21.2C.

See also example no. 101.

211

MOMENTS in history. — [Birmingham] :
    Chad Valley, [19—].
    1 filmstrip (7 fr.) : col. ; 45 mm. —
(Colour slide ; 87).
    Mounted in rigid format for use with
Chad Valley Give-a-show projector.

Description of filmslips in rigid format — Ch.1 and Ch.8. Number of frames included after specific material designation — 8.5B2. Colour and size (i.e. width) recorded — 8.5C4 and 8.5D2. (Dimensions of filmslips and filmstrips, unlike those of other graphic materials, are given in millimetres.) Important physical details not included in physical description area are given in note — 8.7B10. Both a filmstrip and a film-slip are designed to be viewed frame by frame. They differ in that a filmstrip is usually in the form of a roll and a filmslip is a short length of film, sometimes in rigid format.

MONBODDO, James Burnet, <u>Lord</u>
Of the origin and progress of language /
by James Burnet. — Menston [Yorkshire] :
Scolar Press, 1967.
6 v. ; 21 cm. — (English linguistics
1500-1800 : a collection of facsimile
reprints ; no. 48).
Facsim of: 1st ed., London : Cadell,
1773-1792.

1.   Title   2.   Series†

Number of volumes recorded — 2.5B17. Other
title information of series included, as it provides
valuable information identifying series — 1.6D1.

Nobleman who uses his surname in his works
but is better known by his title — 22.6A. Author
was Scottish ordinary lord of session, so 'Lord'
is retained in title — 22.6A2.

MOON landing 1969 : NASA's Apollo
project. — New York : GAF, 1969.
3 stereograph reels (Viewmaster)
(21 double fr.) : col. + 1 booklet.
"Actual moon trip photographs
July 21 1969".
Reels in pocket at back of booklet.

Description of stereographs as graphic materials —
Ch.1 and Ch.8. (Stereographs are slides presented
in pairs, designed to produce a three-dimensional
effect when used with a stereoscope viewer or
projector.) 'Reel' and trade name added to
specific material designation — 8.5B1. Number
of double frames added — 8.5B2. Indication
of colour — 8.5C13. No dimensions given for
stereograph — 8.5D1.

The MUTINY and piratical seizure of the
convict-brig Cyprus when on voyage
from Hobart-Town to Macquarrie Harbour
during August 1829 : being the apprehen-
sion, trial, sentence, of the mutineers, as
reported by The Times of Oct. 14th to
Dec. 14th 1830. — Mitcham : S.A. Spence,
1968.
71 p. in various pagings, 2 leaves of
plates (1 folded) : ill., map ; 27 cm.
Most alternate pages blank.
Limited ed. of 75 copies.

1.   The Times

This publication has an extremely complicated
pagination consisting mainly of leaves numbered
as pages, i.e. 1, 3, 5 . . . 39, 41, 43 . . . through
to 71. A few of the pages are printed on both
sides. One of the leaves is numbered in roman,
i.e. xi, and others in asterisks, i.e. *, **, ***,
etc. and b*, b**, etc. A second sequence of
leaves numbered as pages in arabic, i.e. 13, 15,
precedes p. 39. When a volume has complicated
or irregular paging, the total number of pages
may be given, followed by 'in various pagings' —
2.5B8(a). (Rule 2.5B5 is relevant here too: if
the numbering within a sequence changes, the
first part of the sequence is ignored.) Note on
limited edition — 2.7B10.

Related work which is to be catalogued separately
entered under its own heading — 21.28B.

NATIONAL legislation and treaties relating
to the law of the sea = Législation
nationale et traités concernant le droit de
la mer. — New York : United Nations, 1976.
xxviii, 586 p. ; 24 cm. — (United
Nations legislative series = Série législative
des Nations Unies ; ST/LEG/SER.B/18).
Text partly in English, partly in French.
United Nations publication sales no.:
E/F.76.V.2.

1.   Législation nationale et traités
concernant le droit de la mer
2.   Series
3.   Série législative des Nations Unies

Parallel titles recorded in the order indicated on chief source of information — 1.1D1. Publication details appear in more than one language, so they are recorded in language of title proper — 1.4B5. Parallel titles of series recorded as for parallel titles in a second level description (i.e. if there were three parallel titles, the third would not be recorded unless it were in English) — 1.6C1 and 1.3D2. Important number borne by item other than ISBN recorded in a note — 1.7B19 and 2.7B19.

Compilation of laws governing more than one jurisdiction and collection of treaties consisting of those contracted between more than three parties are both entered as general collections — 21.31B2 and 21.35F3. Collection with collective title entered under title -- 21.7B.

NATIONAL LIBRARY OF CANADA   216

National Library news / National Library of Canada = Nouvelles de la Bibliothèque nationale / Bibliothèque nationale du Canada. — Vol. 1, no. 1 (Jan./Feb. 1969)-   . — [Ottawa] : National Library of Canada, 1969-   .
  v. : ill., ports. ; 28 cm.
  Issued every 2 months.
  Text in English and French.
  ISSN 0027-9633.

1. Title
2. Nouvelles de la Bibliothèque nationale

Description of printed serials — Ch.1, Ch.2 and Ch.12. Parallel titles recorded — 12.1D1. Statement of responsibility appears in abbreviated form as part of the title proper, but it is given as further statement of responsibility as well, since it appears separately in chief source of information — 12.1F2. When item has parallel titles and statements of responsibility in more than one language, each statement is given after the parallel title to which it relates — 1.1F11. Chronological designation appears in two languages, so designation appearing first is recorded — 12.3C3.

Work of administrative nature emanating from corporate body and dealing with body itself, its internal procedures and its staff is entered under heading for body — 21.1B2(a). Name appears in two languages, both of which are official, so entry is under the English form — 24.3A.*

217

NATO

NATO : facts about the North Atlantic Treaty Organisation. — Paris : NATO Information Service, 1962.
  ix, 320 p. ; 25 cm.

Work of administrative nature emanating from corporate body and dealing with body itself is entered under heading for body -- 21.1B2(a). Variant forms of name in chief source of information - NATO is both the predominant form and the brief form — 24.2D.*

The authors appreciate that the choice of heading for this item conflicts with the examples in rules 26.3A4 and 26.3C2, which imply that NATO should be entered under the full form of name. The above heading, however, reflects a correct interpretation of the rules for this particular item.

218

NETWORK analysis : a guide to the use of network analysis in programming and control of the design of construction works / prepared by joint working group of Royal Institute of British Architects ... [et al.]. — London : H.M.S.O., 1967.

vi, 40 p. : ill., form ; 30 cm. — (Research and development building management handbooks ; 3).

Cover title: Network analysis in construction design.

At head of title: Ministry of Public Building and Works, Research and Development.

One ill. on folded leaf in pocket.

1. Royal Institute of British Architects
2. United Kingdom. <u>Ministry of Public Building and Works</u>

Variation of title given in note — 2.7B4. Statement of responsibility not recorded in title and statement of responsibility area is given in note — 2.7B6. Illustrative matter issued in a pocket inside the cover of an item is included in the physical description; number of items and their location recorded in a note — 2.5C7 and 2.7B10.

Work emanating from corporate body but not falling within any of the categories listed at 21.1B2 is entered under title — 21.1C(3). (Despite the wording of the title page, the foreword indicates, by the use of lower case letters etc., that the joint working group lacks a name, and so entry cannot be under name of body as instructed at 24.15A).

219

The NEW Oxford illustrated dictionary. — Sydney, Australia : Bay Books in association with Oxford University Press, 1976.

2 v. (xvi, 1920 p.) : ill. (chiefly col.), maps, ports. ; 29 cm.

Based upon the text of the Oxford illustrated dictionary / edited by J. Coulson ... [et al.]. Additional material derived from the Australian and New Zealand supplement to the Pocket Oxford dictionary, 5th ed., and from other sources ; with many new illustrations.

Published in 40 weekly parts with loose-leaf binders. Distributed in the U.K. by: City Magazines Ltd.

Contents: v. 1. AAC-LEA — v. 2. LEB-ZYM.

Work in more than one volume — 2.5B17. Pagination continuous so given in parentheses, ignoring separately paged sequence of preliminary material in volumes other than first — 2.5B20. Note on edition and history — 1.7B7 and 2.7B7. Note on publication and distribution — 1.7B9 and 2.7B9. Contents note — 1.7B18 and 2.7B18.

It is appreciated that libraries and other agencies may wish to catalogue this work as an incomplete item when they receive the first parts. To do this, the specific material designation would be given alone preceded by three spaces — 1.5B5, i.e. [3 spaces] v. and (<u>loose-leaf</u>) added — 2.5B9. A note about the method of publication would need to be given — 1.7B9, e.g.

In progress. To be published in 40 weekly parts

Work of unknown authorship entered under title — 21.5A.

220

1914-1918 : [war medal awarded to] 147780 Gunner S.W.W. Heaver, R.A. — [1919 (London : Royal Mint)]

1 medal : silver ; 4 cm. diameter.

Recipient's name engraved on rim.

Description of three-dimensional artefacts — Ch.1 and Ch.10. Title transcribed as it appears on item — 1.1B1. Brief explanation added to title — 1.1E6. Artefact not intended primarily for communication has date as first element of publication, etc. area — 10.4F2. None of listed specific material designation terms is appropriate, so specific name of item is given as concisely as possible — 10.5B1. Material recorded in physical description area — 10.5C1. Word added to measurement to indicate which dimension is given — 10.5D1. No authority to give measurement less than 10 cm. in millimetres, as is the case with printed monographs, although this would seem more appropriate, i.e. 37 mm.

Explanatory words added to statement of responsibility — 1.1F8. There are six unnumbered pages at the front of this book. However, unnumbered sequences are disregarded unless they constitute the whole or a substantial part of the work, or unless an unnumbered sequence includes a page or pages referred to in a note — 2.5B3. Illustrations in colour — 2.5C3.

Work consisting of reproduction of works of an artist and text about him is entered under heading for the artist, as he appears to be represented as the author in the chief source of information and the text is a minor element — 21.17B. An added entry is made under the heading for a prominently-named writer not given as main entry heading — 21.30C.

Robert Melville

NED KELLY

27 paintings by

SIDNEY NOLAN

Thames and Hudson · London

221

NOLAN, Sidney
    Ned Kelly : 27 paintings / by Sidney Nolan ; [text by] Robert Melville. — London : Thames and Hudson, 1964.
    60 p. : col. ill. ; 21 cm.

1.   Title   2.   Melville, Robert†

222

NORTH OF SCOTLAND HYDRO
    ELECTRIC BOARD
    Report and accounts / North of Scotland Hydro Electric Board. — 1944-   . — Edinburgh : The Board, 1944-   .
        v. ; 25-28 cm.
        Annual.
        Title varies slightly.
        From 1949 published by H.M.S.O. as a House of Commons paper and includes: Report of the Electricity Consultative Council for the North of Scotland District.

1.   Title
2.   Electricity Consultative Council for the North of Scotland District

Description of printed serials — Ch.1, Ch.2 and Ch.12. Variation in size — 12.5D1 and 2.5D3. Note on change of publisher — 12.7B9. Note on presence within a serial of another serial — 12.7B18.

Serial of administrative nature emanating from corporate body and dealing with body itself and its finances is entered under heading for the body — 21.1B2(a). Entry directly under name — 24.1.

NUFFIELD '460 farm tractor. —
[Oxford?] : Morris Motors, [197-?].
1 mock-up : red.
Sectionalised representation of tractor, powered by electricity to demonstrate operation.
Actual size.

223

Description of three-dimensional artefacts — Ch.1 and Ch.10. Item is treated as 'mock-up', which is defined in AACR 2 as: 'a representation of a device or process that may be modified for training or analysis to emphasise a particular part or function; it usually has movable parts that can be manipulated' (p. 568).

Title transcribed in accordance with rule 1.1B1; quotation marks are retained as the title proper is a quote from the item's content. Work consists of a performance by a comedian who is also responsible for the material; his contribution therefore goes beyond that of mere performance and his name is recorded as a statement of responsibility — 6.1F1.

Entry is under the heading for the single person responsible for the artistic content — 21.1A1, 21.1A2 and 21.4A. Entry under name by which person is commonly identified — 22.1A. Name with prefix which is not article, preposition or combination of the two entered under prefix — 22.5D2.

224

O'BRIEN, Flann
The best of Myles : a selection from 'Cruisheen Lawn' / Myles na Gopaleen (Flann O'Brien) ; edited and with a preface by Kevin O Nolan. — London : Pan, 1977.
400 p. : ill. ; 20 cm.
Articles originally appeared in: The Irish times.
ISBN 0-330-24855-3.

1. Title   2. Irish times

Statement of responsibility recorded as it appears in item — 1.1F1.

Author's works appear under more than one pseudonym (real name is Brian O'Nolan); entry is under predominant name, with references from others — 22.2C2. Added entry under heading for related work — 21.30G.

OKE'S
MAGISTERIAL FORMULIST

(A Companion Volume to Stone's Justices' Manual)

FORMS AND PRECEDENTS

SEVENTEENTH EDITION

BY

WILLIAM SCOTT, LL.B.(Lond.)
SOLICITOR ; CLERK TO THE JUSTICES FOR THE COUNTY
BOROUGH OF TEESSIDE.

225

O'CONNOR, Tom
"Alright mouth" / Tom O'Connor. — Liverpool : Stag Music, 1974.
1 sound disc (ca. 40 min.) : 33⅓ rpm, stereo. ; 12 in.
Stag music: SG.10063.

1. Title

LONDON
BUTTERWORTH & CO. (PUBLISHERS) LTD.
SHAW & SONS, LTD.

1968

OKE, George Colwell
Oke's magisterial formulist . . . : forms
and precedents. — 17th ed. / by William
Scott. — London : Butterworths, 1968.
xii, 1088, 121 p. : forms ; 25 cm.
"Companion volume to Stone's justices'
manual".
Text on lining paper.
ISBN 0-406-32603-7.

1.   Title   2.   Scott, William

Name associated with responsibility for item
transcribed as part of title and so no further
statement relating to that name needed — 1.1F13.
Lengthy other title information omitted from
title and statement of responsibility area and
given in note — 1.1E3 and 1.7B5. Statement of
responsibility relating to edition follows edition
statement — 1.2C1. Two publishers named on
title page, but first only is given, as second is not
given prominence by typography — 1.4D5. Date
in publication area refers to edition named in
edition area — 1.4F1. Number of pages in each
numbered sequence recorded — 2.5B2. Type of
illustration recorded — 2.5C2.

Edition that has been revised, updated, etc. by
someone else is entered under heading for original
if person or body responsible for original is named
in statement of responsibility or title; an added
entry is made under heading for reviser — 21.12A.

1000 makers of the twentieth century /
    edited by Godfrey Smith. — [London] :
Times Newspapers, 1971.
[174] p. : ports. ; 30 cm.
Based on a series of articles published in
the Sunday times weekly colour magazine
in 1969.
ISBN 0-7153-5441-8.

1.   Smith, Godfrey
2.   The Sunday times magazine

Title transcribed exactly — 1.1B1. Only one type of
illustration — 2.5C2. Note on bibliographic
history — 1.7B7 and 2.7B7.

Related work under its own heading — 21.28B.
Work produced under editorial direction entered
under title — 21.7A. Added entry under work to
which item is related — 21.28B.

OWEN, Joseph
[Will] , 1777 May 28 / Joseph Owen.
[4] p. ; 31 cm.
Ms. (transcript, handwritten), original
written in Lydiate, Lancashire.
Title supplied by cataloguer.
Witnesses: Henry Holland, Elizabeth
Holland and John Molyneux.

Description of manuscripts — Ch.1 and Ch.4.
Title supplied for legal document — 4.1B2. Date
of signing legal document included as part of
title — 4.1B2. Date not needed in date area
because included already in title proper — 4.4B1.
Details of copy given as note — 4.7B1. (Location
of original should be added if it can be ascertained.
In this instance, only the place where it was
written is known).

PAINTINGS at Chatsworth : colour post-
    cards of paintings in the Devonshire
Collection. — Derby : English Life
Publications, [196-?] .
8 postcards : col. ; 15 x 11 cm.
In folder.
Contents: Trial by jury / Landseer —
The holy family / Murillo — Georgiano,
Duchess of Devonshire, with her daughter
Georgiano / Reynolds — The flight into
Egypt / Ricci — The Acheson sisters /
Sargent — Portrait of an oriental (King
Uzzich?) / Van Rijn — Arthur Goodwin,
M.P. / Van Dyck — The adoration of the
Kings / Veronese.

1.   Devonshire Collection†

Description of postcards as graphic materials —
Ch.1 and Ch.8. Contents note — 1.7B18 and
8.7B18.

Collection of independent works by different
persons entered under its collective title — 21.7A

and 21.7B. Added entry for the name of the collection from which reproductions of art works have been taken — 21.30H.

230

PALMER, P.G.
     Archbishop Abbot and the woollen industry in Guildford / P.G. Palmer. — [1923?].
          66, a-g leaves ; 25 cm.
          Holograph.
          Bibliography: leaves a-g.

1.   Title

Description of manuscripts — Ch.1 and Ch.4. Pagination recorded as for printed monographs — 4.5B1. Lettered pages or leaves recorded as inclusive lettering — 2.5B2. Designation for manuscript handwritten by the author is 'Holograph' — 4.7B1.

PARIS, Matthew
     La vie de Seint Auban : an Anglo-Norman poem of the thirteenth century / edited by Arthur Robert Harden. — Oxford : Blackwell for the Anglo-Norman Text Society, 1968.
          xxix, 85 p., [1] leaf of plates : facsim. ; 23 cm. — (Anglo-Norman texts ; 19).
          Attributed to Matthew Paris.
          ISBN 0-631-0480-1.

1.   Title   2.   Harden, Arthur
                                       Robert
3.   Series

Statement of responsibility does not appear prominently in item and so is given in note — 1.1F2 and 2.7B6.

Reference sources indicate that Paris is probable author and so entry is made under heading for him — 21.5B.

ENGINEERING WORKSHOP DRAWING

INCLUDING AN INTRODUCTION TO PLANE AND SOLID GEOMETRY WITH SPECIAL REFERENCE TO THE NEEDS OF STUDENTS IN MAJOR AND MINOR COURSES AND IN JUNIOR TECHNICAL SCHOOLS

BY

A. C. PARKINSON

A.C.P. (HONS.), F.COLL.H., ETC.

MEMBER OF THE ROYAL SOCIETY OF TEACHERS

LECTURER IN THE ENGINEERING DEPT., THE TECHNICAL COLLEGE, KINGSTON-UPON-THAMES

SOMETIME INSTRUCTOR, UNIVERSITY OF LONDON GOLDSMITHS' COLLEGE, ETC.

AUTHOR OF "A FIRST YEAR ENGINEERING DRAWING," "INTERMEDIATE ENGINEERING DRAWING"

"ENGINEERING INSPECTION," "BLUEPRINT READING SIMPLIFIED"

"SCREW THREAD CUTTING AND MEASUREMENT," ETC.

JOINT AUTHOR OF "LOGARITHMS SIMPLIFIED" AND "ENGINEERING MATHEMATICS"

FOURTH EDITION

(Thirteenth Impression—Reprinted with Revision and Additions)

LONDON
SIR ISAAC PITMAN & SONS, LTD.
1946

PARKINSON, A.C.

Engineering workshop drawing : including an introduction to plane and solid geometry . . . / by A.C. Parkinson. — 4th ed., 13th impression, repr. with revision and additions. — London : Pitman, 1946.
    viii, 116 p. : ill. ; 22 x 28 cm. — (Technical school series).
    "With special reference to the needs of students in major and minor courses and in junior technical schools".

1.   Title   2.   Series

Other title information which is lengthy is omitted from title and statement of responsibility area and given in a note — 1.1E3 and 1.7B5. Omission indicated by mark of omission (i.e. three dots) — 1.0C and 1.1E3. Omission of qualifications, etc. in statement of responsibility area — 1.1F7. Reissue of a particular edition which contains changes is given as a subsequent edition statement — 2.2D1. Date in publication, etc. area is given as date of reissue only if reissue is specified in edition area (4th ed. was first issued in 1936) — 1.4F3. Width greater than height — 2.5D2.

PARLIAMENTARY AND SCIENTIFIC COMMITTEE

Report on collection, dissemination, storage and retrieval of scientific and technological information / Parliamentary and Scientific Committee. — London : The Committee, 1968.
    24 p. ; 22 cm.

1.   Title

Work emanating from corporate body and recording its collective thought is entered under heading for body — 21.1B2(c). Name of body includes term implying administrative subordination (i.e. 'Committee'), but name of higher body is not required for identification of subordinate body — 24.12 and 24.13 (Type 2).

The PARLOUR song book : a casquet of vocal gems / edited and introduced by Michael R. Turner ; the music edited by Antony Miall. — London : M. Joseph, 1972.
    x, 374 p. : chiefly music ; 27 cm.

1.   Turner, Michael R.
2.   Miall, Antony

Musical work that includes words is entered under heading for composer — 21.19A. This item, however, is a collection with collective title and so is entered under that title — 21.7B

The PENGUIN book of French verse / [edited and introduced by Brian Woledge, Geoffrey Brereton and Anthony Hartley]. — Rev. ed. — Harmondsworth : Penguin, 1975.
    xxxii, 664 p. ; 19 cm.
    Text in French, with prose translations of each poem and introduction in English.
    First published in 4 volumes, 1957-1961.
    Contents: Twelfth to fifteenth centuries / introduced and edited by Brian Woledge — Sixteenth to eighteenth centuries / introduced and edited by Geoffrey Brereton — Nineteenth and twentieth centuries / introduced and edited by Anthony Hartley.
    ISBN 0-14-042-182-3.

1.   Woledge, Brian
2.   Brereton, Geoffrey
3.   Hartley, Anthony

Title including name of publisher that is an integral part of title proper is transcribed in full — 1.1B2. Title page bears both collective title and titles of individual works; former is given as title proper and latter are given in contents note — 2.1B2 and 2.7B18. Statement of responsibility taken from cover, not chief source of information (i.e. title page) and so is enclosed in square brackets — 2.0B2.

Work produced under editorial direction entered under title — 21.1C(2) and 21.7B. Added entries made for up to three editors — 21.30A and 21.30D.

236

PERKINS, Al

Doctor Dolittle and the pirates / Hugh Lofting ; adapted for beginning readers by Al Perkins ; illustrated by Philip Wende. — London : Collins and Harvill, 1968.

61 p. : col. ill. ; 24 cm. — (Beginner books. I can read it all by myself).

Published by arrangement with: New York : Random House.

1. Title 2. Lofting, Hugh
3. Wende, Philip

More than one statement of responsibility — 1.1F6. Series and subseries recorded — 1.6H1. Note on publication — 1.7B9 and 2.7B9

Adaptation under the heading for the adapter — 21.10.

237

PHILIP, Prince, consort of Elizabeth II, Queen of the United Kingdom

The evolution of human organisations / by His Royal Highness the Prince Philip Duke of Edinburgh. — Southampton : University of Southampton, 1967.

27 p. ; 22 cm. — (Fawley Foundation lectures ; 1967).

1. Title 2. Series

Consort of ruler entered under name or title, followed by 'consort of' and heading for ruler — 22.17A4. Title and name of country governed added to name of ruler — 22.17A1. Roman numeral associated with name of ruler added to appropriate name — 22.17A2.

238

PHILIPS' 12" political challenge globe. — Scale 1:42,000,000. — London : Philips, 1970.

1 globe : col., wooden, in metal cradle mounted on wooden stand ; 31 cm. in diam.

Stand contains slot for: Philips' record atlas. 27th ed. London : Philips, 1967. (128, 130 p.) : 142 col. maps.

1. Philips' record atlas

Title proper includes statement of responsibility — 1.1B2. Therefore, no further statement relating to that name is needed — 1.1F13. Dimensions for globe — 3.5D4. 'With' note describing separately titled part of cartographic item lacking collective title — 1.7B21 and 3.7B21.

239

PHOTOGRAPH and slide classification for western art / Photograph and Slide Collection, Fine Arts Library, Fogg Art Museum. — Cambridge, Mass. : Harvard University Library, Microreproduction Dept., [1973?].

1 microfilm reel ; 35 mm.
Low reduction.
Comic mode.
Microreproduction of: Rev. ed., 1973.

1. Fogg Art Museum. Fine Arts Library. Photographic and Slide Collection

Description of microfilms — Ch.1 and Ch.11. Statement of responsibility recorded as it appears on item — 1.1F1 and 11.1F1. There is no specific rule for recording the subordinate bodies of a higher body, but the example at rule 7.1F1 ('Flowering and fruiting of papaya / Department of Botany, Iowa State University') shows that two names in an hierarchy are separated by a comma. Microfilm is positive (i.e. black lettering on white), so this detail is not recorded — 11.5C1.

240

PLANNING for cataloguing : proceedings of a meeting of the Cataloguing and Indexing Group of the Library Association, held at Liverpool on 11th June, 1970. — Liverpool : College of Commerce, Dept. of Library and Information Studies, 1970.

1 sound tape reel (ca. 90 min.) : 3¾ ips, mono. ; 7 in.

J. Watters, S. Fellows and A.C. Bubb, principal speakers.

1. Library Association. Cataloguing and Indexing Group

Description of sound tape reels — Ch.1 and Ch.6. No indication of duration appears on item but approximate time can readily be established — 6.5B2. Number of tracks given only if other than standard — 6.5C6. Diameter of reel given but width of tape only given if other than standard — (¼ in.) — 6.5D6. Note of persons considered to be important who were not named in the statement of responsibility — 1.7B5 and 6.7B6.

Item consists of the proceedings of a meeting but the meetings lacks a name (the name of the organising corporate body is *not* the name of the meeting) and entry is therefore under title — 21.5A.

241

PLANNING outlook. — Vol. 1, no. 1 (July 1948)-v. 6, no. 2 (1964) ; Vol. 1 (Dec. 1966)-   . — London : Geoffrey Cumberlege, Oxford University Press, 1948.
    v. ; 24-30 cm.
    Irregular (1948-1965), 2 issues yearly (1966-   ).
    Journal of the School of Town and Country Planning, King's College, University of Durham (later the Department of Town and Country Planning in the University of Newcastle upon Tyne) and, from 1973 to 1976, of the Department of Town Planning of Oxford Polytechnic.
    Imprint varies; new series 1966- first published by Oriel Press and subsequently by the University of Newcastle.

    1.   University of Durham. King's College. School of Town and Country Planning
    2.   University of Newcastle upon Tyne. Department of Town and Country Planning
    3.   Oxford Polytechnic. Department of Town Planning

Chief source of information for a serial is the title page of the first issue — 12.0B1. An editor is named on the title page but this is not recorded in the statement of responsibility area — 12.1F3. Serial which starts a new designation system without changing its title proper; designation of first and last issues of the old system given, followed by the designation of the first issue of the new system — 12.3G. Serial which changes its size, recorded by analogy with 2.5D3. Note on change of frequency — 12.7B1. Note on statement of responsibility — 12.7B6. Note on publication — 12.7B9.

242

[PLATED tibia and broken fibula] . — Wallasey : Victoria Central Hospital, [197-].
    1 radiograph ; 29 x 24 cm.
    Shows front view and side view.
    Title supplied by cataloguer.

Description of radiographs as graphic materials — Ch.1 and Ch.8. Supplied title enclosed in square brackets — 1.1B7 and 8.1B2. Source of title given in note — 8.7B3. Patient's name has been omitted for reasons of confidentiality but it is recognised that this would be of prime importance to certain collections. In such cases entry might best be made in the form :
    OTHER, A.N. : plated tibia and broken fibula
Alternatively, patient might be identified by number.

243

PLAUTUS, Titus Maccius
    Miles gloriosus / T. Macci Plauti ; edited with an introduction and notes by Mason Hammond, Arthur M. Mack, Walter Moscalew. — 2nd ed. rev. / revised by Mason Hammond. — Cambridge, Mass. : Harvard University Press, 1970.
    x, 208 p. ; 22 cm.
    Latin text with introduction and notes in English.
    ISBN 0-674-57436-2.

    1.   Title   2.   Hammond, Mason
    3.   Mack, Arthur M.
    4.   Moscalew, Walter

Edition statement transcribed as it appears on item, except that standard abbreviations used and numerals in place of words — 1.2B1. Note on language of item — 1.7B2.

Roman living before 476 A.D. entered under part of name most commonly used as entry element in reference sources — 22.9.

PLINY, the Elder
[Naturalis historia. Book 20-23. English]
Natural history : libri XX-XXIII / Pliny ; with an English translation [and introduction] by W.H.S. Jones. — Rev. and repr. — London : Heinemann, 1969.
xxvi, 532 p. ; 17 cm. — (Natural history / Pliny ; v. 6) (Loeb classical library).
Latin text, parallel English translation. Complete work published in 10 v.

1. Title   2.   Natural history
3. Loeb classical library

Numbering of first series as it appears on title page is: 'Volume VI'; this is recorded using standard abbreviations and substituting arabic for other numerals — 1.6G1. Note on language of item — 2.7B2.

Translation entered under heading appropriate to the original — 21.14A. Established English form of name used for Roman of classical times — 22.3B3.* Words normally associated with name added after comma and underlined — 22.8A. Uniform title of work created before 1501 is title in original language — 25.4A. Item consists of consecutive numbered parts of work, so designation of parts is given in singular as subheading of uniform title followed by the inclusive numbers of the parts — 25.6B1. Language added, if other than that of original — 25.5D.

[POD razor = Ensis siliqua].
1 shell ; 18 cm. long.
Title supplied by cataloguer.

1. Ensis siliqua

Description of naturally occurring objects as three-dimensional artefacts and realia — Ch.1 and Ch.10.

Place of publication, name of publisher and date of publication omitted, unless object is mounted for viewing or packaged for presentation (see example no. 348) — 10.4C2, 10.4D2 and 10.4F2. Specific name of item given as concisely as possible in physical description area — 10.5B1. Dimension given — 10.5D1. Note on source of title — 10.7B3.

POLETTE, Nancy
Library skills for primary grades / Nancy Polette ; illustrated by Helen Hausner and Associates. — St. Louis : Milliken, 1973.
12 p., [36] leaves of plates : ill. (some col.) ; 28 cm. — (Milliken full-color transparency-duplicating books).
Plates consist of 12 full colour transparencies and 24 duplicating masters which may be detached and used to provide a complete and adaptable library programme for pupils in kindergarten and the primary grades.

1. Title   2.   Helen Hausner and Associates
3. Series

Item which consists of text and a number of detachable graphics bound together in book format, here treated as a printed monograph. The detachable leaves are described as plates according to rule 2.5B10 and a note used to amplify the physical description (2.7B10) and to indicate the nature and scope of the item (1.7B1 and 2.7B1). It might be considered more appropriate to treat this item as a graphic (see example no. 364).

It is unclear whether this is a work for which an artist has provided illustrations (21.11A) or a work that is a collaboration between a writer and an artist (21.24). In either case the main entry heading would be 'Polette', under the former rule as the author of the text and under the latter as the first named (the artist is not given greater prominence).

247

A POLLUTED beach. — [Liverpool : City of Liverpool Museums, 197-] .

1 diorama (various pieces) : col. ; in glass-fronted container, 238 x 80 x 105 cm.

Items picked up along a 100-yard stretch of beach in March 1972: oil-polluted guillemots (stuffed), rusty cans, plastic bag, cartridge cases, tyres, etc., in front of b&w photo. of wrecked "Torrey Canyon".

Prepared for display by the Museum.

Description of dioramas — Ch.1 and Ch.10. Pieces cannot be named concisely in physical description area — 10.5B2. Container named and its dimensions recorded — 10.5D2. Note relating to history of item — 10.7B7. Brief summary of content of item — 10.7B17.

248

POTTER, Beatrix

A jig-saw puzzle of Jemima Puddleduck : Beatrix Potter's famous character. — London : Warne, [197-?] .

1 jigsaw puzzle (43 pieces) : wood, col. ; in box, 22 x 22 x 4 cm.

   1.   Title

Description of three-dimensional artefacts — Ch.1 and Ch.10. None of listed terms is appropriate as specific material designation, so specific name is given as concisely as possible — 10.5B1.

Material and colour recorded — 10.5C1 and 10.5C2. If object is in container, container is named and its dimensions given, either after those of the object or as the only dimension — 10.5D2.

Reproduction of art work entered under heading for original work — 21.16B.

249

POWELL, Sandy

The lost policeman : a humorous sketch / Sandy Powell (comedian) ; assisted by Little Percy. — [London?] : Broadcast, [193-?] .

1 sound disc (ca. 5 min.) : 78 rpm, mono. ; 8 in.

Broadcast: 429.

   1.   Title   2.   Percy, <u>Little</u>

Statement of responsibility recorded in the form in which it appears on the item — 1.1F1. Contribution of person which goes beyond that of mere performance and so name can be recorded as a statement of responsibility — 6.1F1. Probable place of publication — 1.4C6 and probable date — 1.4F7.

Entry under the heading for the principal person responsible, which is indicated by the wording and the layout of the chief source of information — 21.1A2 and 21.6B1. Entry under name by which person is commonly identified — 22.1A. Added entry under collaborating person — 21.30B and heading for that person involves entry under phrase — 22.11A. Phrase consists of forename with another word, so entry is under forename with a reference from the name in direct order — 22.11B.

[PRAJNAPARAMITA. <u>English</u>. <u>Selections</u>]
Selected sayings from the Perfection
of Wisdom / chosen, arranged and
translated by Edward Conze. — 2nd ed. —
London : Buddhist Society, 1968.
131 p., [1] leaf of plates : ill. ; 23 cm.
Translation from the Sanscrit.
ISBN 0-901032-00-X.

1.   Title   2.   Conze, Edward
3.   Buddhist Society

Work accepted as sacred scripture by religious
group entered under title — 21.1C(4) and 21.37A.
Uniform title is title by which scripture is most
commonly identified in English language
sources — 25.17. Language and 'Selections'
added after uniform title by analogy with
rules for other sacred scriptures in accordance
with general rules for uniform titles — 25.5D
and 25.6B3. Added entry under heading for
translator because main entry is under title and
because main entry heading may be difficult
for catalogue-users to find — 21.30K1 and
21.30K1(e).

PREVIN, André
The good companions : the musical of
the novel by J.B. Priestley : [vocal selection / music by André Previn ; lyrics by
Johnny Mercer]. — London : Chappell,
c1974.
52 p. of music : ill. ; 28 cm.

1.   Title   2.   Mercer, Johnny
3.   Priestley, J.B.

Description of music — Ch.1 and Ch.5.

Musical work which contains words entered under
heading for composer — 21.19A.

PRIESTLEY, Joseph
[Historical account of the navigable
rivers, canals and railways of Great
Britain]
Priestley's navigable rivers and canals :
Historical account of the navigable rivers,
canals, and railways throughout Great
Britain / by Joseph Priestley ; with a new
introduction by Charles Hadfield. —
Newton Abbot : David and Charles, 1969.
xv, 703, viii p., [1] folded leaf of
plates : map ; 23 cm.
Facsim. of: 1st ed., London : Longman,
Rees, Orme, Brown and Green, 1831.
ISBN 0-7153-4395-5.

1.   Title

Description of facsimiles — 1.11. Data relating to
the original given in the note area only — 1.11A.
If the facsimile has a title different from that of
the original, the title of the facsimile is given as
the title proper, and the original title is recorded
as other title information if it appears on the chief
source of information of the facsimile — 1.11B.
Facsimile has publication details of both original
and facsimile, but only those of facsimile are
given in the publication area — 1.11C. Physical
description of facsimile given in physical description area — 1.11D. ISBN of facsimile given in
standard number and terms of availability area —
1.11E. All details of the original given in single
note in the order of the areas of description —
1.11F.

For work created after 1500 and known by more
than one title, uniform title is title in original
language by which work is best known — 25.3A.
If no one title predominates, the title of the
original edition is used — 25.3B.

PROLE, Lozania
The greatest nurse of them all / by
Lozania Prole. — London : Hale, 1968.
184 p. ; 21 cm.
Based on the life of Florence Nightingale.

1.   Title

Work is the result of collaboration between two people (i.e. Ursula Bloom and Charles Eade) who have shared a pseudonym. Entry is under pseudonym with references from real names. *
(If other works by either writer were entered under real name, a reference would have to be made to that name from this heading.) — 21.6D. *

254

PUTNAM, Sallie A.
    [Richmond during the war]
    In Richmond during the Confederacy / by a lady of Richmond (Sallie A. Putnam). — New York : McBride, 1961.
        389 p. ; 21 cm.
        Subtitle on facsim. of original t.p.: Four years of personal observation.
        First published: New York : Carleton, 1867.

    1.   Title   2.   In Richmond during
                              the Confederacy

Numbering within sequence of pages changes from roman to arabic (i.e. i-xiv, 15-389 p.); numbering of first part of sequence is ignored — 2.5B5. Other title information not recorded in title and statement of responsibility area is given in note if considered important — 2.7B5.

Person commonly identified in reference sources by proper name is entered under that name, even if characterising phrase appears in chief source of information. A reference would be made from that phrase — 22.11D. * (See also example no. 124). No single title established as being the one by which the work is best known, so uniform title is title proper of original edition — 25.3B.

QUIN, Vera
    Quin's reading games. — Peppard Common, Oxfordshire : Cressrelles, 1976.
        1 game (various pieces).
        Lotto-type game.
        Contains 36 9-word cards, 324 single-word cards, 4 boards, 6 counters, 2 dice and explanatory leaflet.
        Exercises in pairing words to discriminate between sounds, and games to familiarise users with commonest printed notices, forms and posters.

    1.   Title

Description of games — Ch.1 and Ch.10. If pieces cannot be named concisely, term 'various pieces' is added to specific material designation — 10.5B2. If more detailed description is considered useful, this is given in a note — 10.7B10.

256

RAISING the "Empress of Canada" in Gladstone Dock, Bootle, 3 March, 1954 / made by Bootle Fire Brigade. — Bootle : The Brigade, 1954.
        1 film reel (10 min.) : si., b&w ; 16 mm.
        Summary: Shows how the ship was raised after she rolled over and sank owing to the effects of a fire on board.

    1.   Bootle (Lancashire) Fire Brigade

Description of films — Ch.1 and Ch.7.

Work emanating from corporate body but not falling within any of the categories listed at 21.1B2 is therefore entered under title — 21.1C(3). Heading for added entry distinguishes Bootle, Lancashire (now Sefton, Merseyside) from Bootle, Cumbria — 23.4D1.

RASMUS, Carolyn J.
  Agility / Carolyn J. Rasmus. —
Cambridge, Mass. : Ealing, 1969.
  1 film loop (3 min., 35 sec.) : si., col. ;
Super 8 mm. — (Functional fitness).
  Consultants: The American Associa-
tion for Health, Physical Education and
Recreation.
  "Licensed only for direct optical
projection before a viewing audience"—Box.
  Notes on box.

1.   Title   2.   Series

Description of film loops — Ch.1 and Ch.7.
Duration added to specific material designation;
as this is less than five minutes, it is given in
minutes and seconds — 7.5B2. Sound character-
istic given — 7.5C3. Indication of colour —
7.5C4. Gauge given in millimetres; 'Super' or
'standard' added as appropriate, since the film
is 8 millimetres — 7.5D2. Note on restrictions
that apply to the showing of a film. This is not
specifically covered in AACR 2, but has been
recorded by analogy with rules for manuscripts —
4.7B14.

The READER'S digest great world
    atlas / planned under the direction
of the late Frank Debenham. — Rev. and
updated ed. — London : Reader's Digest
Association, 1974.
  1 atlas (179 p.) : 170 col. maps ; 40 cm.
  First ed. published: 1961.

1.   Debenham, Frank

Description of atlases as cartographic materials —
Ch.1 and Ch.3. Title transcribed exactly as to
wording — 1.1B1. (Initial articles are omitted only
in the main entries for corporate bodies — 24.5A.)
If the first word of the title of a work entered
under its title proper is an article, the next word
is capitalised — A.4D. Pagination and number of
maps recorded — 3.5B3 and 3.5C2.

Entry under title for work produced under
editorial direction — 21.1C(2).

REMINGTON, J.M.
  Algebra / J.M. Remington. — 3rd ed. —
London : Intercontinental Book
Productions in conjunction with Seymour
Press [distributor] , 1974.
  56 p. ; 13 cm. — (Pass GCE O level and
CSE exams. Key facts ; 10).
  Twenty-nine loose cards in plastic wallet.
  ISBN 0-85047-201-6.

1.   Title   2.   Series

Description of item which, although containing
numbered pages, actually consists of a series of
cards. Note made of important physical details
not already included in physical description
area — 2.7B10.

RETROSPECTIVE UK MARC file,
    1950-1975 / British Library,
Bibliographic Services Division. — [1976
ed.] . — London : B.L.B.S.D., 1976.
  1 data file (519,653 logical records) +
microfiche index (82 microfiches : negative ;
10 x 15 cm.).
  Records relate to books published in
the U.K.
  ASCII characters.
  Updated and revised version of file
first issued in 1975.
  27 tape reels : 9 tracks, 800 bpi, NRZI.

1.   British Library. Bibliographic
                       Services Division

Description of machine-readable data files — Ch.1
and Ch.9. Specific material designation chosen
from one of three terms given in rule 9.5B1. For
a data file, number of logical records is added in
parentheses — 9.5B2. Name, and optionally the
physical description, of accompanying material
recorded in file description area — 1.5E1(d) and
9.5D2. Note on nature and scope of item — 9.7B1.
Note on type of characters that make up file —
9.7B2. Note on edition and history — 1.7B7
and 9.7B7. Note on physical description of
the medium of the file if judged necessary —
9.7B10.

Work emanating from corporate body but not falling within any of the categories listed at 21.1B2 is treated as if no corporate body were involved (21.1B3) and entered under title — 21.1C(3).

261

RIMBAULT, Edward F.
New instructions on the art of singing : comprising directions for the formation and cultivation of the voice after the methods of the best Italian masters . . . chiefly selected from the celebrated tutor of Lablache / arranged and edited by Edward F. Rimbault. — New & rev. ed. — London : Chappell, [19—].
81 p. : chiefly music ; 36 cm.
Cover title: Rimbault's new singing tutor for soprano or tenor adapted from the valuable work of Lablache.

1.   Title   2.   Lablache, Luigi

Other title information abridged — 1.1E3. Physical description of item consisting mainly of music not dealt with in rule 5.5B, so rule 2.5C6 applied.

Adaptation of music under heading for the adapter — 21.18C.

Roads to Freedom

Essays in Honour of Friedrich A. von Hayek

Edited by
Erich Streissler
Managing Editor

Gottfried Haberler

Friedrich A. Lutz

Fritz Machlup

London   Routledge & Kegan Paul

262

ROADS to freedom : essays in honor of Friedrich A. von Hayek / edited by Erich Streissler . . . [et al.]. — London : Routledge & K. Paul, 1969.
xix, 315 p., 1 leaf of plates : port. ; 26 cm.
Bibliography: p. 309-315.
ISBN 0-7100-6616-3.

1.   Streissler, Erich
2.   Hayek, Friedrich A. von†*

More than three persons have same degree of responsibility for work, so all but first are omitted and mark of omission and [et al.] added — 1.1F3.

An example of a festschrift, here treated as a work produced under editorial direction and entered under title — 21.7B. Added entry for person honoured by festschrift — 21.30F.

ROBERTS, James L.
  Hamlet : notes / James L. Roberts. —
Toronto : Coles, 1976.
  112 p. ; 22 cm. — (Coles notes ; 406).
  Cover title: Shakespeare Hamlet : notes.

  1. Title   2. Series

This work presents a discussion and interpretation
of 'Hamlet' but does not contain any of the text
of the play. It cannot therefore be considered as
a commentary (21.13) but simply as a work of
single personal authorship — 21.1A1, 21.1A2
and 21.4A.

ROBINSON, John A.T.
  Honest to god / John A.T. Robinson. —
London : SCM Press, 1963.
  143 p. ; 19 cm.

  1. Title

Author is referred to on title page as 'John A.T.
Robinson, Bishop of Woolwich' but the title is
omitted from the statement of responsibility
and no mark of omission is necessary — 1.1F7.

Title is also omitted from heading — 22.15C.

RODGERS, Richard
  Slaughter on tenth avenue : piano
solo / by Richard Rodgers. — London :
Chappell, c1956.
  1 piano score (12 p.) ; 28 cm.

  1. Title

Description of music — Ch.1 and Ch.5. Specific
material designation chosen from list of terms
given in rule 5.5B1.

RODIN MUSEUM
  Rodin Museum : handbook / by
John L. Tancock. — Philadelphia :
Philadelphia Museum of Art, 1969.
  103 p. : ill. ; 18 cm.

Work of administrative nature emanating from
corporate body and dealing with its resources
is entered under heading for body — 21.1B2(a).
As indicated in example no. 56, the phrase 'of
an administrative nature' is a little ambiguous
but the examples: 'National Gallery'; 'First
National Bank of Chicago'; and 'Royal Ontario
Museum'; included in rule 21.4B appear to
corroborate this interpretation.

The ROMAUNT of the rose / edited by
  Frederick J. Furnivall. — London :
K. Paul, Trench, Trübner for the Chaucer
Society, 1911.
  ix, 101 p. ; 22 cm.
  "A reprint of the first printed edition
by William Thynne A.D. 1532".

  1. Furnivall, Frederick J.
  2. Chaucer Society
  3. [Roman de la rose. English
        (Middle English)]

If added entry is required for basic story found in
many versions, uniform title is title that is
established in English-language reference sources;
name of language is added — 25.12A. Initial
article omitted — 25.4A. If language of item is
in an early form of a modern language, name
of modern language is added to uniform title,
followed by that of the early form in
parentheses — 25.5D.

ROSSINI, Gioacchino
[Il barbiere di Siviglia. Vocal score.
English & Italian]
The barber of Seville = Il barbiere
di Siviglia : a lyric comedy / adapted from
the French of Pierre Augustin Caron de
Beaumarchais ; and rendered into English
from the Italian by J. Wrey Mould ; the
music composed by Gioacchino Rossini ;
revised from the orchestral score by
W.S. Rockstro. — London : Boosey, 1848.
1 vocal score (viii, 16, 370 p.) ;
24 cm. — (The standard lyric drama ; v. 3).
Preface and libretto in English, followed
by the music with words in English and
Italian.

1.   Title   2.   The barber of
                         Seville
3.   Beaumarchais, Pierre Augustin
        Caron de
4.   Mould, J. Wrey
5.   Rockstro, W.S.   6.   Series

Opera entered under heading for composer —
21.19A. Uniform title for musical work is
composer's original title in language in which it was
formulated — 25.27A. 'Vocal score' added to
uniform title — 25.31B3. Names of languages
added — 25.31B7 and 25.5D.

ROYAL COLLEGE OF SURGEONS.
   Museum
   Illustrated guide to the Museum of the
Royal College of Surgeons, England / by
Arthur Keith. — London : Printed for The
College and sold by Taylor and Francis,
1910.
   vi, 132 p., [1] leaf of plates : ill., plans,
port. ; 22 cm.

1.   Title   2.   Keith, Arthur

Inclusion in publication area of words indicating
the function (other than solely publishing)
performed by a body — 1.4D3.

Work of an administrative nature emanating from
corporate body and dealing with its resources is
entered under heading for body — 21.1B2(a).
As indicated in example no. 56, the phrase 'of
an administrative nature' is a little ambiguous
but the examples noted in the annotation to this
example and to example no. 266 appear to
corroborate this interpretation. Name that
includes the entire name of the higher body —
24.13(Type 5). Name of the higher body
omitted from subheading — 24.13.

ROYAL COMMISSION ON LOCAL
   GOVERNMENT IN ENGLAND
   Local government reform : short version
of the report of the Royal Commission on
Local Government in England / presented
to Parliament by command of Her Majesty
June 1969. — London : H.M.S.O., 1969.
   vi, 22 p. : map ; 25 cm. — (Cmnd. ;
4039).
   Chairman: The Rt. Hon. Lord
Redcliffe-Maud.

1.   Title
2.   Redcliffe-Maud, John Primatt
         Redcliffe Redcliffe-Maud, Baron

Abridgment under the heading for the original —
21.12A. Work emanating from corporate body
and recording its collective thought (in this case,
the report of a commission) is entered under
heading for body — 21.1B2(c). Body created
by a government which does not need the name
of the government for identification purposes
entered under its own name — 24.17 and
24.18(Type 2).

S.R. Ranganathan, 1892-1972 : papers
   given at a memorial meeting on
Thursday 25th January 1973 / edited
by Edward Dudley. — London : Library
Association, 1974.
   40 p. : port. ; 22 cm.
   ISBN 0-85365-197-3.

1.   Dudley, Edward

If title proper includes initials with full stops between them, initials are recorded with full stops, but without spaces between them — 1.1B6.

Work emanating from body which is considered to lack a name (the indefinite article is used and 'memorial meeting' is relatively meaningless by itself) entered under title — 21.5A.

272

SALCOMBE and Kingsbridge : Dartmouth, Brixham, Paignton, Torquay and South Devon. — 5th ed. — London : Ward Lock, [1963].
160 p., 11 p. of plates (some folded) : ill., maps, plans ; 18 cm. — (Red guides).

1.   Series

Volume which contains both leaves and pages of plates; number is recorded in terms of whichever is predominant — 2.5B10.

Work of unknown authorship entered under title — 21.5A.

273

SAN ANTONIO
[La fin des haricots. English]
The strangler / by San Antonio ; translated by Cyril Buhler. — London : Duckworth, 1968.
144 p. ; 19 cm.
Originally published: Paris : Editions Fleuve, 1961.
ISBN 0-7156-0397-3.

1.   Title   2.   The strangler

Entry under phrase — 22.11A. Apart from references needed in connection with the use of uniform title, a further reference would be required from the author's real name (Frederic Dard) — 26.1 and 26.2A1. No added entry under heading for translator because work does not fall into one of categories listed at 21.30K1.

274

SANGHARAKSHITA, Bhikshu
The Three Jewels : an introduction to Buddhism / by Bhikshu Sangharakshita (Sthavira). — London : Rider, 1967.
xi, 276 p. ; 22 cm.

1.   Title

Vernacular term of address, etc. added to name of person of religious vocation — 22.17D.

275

SANTEE, Walt
Mark of vengeance / by Walt Santee. — London : Hale, 1968.
156 p. ; 20 cm.

1.   Title

Author who uses several pseudonyms, but is not known predominantly by one name. Each item therefore entered under heading for name appearing on it — 22.2C3. (Reference needed from real name — King, Albert and other pseudonyms).*

276

SCHOLA HUNGARICA ENSEMBLE
Magyar Gregorianum : a karácsonyi ünnepkör dallamai. — [Budapest] : Hungaraton, [1976].
1 sound disc : 33 ⅓ rpm, stereo. ; 12 in.
Container notes in Hungarian, English, German and Russian.
Container title: Gregorian chants from Hungary : medieval Christmas melodies.
Schola Hungarica Ensemble, Janka Szendrei, László Dobszay, leaders.
"This recording was made at the medieval church at Besa"—Container.
Hungaraton: LPX 11477.

1.   Title
2.   Gregorian chants from Hungary†

Title proper appears in two languages but the version chosen is that which appears on the chief source of information (i.e. the label) — 6.0B2.

Note made of container title[1] — 1.7B4 and 6.7B4. When the participation of a body found in a statement in the chief source of information is confined to performance, such a statement is given in a note — 6.1F1 and 6.7B6. (But see also example no. 66).

Sound recording containing musical works by different persons entered under the heading for the principal performer — 21.23C.

277

SCOTT, Robert
    The diaries of Captain Robert Scott : a record of the second Antarctic Expedition, 1910-1912. — High Wycombe : University Microfilms, 1968.
      6 v. (ca. 2000 p.) : ill., ports. ; 21-26 cm.
    Facsim. of: B.M. Add. Ms. 51024-41.
    Includes facsim. of: South polar times. 1911.

1.   Title
2.   Scott Antarctic Expedition (<u>2nd</u> : <u>1910-1912</u>)
3.   South Polar times

Rules for monographs in more than one volume do not give instructions on recording number of pages where work is printed without pagination — 2.5B17 to 2.5B22. However, estimate has been made in accordance with rule for single volumes — 2.5B7. If volumes in multivolume set differ in height by more than two centimetres, the smallest and largest size are given, separated by a hyphen — 2.5D3.

It might become necessary to distinguish this author from others with the same name. Once 'Robert Scott' has been chosen as the form by which this author is commonly identified, the full form ('Robert Falcon Scott') could not be used, but some other method. Possibilities are: addition of dates of birth and death — 21.18 — or addition of title (i.e. 'Captain') — 22.19B. An added entry under 'South polar times', as a related work, would be needed — 21.30G — unless it were decided to make an analytical entry — 13.5A. The added entry for the expedition is formulated by analogy with the rules for conferences. The footnote to the 'Challenger Expedition' example in rule 24.1 indicates that this is the method to follow.

278

SCOTT, Tom, <u>b</u>. 1906
    Golf secrets of the masters / by Tom Scott and Geoffrey Cousins. — London : S. Paul, 1968.
      136 p., 16 p. of plates : ill., ports. ; 22 cm.
      ISBN 0-09-085930-8.

1.   Title   2.   Cousins, Geoffrey

Dates added to distinguish between different persons of same name -- 22.18. Optionally, dates may be added to all personal names, even if there is no need to distinguish between headings.

See also examples no. 87, 88, 136, 137, 277, 305, 306

279

SCOTT, Tom, <u>b</u>. 1918
    At the shrine o the unkent sodger : a poem for recitation / by Tom Scott. — Preston : Akros, 1968.
      22 p. ; 22 cm.

1.   Title

See annotation following previous example.

---

[1] "Container" seems to be the umbrella term for a sound recording's sleeve, box, etc. and this is the term which appears in the examples included in rules such as 6.7B4

280

SCOTT, Sir Walter
    [Novels. Selections]
    The Waverley pageant : the best passages
from the novels of Sir Walter Scott ;
selected, with critical introductions, by
Hugh Walpole ; with notes by Wilfred
Partington. — London : Eyre and
Spottiswoode, 1932.
    662 p. ; 20 cm.

1.   Title   2.   The Waverley
                            pageant
3.   Walpole, Hugh

Name associated with responsibility for the item is
transcribed as part of other title information —
1.1F13. Subsequent statements of responsibility
recorded — 1.1F6 and preceded by semi-colons —
1.1A1.

Selections from the works of one personal author —
21.4A. British title of honour inserted in heading —
22.12B. If item consists of extracts from works of
one person in a particular form, 'Selections' is
added to collective title — 25.10.

281

SELECTIONS from the English novel-
    ists : an anthology of representative
passages, Henry Fielding to D.H. Lawrence /
edited by C.J. Lowe and R.J. Gates. —
London : Routledge and K. Paul, 1967.
    ix, 211 p. ; 20 cm.
    ISBN 0-7100-6031-9.

1.   Lowe, C.J.   2.   Gates, R.J.

Collection or a work produced under editorial
direction entered under title — 21.1C(2).

282

SEMINAR ON THE DEVELOPMENT
    OF PUBLIC LIBRARIES IN ASIA
    (1955 : Delhi)
    Public libraries for Asia : the Delhi
Seminar. — Paris : Unesco, 1956.
    165 p., [9] p. of plates : ill. ; 22 cm. —
(Unesco public library manuals ; 7).

1.   Title   2.   Series

Conference not named on title page but name is
given in introduction and use of definite article
is taken as evidence of presence of name — 21.1B1.
Access points are normally determined from the
chief source of information for the item being
catalogued but other statements prominently
stated may be taken into account (21.0B).
'Prominently stated' is defined (0.8) as a formal
statement found in one of the prescribed sources
of information for areas 1 and 2 of the item
being catalogued. However, information appearing
in the content of an item (e.g. the text of a book)
may be used when a statement appearing in the
chief source of information is ambiguous or
insufficient (21.0B). 'The Delhi Seminar' seems
to be such an ambiguous or insufficient statement
and the name of the conference given in the introduction is therefore used. 'The Delhi Seminar' is,
however, a possible alternative name from which a
reference might be required — 26.3A1.* The
heading for this reference would be:
    Delhi Seminar (1955)
If the location is part of the name of a conference,
it is not repeated — 24.7B4.

283

SEUSS, Dr.
    One fish two fish red fish blue fish / by
Dr. Seuss. — London : Collins and Harvill,
1960.
    63 p. : col. ill. ; 24 cm. — (Beginner
books. I can read it all by myself).
    Published by arrangement with:
New York : Random House.

1.   Title   2.   Series
3.   I can read it all by myself

Title included in statement of responsibility if
omission would leave only surname — 1.1F7(b).

Word or phrase associated with name added
when name consists only of a surname — 22.15A.
A reference would be required from the name
in direct order. * If Seuss was not a real name
entry would be under the phrase in direct
order, e.g. Dr X — 22.11A.

SHACKLETON, Keith
    Birds of the Atlantic Ocean / paintings
by Keith Shackleton ; text by Ted Stokes ;
foreword by H.R.H. The Prince Philip,
Duke of Edinburgh. — Hamlyn for Country
Life Books, 1968.
    156 p. : ill. (chiefly col.), maps ; 29 cm.

1.   Title   2.   Stokes, Ted

Work of mixed responsibility resulting from the
collaboration between an artist and a writer
entered under the one named first unless the
other's name is given greater prominence — 21.24.

area — 1.5E1(d) and 6.5E1 (rules 1.9B and 1.10B
are also relevant). Optionally, the physical description of the accompanying material is added. Notes
on cast and credits — 1.7B6, 6.7B6 and by
analogy with 7.7B6. Note on accompanying
material — 1.7B11 and 6.7B11.

Sound recording of one literary work under the
heading appropriate to that work — 21.23A. Item
is treated as an abridgment - not an adaptation - and
entry is made under the heading for the original
author — 21.12A. No added entry for series as
all of the parts are under the heading for one
person — 21.30L(3).

SHAKESPEARE, William
    Hamlet / [directed by Michael Red-
grave ; script adapted by Michael
Benthall]. — Modern abridged version. —
London : Oldbourne Press, c1964.
    1 sound disc (ca. 50 min.) : 33 ⅓
rpm, mono. ; 12 in. + 1 text (42 p. ;
31 cm.). — (Living Shakespeare).
    Cast: Michael Redgrave, Margaret
Rawlings, John Phillips.
    Credits: Musique concrete, Desmond
Leslie ; narrator Michael Benthall.
    Text includes acting version, complete
play, notes and glossary.
    Oldbourne: DEOB 1AM.

1.   Title*   2.   Redgrave, Sir
                            Michael
3.   Benthall, Michael

No statement of responsibility in the chief source
of information of a sound recording (i.e. the label)
so information taken from the container, i.e. the
sleeve, and enclosed in square brackets — 6.0B2
and 1.0A1. Shakespeare is not given as a statement
of responsibility on either the label or the sleeve and
cannot therefore be included — 1.1F2. The
presence of the word *version* is taken as evidence of
edition statement — 1.2B3. Two names appear on
the label but the trade name "Living Shakespeare"
appears to be the name of a series rather than a
publishing subdivision — 6.4D3. It is also presented
as a series on the accompanying text. Accompanying material recorded in physical description

SHAKESPEARE, William
    [Plays. Selections]
    Shakespearian quotations in everyday
use : a key to their source and context / by
L.L.M. Marsden. — London : Witherby,
1927 (1964 printing).
    156 p. ; 18 cm.

1.   Title
2.   Shakespearian quotations in every-
        day use
3.   Marsden, L.L.M.

Optionally, date of printing can be given if found on
the item and if considered important by the cataloguing agency — 2.4G2.

If item consists of extracts from works of one
person in a particular form, uniform title consists of appropriate collective title, with the
addition of 'Selections' — 25.10.

SHAKESPEARE, William
   [Works]
   The complete works of William
Shakespeare arranged in their chronological
order ; edited by W.G. Clark and W. Aldis
Wright ; with an introduction to each play,
adapted from the Shakespearian primer of
Professor Dowden. — Garden City, N.Y. :
Nelson Doubleday, [19—].
   2 v. (1140 p.) ; 22 cm.
   Two columns per page.

1.   Title
2.   The complete works of William
       Shakespeare
3.   Clark, W.G.   4. Wright, W. Aldis

Number of volumes recorded — 2.5B17. Pagination
given in parentheses if volumes continuously
paged — 2.5B20. Note on important physical
details not included in physical description
area — 1.7B10 and 2.7B10.

Uniform titles — collective title 'Works' used for
an item which consists of, or purports to be, the
complete works of a person — 25.8.

SHANKLAND, COX AND ASSOCIATES
   Ipswich draft basic plan : a consultants'
proposals for the expanded town : a report
to the Minister of Housing and Local
Government and Ipswich County Borough /
by Shankland, Cox and Associates. —
London : H.M.S.O., 1968.
   151 p., [1] folded leaf of plates : ill.
(some col.), maps, plans ; 30 cm.

1.   Title   2.   Ipswich. Council
3.   United Kingdom. Ministry of
       Housing and Local Government

Work emanating from corporate body and recording its collective thought is entered under heading
for body — 21.1B2(c). Ministry entered subordinately (in added entry heading) — 24.18(4).
Ipswich is no longer a county borough; the
Ministry of Housing and Local Government no
longer exists. Appropriate references would have
to be made — 26.0.

[SHOE-HORN] . — 1912 (Birmingham :
   H.V.P. & Co.).
   1 shoe horn : silver ; 28 cm.
   Title supplied by cataloguer.
   Blade is silver plated.
   Date and place of manufacture derived
from hall-mark on handle.

Description of three-dimensional artefacts — Ch.1
and Ch.10. Artefact not intended primarily for
communication has date as first element of
publication, etc. area — 10.4F2 — followed, as
name of publisher is not applicable, by place
and name of manufacturer in parentheses — 1.4G1
and 10.4G1. Note on source of title — 10.7B3.
No specific rule for making note on source of
details of manufacture. However, this seems
important and so has been included as 'useful
descriptive information that cannot be fitted
into other areas of the description' — 1.7A5.

Shop Stewards and Industrial Relations

by

T. W. Burrow   M. F. Somerton   T. G. Whittingham

N. Williams

Published by : The Department of Adult Education, University of Nottingham
and the Workers' Educational Association, East Midland District.

Printed by John Clough & Son, (Printers)
Blackstone Street Works
Nottingham
Tel. 83419

290

SHOP stewards and industrial relations /
by T.W. Burrow . . . [et al.]. —
Nottingham : University of Nottingham,
Dept. of Adult Education, 1968.
98 p. ; 22 cm.
Published jointly with the Workers'
Educational Association, East Midland
District.
ISBN 0-802031-06-6.

1. Burrow, T.W.
2. University of Nottingham.
   Department of Adult Education
3. Workers' Educational Association.
   East Midland District

More than three persons have same degree of responsibility, so first only is recorded — 1.1F5. Two publishers named on title page, but second not recorded in publication area as it is not given prominence by typography — 1.4D5. No rule for recording publishing agency that includes subordinate body, but example for motion pictures and sound recordings has been used as authority and subordinate and higher body have been separated by comma — 7.4E1. Note on publication details not included in publication area — 2.7B9.

Responsibility is shared between more than three persons and principal responsibility is not attributed to any one, two or three, so entry is under title — 21.6C2. Added entries for prominently named publishers whose responsibility extends beyond merely publishing the work — 21.30E.

291

SHOPPING in the United States / U.S.,
Department of Commerce, United
States Travel Service. — [Washington?] :
USTS, 1976.
64 p. : ill. ; 23 x 11 cm.
USTS-763 E.

1. United States Travel Service

Work emanating from corporate body which does not fall within any of the categories listed in rule 21.1B2 and is therefore entered under title —

21.1C(3). In added entry, body created or controlled by a government is entered under its own name as it does not belong to any of the types listed in 24.18 — 24.17.

292

SIMON Simon / Denouement Films ;
producer, Peter Shillingford ; director,
Graham Stark. — London : Tigon Film
Productions [distributor], 1970.
1 film reel (30 min.) : sd., col. ; 35 mm.
Cast: Graham Stark, John Junkin,
Norman Rossington, Julia Foster.
Credits: Photography, Derek van Lynt
and Harvey Harrison, Jr. ; sound, John
Wood ; editor, Bunny Warren ; music,
Denis King.
Summary: Mixed comedy involving
two municipal workmen, a blonde typist
and a hydraulic platform truck.

1. Shillingford, Peter
2. Stark, Graham

Persons or bodies credited in the chief source of information with participation in the production of a film who are considered to be of major importance to the film and in the interests of the cataloguing agency are recorded in the statement of responsibility area — 7.1F1. Alternatively, a production company, releasing agency, etc. may be named in the publication, distribution, etc. area — 7.4D1 (see example no. 6). Other statements of responsibility are given in notes, i.e. notes on cast and credits — 7.7B6.

If a film emanates from a corporate body it is unlikely to fall within the categories listed in 21.1B2. The producers, by definition (see Appendix D) are not responsible for the artistic or intellectual content. Personal authorship is usually, as in this case, uncertain or diffuse and entry is therefore under title — 21.1C. Further added entries could be made under any of the other bodies or persons named in the entry if the cataloguing agency considered that they provide important access points.

SINHA, Dharnidhar Prasad
    Culture change in an intertribal market : the role of the Banari intertribal market among the hill people of Chatanagpur / by Dharnidhar Prasad Sinha. — London : Asia Publishing House, 1968.
    xvi, 117 p., 14 p. of plates : ill., 4 maps ; 22 cm.
    Bibliography: p. 109-112.
    ISBN 0-210-27031-4.

    1.   Title

Entry under element of name which identifies individual and functions as surname — 22.5B. Also applicable is rule for Indic name of person flourishing after the middle of the nineteenth century. Entry is under surname or the name that the person is known to have used as a surname — 22.25B.

[SLOVO o polku Igoreve. English]
    The tale of the armament of Igor, A.D. 1185 : a Russian historical epic / edited and translated by Leonard A. Magnus. — London : Oxford University Press, 1915.
    lxiii, 122 p., [1] leaf of plates : map ; 23 cm. — (Publications of the Philological Society).
    "With revised Russian text, notes, introduction and glossary".
    Bibliography: p. 119-122.

    1.   Magnus, Leonard A.
    2.   The tale of the armament of Igor†
    3.   Series

Words in quoted notes not abbreviated — B.5.

Original language of anonymous work created before 1501 is not written in Greek nor in roman script, so original title is used as uniform title, since no established title exists in English — 25.4C. Name of language added to title as it is different from original — 25.5D.

SMELTZER, Victor R.
    Sound / devised by Victor R. Smeltzer and Arthur G. Waring. — Manchester : T. Hope & Sankey Hudson, [197-?].
    1 portfolio (10 lesson cards : ill., b&w ; 21 x 17 cm.). — (Brightway science cards for juniors. Introductory series).
    Cards printed on 1 side only.

    1.   Title   2.   Waring, Arthur G.
    3.   Series

No authority for using term 'Lesson cards' after 'portfolio' (not listed at 2.5B2), but it would seem desirable to class them as printed material.

See also examples no. 157 and 368.

SMITH John L.
    Rail to Tenterden / by John L. Smith. — Sutton [Surrey] : Lens of Sutton, 1967.
    80 p. : chiefly ill., facsims., map ; 25 cm.

    1.   Title

Name of county given after place of publication if considered necessary for identification — 1.4C3. (Name is not abbreviated, because list of stipulated abbreviations of place-names does not include places in United Kingdom — B.14.)

SOUVENIR playing cards [of] Montreal and Quebec. — Montreal : Canadian Playing Card Co., [192-?].
    1 game (54 cards) ; 9 x 7 cm. in case, 10 x 8 x 3 cm.
    Faces of cards contain various b&w views of Montreal, Quebec and Ottawa + ill. of Caughnawaga Indian and map: The principal highways of the Province of Quebec.

Description of games as three-dimensional artefacts — Ch.1 and Ch.10. Number of pieces given after specific material designation — 10.5B2. Dimensions of objects and container given — 10.5D1 and 10.5D2. Important physical details not included in physical description area given in note — 10.7B10.

298

The SPANISH Inquisition : a collection of contemporary documents / compiled and edited by John Langdon-Davies. — London : Jackdaw : Distributed by J. Cape, 1966.
16 pieces : ill. ; 21 x 22-42 x 37 cm. + notes (1 sheet), in folder, 24 x 37 cm. — (Jackdaw ; no. 44).
Partial contents: A procession to an auto de fe : engraving / by B. Schoonebeck — A bond written by a nun making a pact with the devil — The loyal martyrs : an English ballad sheet.

1. Langdon-Davies, John
2. Series

Inclusion, in publication area, of phrase indicating function (other than solely publishing) performed by a body — 1.4D3(a). Multipart item described in terms of 'pieces' — 1.10C2(c) and 2.5B18. Sizes of parts in multipart set differing in size given in similar manner to differing volumes in multivolume set, i.e. smallest size and largest size (when difference is more than two centimetres) — 2.5D3. Accompanying material recorded in physical description — 2.5E1. No authority in Ch.2 or in rule 1.10C2(c) for giving details of container in physical description area but recorded here by analogy with rules 1.10C2(a) and 10.5D2.

299

SPEED, John
The Countie Pallatine of Lancaster described and divided into hundreds, 1610. — Scale ca. 1:500,000. — Ireland : Irish Cabin Linens, [197-].
1 map : col., linen ; 71 x 45 cm.
Probable cartographer: John Speed.
Reproduction of original, intended for use as a tea towel.
Insets: Map of Lancaster and ports. of Kings and Queens of England.

1. Title

Description of maps — Ch.1 and Ch.3.

Item which may be described in terms of either one medium or another — see annotation of example no. 316.

Entry under probable author — 21.1A2 and 21.5B. Cartographers are the authors of their maps — 21.1A1.

300

SPENCER'S decimal percentage and discount reckoner. — London : J. Spencer, 1970.
176 p. ; 18 cm.
ISBN 0-85436-003-4.

1. John Spencer & Co. (Publishers)

Publisher recorded in shortest form in which it can be understood and identified internationally — 1.4D2. (Appears on title page as: John Spencer & Co. (Publishers) Ltd.)

Work which appears to emanate from a corporate body but which does not fall into any of the categories listed in 21.1B2 is entered under title — 21.1C(3). An alternative interpretation of the rules would be to treat it as an anonymous work, but this would not alter the entry — 21.1C(1). If the first interpretation is adopted, an added entry is needed under 'John Spencer & Co. (Publishers)' as a prominently-named corporate body ; this entry would also be needed for the second interpretation, as the firm is a publisher whose responsibility extends beyond that of merely publishing the work — 21.30E.

301

SPINK, Michael
The 1-2-3 frieze / Michael Spink. — London : Cape, 1969.
2 pictures : col. ; 21 x 152 cm. folded to 21 x 16 cm.
One frieze has individual pictures numbered 1 to 10, each showing the appropriate number of a particular animal or tree. Second frieze shows them integrated into single country scene.
ISBN 0-224-61746-X.

1. Title

Using the nearest related term in Ch.8, 'picture', as the specific material designation is not particularly helpful. It might be better, by analogy with Ch.10, to use the specific name of the item, i.e. 2 friezes.

STANBURY, Jacqueline
    Come love with me : poems for people in love / selected by Christine Westwood. — [London] : Times Newspapers, 1975.
    1 sound cassette (55 min.) : 1⅞ ips, stereo. — (World of literature).
    Read by Jacqueline Stanbury, Peter Jeffrey and Ian Gelder.
    Times Newspapers: WLA 003.

    1. Title   2. Westwood, Christine
    3. Jeffrey, Peter   4. Gelder, Ian
    4. Series

Description of sound cassettes — Ch.1 and Ch.6. Title transcribed as it appears in the chief source of information (i.e. the cassette and label — 6.0B1) — 1.1F6. Statement of responsibility recorded in the form in which it appears on item — 1.1F1. Where a sound recording is concerned, if the participation of persons found in a statement in the chief source of information

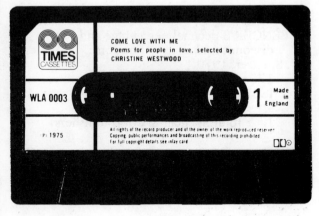

is confined to performance, such a statement is given in a note — 6.1F1 and 6.7B6. (But see also example no. 66). Playing speed given in inches per second — 6.5C3. Number of tracks not required as it is standard (i.e. 4) — 6.5C6. Cassette is of standard dimensions ($3\frac{7}{8}$ x 2½ in.) and tape is of standard width (⅛ in.), so this information is also omitted — 6.5D5. Tape is Dolby processed; it is optional whether to include this following "stereo" in the physical description — 6.5C8.

Sound recording of literary works by different persons entered under the principal performer or, as in this instance, under the first named when there are two or three principal performers — 21.23C.

303

STANDARD TELEPHONES AND
  CABLES
  What everyone who uses a telephone
should know about telecommunications /
Standard Telephone and Cables Limited. —
London : STC, [1976].
  [8] p. : col. ill. ; 30 cm.
  Also available as wallchart (col. ;
62 x 89 cm.).
  Brief survey of telecommunications
in general and STC's part in it in particular.

1.   Title

Same item available in different formats. Note on the other format — 1.7B16.

Work is of an administrative nature in that it serves as an advertisement for the operations of the corporate body from which it emanates. It is therefore entered under the heading for the body — 21.1B2(a). Entry directly under name — 24.1. 'Ltd' omitted from heading — 24.5C1.

304

STATISTICAL package for the social
  sciences / Statistical Package for the
Social Sciences Incorporated. — [S.l] :
Stat. Pack. for the Soc. Sc., [197-].
  1 object program (IBM 360, UNIVAC,
ICL 1900, Honeywell, PRIME) + 1 manual.

1.   Statistical Package for the Social
      Sciences Incorporated

Description of machine readable data files — Ch.1 and Ch.9. No place or probable place of publication can be given so the abbreviation 's.l.' (sine loco) is used — 1.4C6. Specific material designation chosen from list of three possible terms — 9.5B1. For an object program, the name, number, etc. of the machine on which it runs is added in parentheses — 9.5B4. Name of accompanying material recorded in file description area — 1.5E1(d) and 9.5D2.

305

STEVENSON, D.E. (Donald Edward)
  Metabolic disorders of domestic
animals / D.E. Stevenson and A.A. Wilson. —
Oxford : Blackwell Scientific, 1963.
  xiv, 198 p. : ill. ; 23 cm.

1.   Title   2.   Wilson, A.A.

Work of shared responsibility between two persons. Principal responsibility is not attributed to either, so entry is under the heading for the one named first, with an added entry under the heading for the other — 21.6C1. Writer is known by surname and initials, but forenames in spelled out form are added and enclosed in parentheses to distinguish between names that are otherwise identical (see also next example) — 22.16A. Optionally, such additions may be made to other names containing initials.

STEVENSON, D.E. (Dorothy Emily)
   The house on the cliff / D.E. Stevenson. — 1st large print ed. — Anstey,
Leicestershire : Thorpe, 1977.
   480 p. ; 23 cm. — (Ulverscroft large
print series).
   First published: London : Collins,
1966.
   ISBN 0-85456-537-X.

   1.   Title   2.   Series

There are no rules for the treatment of large
print books (unlike for braille and other tactile
books — see example no. 149). However all the
necessary details appear in the description, so
an additional note is unnecessary. Edition
statement transcribed as found on the item,
using standard abbreviations — 1.2B1.

An added entry is not normally required for
a series in which the items are related to each
other only by common physical characteristics
— 21.30L(1). However, such an entry in this
instance might well prove of convenience to users.

See also annotation following previous example.

STREATFIELD, Noel
   Nicholas / by Marlie Brande ; translated by Elizabeth Boas ; adapted by Noel
Streatfield. — London : Benn, 1968.
   [29] p. : ill. (some col.) ; 20 x 24 cm.
   Originally published as: Nat ned
Nikolaj. Copenhagen : Gyldendal, 1966.

   1.   Title   2.   Brande, Marlie
   3.   Nat ned Nikolaj

Pages are unnumbered so number is given in square
brackets — 2.5B7. Width recorded as it is greater
than height — 2.5D2. Note on other manifesta-
tion of same work — 1.7A4.

Adaptation entered under heading for adapter —
21.10.

The SUNDAY Telegraph chart of freshwater fish : angler's guide. — London :
Sunday Telegraph, [1966?].
   1 chart : col. ; 27 cm. diam.
   Circular chart with apertured rotating
overlay. By pointing arrow to figure relating
to a numbered illustration, the name of the
fish illustrated, together with its general
haunts, classification, average length and
record weight, will appear in the apertures.
   On verso: British freshwater fish : a
description classified by family.

Description of charts as graphic materials — Ch.1
and Ch.8. Word added to indicate which
dimension is being given by analogy with 10.5D1.

SUTCLIFFE, Frank Meadow
   Boats in Whitby Harbour / Frank
Meadow Sutcliffe. — London : Camden
Graphics, 1977.
   1 photograph : sepia ; 23 x 31 cm.
   Reproduction of original taken:
ca. 1875.

   1.   Title†

Description of photographs as graphic materials —
Ch.1 and Ch.8. Publication details of reproduction
given in publication area, details of original given
in note — 1.4B6.

Reproduction of art work (including photographs)
entered under heading for original work — 21.16B.

SYMPOSIUM ON ADVANCED MEDICINE (4th : 1968 : Royal College of Physicians of London)
Fourth Symposium on Advanced Medicine : proceedings of a conference held at the Royal College of Physicians of London, 26th February-1st March, 1968 / edited by Oliver Wrong. — London : Pitman Medical in association with the Journal of the Royal College of Physicians of London, 1968.
xii, 420 p. : ill. ; 23 cm.
Bibliography: p. 419-420.
ISBN 0-272-79267-5.

1. Wrong, Oliver
2. Royal College of Physicians of London

Conference as corporate body — 21.1B1 and 21.1B2(d). Word denoting number omitted from heading (i.e. not 'FOURTH SYMPOSIUM ON . . .') — 24.7A. To heading are added: number (24.7B2), date (24.7B3) and location (24.7B4).

SYMPOSIUM ON HEAVY-WATER POWER REACTORS (1967 : Vienna)
Heavy-water power reactors : proceedings of The Symposium on Heavy-Water Power Reactors / held by the International Atomic Energy Agency in Vienna, 11-15 September 1967. — Vienna : International Atomic Energy Agency, 1968.
981 p. : ill. ; 24 cm. — (Proceedings series).
Papers in English and French with English abstracts. Discussions in English.

1. Title
2. International Atomic Energy Agency

Conference as corporate body — 21.1B1. Work which records the collective activity of a conference entered under heading for that body — 21.1B2(d). Entry directly under name — 24.1. Addition of date and location — 24.7B3 and 24.7B4. No added entry for series as it does not provide a useful collocation — 21.30L.

T.J. SMITH & NEPHEW LTD. Medical Division
Elastoplast technique : a classified reference to the use of elastoplast in modern surgery. — 10th ed. — Hull : T.J.S. & N., 1942.
87 p. : 86 ill. ; 22 cm.
Prepared by: T.J. Smith & Nephew Ltd., Medical Division.
Issued to the medical profession only.

1. Title

Number of illustrations recorded if it can be easily ascertained — 2.5C4. Optional note on terms of availability — 1.8D1.

Work emanating from a corporate body which is concerned with the use of one of its products. It seems reasonable, therefore, to consider the item as being of an administrative nature and to enter it under the heading for the body in accordance with 21.1B2(a). 'Ltd' required to make it clear that name is that of a corporate body — 24.5C1. Subordinate body as subheading of name of body to which it is subordinate because name contains a term that by definition implies that the body is part of another — 24.13(Type 1).

[TABLE mat] . — Wisconsin : Wisconsin Tissue Mills, 1974.
1 sheet of col. ill. ; 26 x 36 cm.
Commemorates the U.S. bicentennial.
Title supplied by cataloguer.

This item is here treated as a printed sheet, although it cannot really be said to constitute textual matter. The alternative — to catalogue it as a realia — is probably preferable, as illustrated in example no. 349. Supplied title enclosed in square brackets — 1.1A2. Number of sheets recorded — 2.5B2. Note on nature of item — 2.7B1. Source of title given in note — 2.7B3. British usage has been followed in the supplied title. In North America, 'Place mat' might be more appropriate.

314

TANNER, Ogden
Stress / by Ogden Tanner and the editors
of Time-Life Books. — Authorised British
ed. — Nederland : Time-Life International,
1977.
176 p. : ill. ; 27 cm. — (Human
behaviour).
Previously published: U.S. : Time-Life
Books, 1976.

1.   Title   2.   Time-Life Books
3.   Series

Work of shared responsibility resulting from the
collaboration between a person and a corporate
body — 21.6A(6). Principal responsibility is not
attributed to either one so entry is under the
heading for the one named first — 21.6C1.

315

TAYLOR, Frank
The Comaneci story / by Frank Taylor ;
edited by Don Bate ; cover and poster photographs by Don Morley, Allsport ; [other]
photographs by Daily Mirror photographers . . . [et al.]. — London : Mirror
Group Newspapers, 1976.
44 p. : ill., ports. ; 30 cm. + 1 poster
(col. ; 60 x 42 cm.).
Cover title: Daily Mirror presents the
Comaneci story.

1.   Title   2.   Bate, Don
3.   Morley, Don   4.   Daily Mirror

Statements of responsibility recorded in the order
of their sequence in the chief source of information — 1.1F6. Explanatory word added — 1.1F8.
Accompanying material recorded in physical
description area — 1.5E1 and 2.5E1. Note on
variant title — 2.7B4.

316

[TEA towel] . — Ireland : Irish Cabin
Linens, [197-] .
1 tea towel : linen, col. ; 78 x 49 cm.
Reproduction of map: The Countie
Pallatine of Lancaster, 1610.
Title supplied by cataloguer.
Probable cartographer: John Speed.

1.   Speed, John

Description of realia — Ch.1 and Ch.10. Title
supplied — 1.1B7.

Occasionally an item may be described in terms
of either one medium or another; AACR 2
does not give any specific instructions as to
how a choice is to be made. When an item is
reproduced in another format, rule 1.1C3
appears to indicate that the latter must form
the basis of the description. However, this may
not always be the best solution. This particular
item for instance could, in some circumstances,
be more usefully described as a cartographic
material (as illustrated in example no. 299).
British usage has been followed in the supplied
title. In North America, 'Dish towel' or 'Dish
cloth' would be more appropriate.

317

TECHNICAL services for industry :
technical information and other
services available from government departments and associated organisations /
Department of Trade and Industry. —
London : The Department, 1970.
302 p. ; 21 cm.

1.   United Kingdom. Department of
Trade and Industry

Work emanating from corporate body but not
falling within any of the categories listed at
21.1B2 is entered under title — 21.1C(3).
Added entry under corporate body — 21.30E.
The Department of Trade and Industry was
formed by an amalgamation of the Ministry
of Technology and the Board of Trade in 1971.
In 1974 the Department of Trade and Industry
was replaced by four separate bodies including
the Department of Industry and the Department
of Energy. This is a complex situation which
would require explanatory references to link
the various names — see 26.3C1(b) particularly
the United Kingdom. Ministry of Technology
example.

TEXAS country / Willie Nelson . . . [et al.]. — Los Angeles : United Artists, c1976.

2 sound discs : 33⅓ rpm, stereo.̈ ; 12 in.

Recordings by Willie Nelson (side 1), Bob Willis and his Texas Playboys (side 2), Asleep At The Wheel (side 3), and Freddie Fender (side 4).

United Artists : LA574-H2.

1.   Nelson, Willie

This item is included in AACR 2 as an example of a performing body whose contribution goes beyond that of mere performance and which is therefore recorded as a statement of responsibility — 6.1F1. All but the first body omitted when more than three bodies are named; omission is indicated and "et al." added in square brackets — 1.1F5. Duration may be omitted if it cannot readily be established — 6.5B2. Note of names of performers not already named in the statement of responsibility — 6.7B6.

Sound recording containing musical works by different persons or bodies performed by more than three principal performers entered under title — 21.23D. If four or more persons or bodies are involved an added entry is stipulated for the first named only — 21.30B. However, in this instance, the names of the other performers could be considered to provide "important access points" — 21.30H. Headings such as Asleep At The Wheel would require the addition of a suitable designation in order to convey the idea of a corporate body (as illustrated in example no. 66).

The Open University

Social Sciences : a second level course Urban development Unit 26

The new town idea

Prepared for the Course Team
by Ray Thomas and Peter Cresswell

The Open University Press

THOMAS, Ray

The new town idea / prepared for the Course Team [of] The Open University by Ray Thomas and Peter Cresswell. — Milton Keynes : Open Univ. Press, 1973.

64 p. : ill. ; 30 cm. — (Social sciences : a second level course. Urban development ; Unit 26) (DT 201 26).

ISBN 0-335-01751-7.

1.   Open University
2.   Cresswell, Peter   3.   Series
4.   Urban development
5.   DT 201 26

Other title information of series included if it provides valuable information identifying the series; it is preceded by colon – 1.6D1. Subseries named and preceded by full stop – 1.6H1. Item belongs to two series; each statement enclosed in parentheses – 1.6J1.

Responsibility shared between two persons, neither of whom is attributed with principal responsibility. Entry is therefore under first-named – 21.6C1. Rules instruct that added entry be made under heading for series if it provides useful collocation – 21.30L. For this example, an entry would appear to be useful under each series title and the subseries title.

See also example no. 373.

320

THOMAS HILL AND CO.
[Papers / by and relating to] Thomas Hill and Co. [and members of the firm]. – 1776-1849.
22 items ; 43 cm. or smaller.
Pot ash makers of Everton. Tax and rate bills, receipts, etc., indentures of apprenticeship, records of jury service and exemption from militia service, fire insurance papers, letter on sale of share in Liverpool Library, state lottery ticket, financial account for journey by stage coach, documents from London and North Western Railway Co. re. compensation for damage to firm's property by building of tunnel.
Title supplied by cataloguer.
With: cutting from Liverpool daily post, 28 Feb. 1966, on discovery of foundations of firm's chimney.

1. Title

Description of manuscripts – Ch.1 and Ch.4. Title supplied for collection of manuscripts. Materials relating to corporate body would be described as 'Records', but some of these items are personal and so term for miscellaneous personal or family material (i.e. 'Papers') is used – 4.1B2. Inclusive dates of manuscript collection – 4.4B1.

Shared responsibility, but principal responsibility can be attributed in chief source of information (i.e. the whole collection – 4.0B1) to the corporate body – 21.6B1. As many of the items are of an administrative nature dealing with the corporate body itself, entry is therefore under the body – 21.1B2(a).

STORIES FROM DICKENS

OLIVER TWIST, DAVID COPPERFIELD,

THE OLD CURIOSITY SHOP,

AND GREAT EXPECTATIONS

RETOLD FOR BOYS AND GIRLS

BY

RUSSELL THORNDIKE

RAPHAEL TUCK & SONS LTD.

Fine Art Publishers to Their Majesties the King and Queen and to Her Majesty Queen Mary

LONDON · NEW YORK · TORONTO

321

THORNDIKE, Russell
Stories from Dickens / retold for boys and girls by Russell Thorndike. – London : R. Tuck, [194-].
125 p. : ill. ; 20 cm.
Contents: Oliver Twist – David Copperfield – The Old curiosity shop – Great expectations.

1. Title   2. Dickens, Charles
3. Optionally, analytical title entries for each part

Title page bears both collective title and titles of individual works, so former is given as title proper and latter are recorded in note — 2.1B2. In the United States, the publication, distribution, etc. area would be given as:

London ; New York : R. Tuck

and, in Canada, as:

London ; Toronto : R. Tuck

— 1.4C5. Name of publisher given in shortest form in which it can be understood and identified — 1.4D2.

Adaptation for children entered under the heading for the adapter — 21.10.

Compare with examples no. 14, 90, 331.

322

THOSE Dutch Catholics / edited by
    Michel van der Plas and Henk Suer ; preface by Desmond Fisher ; translated from the Dutch by Theo Westow. — London : Chapman, 1967.
    164 p. ; 23 cm. — ([Here and now]).

1.   Plas, Michel van der
2.   Suer, Hank   3.   Series

Chief source of information for series of printed monograph is the whole publication — 2.0B2. However, series statement has been taken from a source other than the item, and so is enclosed in square brackets within parentheses — 1.6A2.

Work produced under editorial direction entered under title — 21.1C(2). For Dutch surname with prefix, entry is under part following prefix unless prefix is 'ver' — 22.5D1.

323

THREE Restoration comedies / edited with
    an introduction by Gamini Salgado. — Harmondsworth : Penguin, 1968.
    365 p. : 3 facsims. ; 18 cm. — (English library).
    Contents: The man of mode / Sir George Etherege — The country wife / William Wycherley — Love for love / William Congreve.

1.   Salgado, Gamini
2.   Optionally, author and title
        analytical entries for each part

Contents note — 1.7B18. Analytical added entries may be made for parts when comprehensive entry for larger work shows parts either in title and statement of responsibility area or in note area — 13.4.

Entry under title for collections produced under editorial direction — 21.1C(2).

324

TOLSTOI, Alexei Nikolaevich, Count
    [Petr Pervyi : roman / A.N. Tolstoi ; redaktor E. Romashkina]. — [Moskva : Pravda], 1968.
    743 p. : ill. ; 21 cm. — ([Shkolnaya biblioteka]).

1.   Title   2.   Romashkina, E.
3.   Series

This item is printed in Cyrillic, in this case Russian. The rules give no authority for romanising a title proper. The only relevant statement appears in rule 1.1B1, where it instructs that symbols in a title proper that cannot be reproduced by the typographical facilities available are replaced by a cataloguer's description in square brackets. The same applies to the statement of responsibility (1.1F9), the publication details and the series statement (see also 1.0E). Although square brackets have been used in the above entry, in practice some cataloguing agencies may wish to omit them.

Heading for name written in nonroman script is romanised — 22.3C2. Title of nobility included in heading if title commonly appears with name in works by the person or in reference sources — 22.12A.

The rules do recognise that there may be a need for romanisation and make use of the ALA/LC rules when this is called for. The above example, however, has been formulated using British Standard BS 2979 : 1958.

See also example no. 149.

325

The TOWER of London / Ministry of
    Public Building and Works. — London :
H.M.S.O., 1967.
    55 p. : ill. ; 20 cm. + 1 plan (39 x 58 cm. folded to 20 x 12 cm.). — (Ministry of Public Building and Works official guide).
    Plan, scale 1:900, attached to inside cover.

1.   United Kingdom. <u>Ministry of
            Public Building and Works</u>
2.   Series

Accompanying material recorded in the physical description area — 1.5E1(d). Optionally, dimensions of accompanying material given — 1.5E1. Note on the location of accompanying material and note on details not given in physical description area — 2.7B11.

Work emanating from a corporate body but not falling within any of the categories listed at 21.1B2 is entered under title — 21.1C(3).

Compare with example no. 153.

326

TRANSPORT Act 1968 : a C.B.I.
    summary and assessment. — London :
C.B.I., 1969.
    42 p. ; 21 cm.
    ISBN 0-85201-001-X.

1.   C.B.I.
2.   United Kingdom
            [Transport Act (1968)]

Work emanating from corporate body but not falling within any of the categories listed at 21.1B2 is entered under title — 21.1C(3). Variant forms of name appear on items issued by body (i.e. 'C.B.I.' or 'Confederation of British Industry'), but name as it appears in chief source of information is given as added entry heading — 24.2B. (A reference would be needed from form not used — 26.3A3.)

327

TRAQUAIR, Phoebe Anna
    Dante : illustrations and notes / [the illustrations by Phoebe Anna Traquair ; the notes by John Sutherland Black]. — Edinburgh : T. & A. Constable, 1890.
    xcv, 83 p. : 21 ill. ; 23 cm.
    Ill. for Dante's Divine comedy.
    Notes comprise: A Dante chronology — A short bibliography — Dante's library — Index.

1.   Title
2.   Black, John Sutherland
3.   Dante Alighieri
            [Divina commedia]

This work consists principally of one artist's illustrations for a text, and they are entered under the heading for the artist as they are published separately from the text. A name-title added entry is made under the heading for the writer of the original work — 21.11B. The work is also one of mixed responsibility resulting from a collaboration between artist and writer. Again, entry must be under the heading for the artist, as the one named first in the source of information. An added entry is made under the heading for the writer — 21.24.

Miscellaneous No. 5 (1972)

Treaty

establishing

The European Economic
Community

Rome, 25 March 1957

[The United Kingdom is not a party to the Treaty]

*Presented to Parliament
by the Secretary of State for Foreign and Commonwealth Affairs
by Command of Her Majesty
January 1972*

LONDON
HER MAJESTY'S STATIONERY OFFICE

£1 net

Cmnd. 4864

328

[TREATY OF ROME (1957)]
Treaty Establishing the European Economic Community : Rome, 25 March 1957 / presented to Parliament by the Secretary of State for Foreign and Commonwealth Affairs by command of Her Majesty, January 1972. — London : H.M.S.O., 1972.
vii, 170 p. ; 25 cm. — (Miscellaneous ; no. 5 (1972)) (Cmnd. ; 4864).
At head of title: European communities.
Signatories: Belgium, West Germany, France, Italy, Luxembourg, Netherlands.
ISBN 0-10-148640-5.

1. Treaty Establishing the European Economic Community

Names of treaties capitalised — A.20. Statement of responsibility may include words or phrases which are neither names nor linking words — 1.1F15. Two series statements recorded separately, the more specific one first — 1.6J1. Numbering within series recorded in terms given in the item — 1.6G1 and 2.6B1. Note on additional title borne by item — 2.7B4.

Treaty between more than three national governments entered under title — 21.35A2. Uniform title for treaty between more than three parties is name by which treaty is commonly known, with year of signing added in parentheses — 25.16B2. No added entry under 'United Kingdom', because, although it is both the home government and the publishing government, it is not a signatory of the treaty — 21.35A2.

329

TURNER, J.M.W.
The fighting Temeraire / J.M.W. Turner. — [London] : Athena, [196-?].
1 art reproduction : col. ; 55 x 75 cm.
Shows the Temeraire being towed to the breaker's yard.

1. Title

Description of art reproductions as graphic materials — Ch.1 and Ch.8. Method of reproduction should be included in physical description area — 8.5C3. However, method could not be ascertained from item itself and publishers were not prepared to divulge it. Note on the nature of the item — 8.7B1.

Entry under person responsible for artistic content — 21.1A1 and 21.1A2. Rule 21.16B is also relevant: reproduction of art work is entered under heading for original work.

HARALDR THE HARD-RULER AND HIS POETS

By

G. TURVILLE-PETRE

VIGFUSSON READER AND TITULAR PROFESSOR
OF ANCIENT ICELANDIC LITERATURE AND ANTIQUITIES
IN THE UNIVERSITY OF OXFORD

*The Dorothea Coke Memorial Lecture
in Northern Studies
delivered at University College London
1 December 1966*

PUBLISHED FOR THE COLLEGE
BY H. K. LEWIS & CO. LTD LONDON

330

TURVILLE-PETRE, G.
Haraldr the Hard-Ruler and his poets /
by G. Turville-Petre. — London : H.K. Lewis
for the [University] College, 1968.
20 p., 1 leaf of plates ; 26 cm. —
(Dorothea Coke memorial lecture in
northern studies ; 1966).

1.   Title   2.   Series

Two bodies named in publication area; both are
included in accordance with rule authorising
addition of words indicating function of
publisher — 1.4D3. (See also last example in
rule 1.4B8). Numbering of series (in this instance,
a chronological designation) given in terms used
in item — 1.6G1.

Hyphenated surname entered under first element —
22.5C3. *

TWO satyr plays / translated with an
     introduction by Roger Lancelyn Green. —
Harmondsworth : Penguin, 1957.
     95 p. ; 18 cm. — (The Penguin classics).
     Contents: The cyclops / Euripedes —
The searching satyrs / Sophocles.
     With: Appendix : two dithyrambs.

1.   Green, Roger Lancelyn
2.   Euripedes
     The cyclops
3.   Sophocles
     The searching satyrs
4.   The cyclops
5.   The searching satyrs

Title page has both collective title and titles of
individual works, so former is given as title
proper and latter are recorded in note — 2.1B2.
Sophocles' play is named on collective title
page as 'Ichneutai', but when a title is recorded
formally in a note, the heading of the part of
the item to which it refers is recorded — 2.7B18.

Collection of translations of works by different
authors treated as general collections — 21.14B.
Collections with collective title entered under
title; added entry made for editor, and name-title
added entries (see 21.30G) made for independent
works, as there are not more than three — 21.7B.

332

TWO stroke cycle. — Huddersfield :
     C.W. Engineering, [197-?].
     1 transparency (3 attached overlays) :
col. ; 26 x 22 cm. — (Viewpack o.h.p.).
     Overlays can be moved up and down
to demonstrate action of cycle.
     On solid plastic base with rubber feet.

1.   Series

Description of transparencies — Ch.1 and Ch.8.
Number of overlays added to specific material
designation; if they are attached, this is indicated
— 8.5B4. Colour and dimensions given —
8.5C16 and 8.5D4. No provision for describing
transparencies mounted on solid base in physical
description area, so details recorded in note —
8.7B10.

333

UNITED KINGDOM
   [British Library Act]
   British Library Act 1972. — London :
H.M.S.O., 1972
     9 p. ; 24 cm.
     ISBN 0-10-545472-9.

   1.   Title

Formal name of legislative act capitalised — A.20.

Laws governing one jurisdiction entered under
heading for jurisdiction governed by them —
21.31B1. Official short title used as uniform
title; date omitted because no other laws
entered under same heading — 25.15A2.

334

UNITED KINGDOM
   [Public Libraries and Museums Act
(1964)]
   Public Libraries and Museums Act
1964 : Chapter 75. — London : H.M.S.O.,
1964.
     ii, 22 p. ; 25 cm.

   1.   Title

Formal name of legislative act capitalised — A.20.

Laws governing one jurisdiction entered under
heading for jurisdiction governed by them —
21.31B1. Official short title used as uniform
title; date added if several laws entered under
same heading — 25.15A2.

335

UNITED KINGDOM. Army
   Drill (all arms) / prepared under the
direction of the Chief of General Staff. —
London : H.M.S.O., 1965.
     vi, 159 p. : ill. ; 19 cm.

   1.   Title

Work of administrative nature emanating from
corporate body and dealing with its procedures
is entered under heading for body — 21.1B2(a).

Principal armed service entered as direct subheading of name of government — 24.18(Type 7)
and 24.24A. Subheading for government official
not mentioned at 24.20 is that of agency that
official represents — 24.20E.

336

UNITED KINGDOM. Army. Lancashire
   Rifle Volunteer Regiment, Fifteenth
   Fifteenth Lancashire Rifle Volunteer
Regiment : prize list for 1877. —
[Liverpool], 1877.
     [12] p. ; 21 cm.

Work of administrative nature emanating from
corporate body and dealing with its staff is
entered under heading for body — 21.1B2(a).
Principal armed service entered as direct subheading of name of government — 24.18(Type 7)
and 24.24A. Component branch entered as
direct subheading of heading for principal armed
service; numbering added after name in style
found on item — 24.24A.

337

UNITED KINGDOM. Committee
   of Inquiry into Trawler Safety
   Trawler safety : final report of the
Committee of Inquiry into Trawler
Safety. — London : H.M.S.O., 1969.
     x, 167 p. : ill., map ; 25 cm. —
(Cmnd. ; 4114).
   Committee appointed by the
President of the Board of Trade and
chaired by Sir Deric Holland-Martin.
     ISBN 0-10-141140-5.

   1.   Title
   2.   Holland-Martin, Sir Deric

Work emanating from corporate body and
recording its collective thought (in this case,
the report of a committee) is entered under
heading for corporate body — 21.1B2(c).
Government agency containing name implying
administrative subordination (i.e. 'Committee')
entered subordinately — 24.18(Type 2).* No
specific rule for making added entry under
heading for chairman of committee, but rule
instructing that one be made for name having
relationship to work that would provide
important access point has been used as
authority — 21.30F.

UNITED KINGDOM. General
Register Office
A digest of the results of the census
of England and Wales in 1901 : arranged
in tabular form, together with an explanatory introduction / compiled by William
Sanders and produced under the general
supervision of Thomas G. Ackland. —
London : Layton, 1903.
xxxi, 131 p. ; 23 cm.

1.   Title†   2.   Sanders, William
3.   Ackland, Thomas G.

Title page indicates that item is a digest of the
1901 census and the introduction repeats that
the work 'claims to be nothing more than this;
condensed from the voluminous folios recently
issued by the Census office'. Entry is therefore
under the heading for the original work — 21.12A.
The census was carried out by the Registrar-General
and entry would therefore be made under the
corporate heading for this official — 21.4D1
in the form indicated by rule — 24.20E. Body
entered subordinately, as name might be used
by another agency — 24.18(3).*

UNITED KINGDOM. Office of the
Registrar of Restrictive Trading
Agreements
Guide to the registration of goods
under the Resale Prices Act 1964 : notes /
by the Registrar of Restrictive Trading
Agreements. — London : H.M.S.O., 1964.
5 p. ; 24 cm.

1.   Title

Capitalisation for legislative acts — A.20.

Work emanating from corporate body and recording its collective thought is entered under heading
for body — 21.1B2(c). Government agency whose
name normally implies administrative subordination entered as subheading of heading for government, providing name of government is required
for identification of agency — 24.18(Type 2).

Public Libraries and Museums

A
B I L L

To place the public library service
provided by local authorities in England
and Wales under the superintendence
of the Minister of Education, to make
new provision for regulating and im-
proving that service and as to the
provision and maintenance of museums
and art galleries by such authorities,
and for purposes connected with the
matters aforesaid.

Presented by Sir Edward Boyle
Supported by
Mr. Quintin Hogg, Mr. Secretary Heath,
Sir Keith Joseph, Mr. Alan Green and
Mr. Chataway

Ordered, by The House of Commons,
to be Printed, 24 *January,* 1964

LONDON
PRINTED AND PUBLISHED BY
HER MAJESTY'S STATIONERY OFFICE
Price 1*s.* 6*d.* net
[Bill 67]   (37807)   42/5

UNITED KINGDOM. Parliament.
House of Commons
Public Libraries and Museums : a bill
to place the public library service provided
by local authorities in England and Wales
under the superintendence of the Minister
of Education . . . / presented by Sir Edward
Boyle ; supported by Quintin Hogg . . .
[et al.]. — London : H.M.S.O., 1964.
iii, 17 p. ; 25 cm. — ([H.C.] Bill ;
[1963-64] 67).

1.   Title   2.   Boyle, Sir Edward

Long title may be abridged if this can be done without loss of essential information — 1.1B4.

Legislative bill entered under heading for appropriate legislative body — 21.31B3. Legislative body entered as subheading of heading for government — 24.18(5). For legislature with more than one chamber, chamber is entered as subheading of heading for the legislature — 24.21A. No added entry is required for Quintin Hogg but, if it were, the heading would be:

> Hailsham of St. Marylebone, Quintin Hogg, Baron

and references would be required for changes of name. See example in rule 22.6A3.

341

UNITED KINGDOM. Parliament. House of Lords

Architects Registration (Amendment) : a bill intituled An act to amend section 14 of the Architects (Registration) Act 1931 ... — London : H.M.S.O., 1969.

4 p. ; 25 cm. — ([H.L.] Bill ; [1968-69] 129).

Brought from the Commons 2nd July 1969.

1. Title

Legislative bill entered under heading for appropriate legislative body — 21.31B3. For legislature with more than one chamber, chamber is entered as subheading of heading for the legislature — 24.21A.

342

UNITED KINGDOM. Prime Minister

Statement on the findings of the Conference of Privy Councillors / presented to Parliament by the Prime Minister. — London : H.M.S.O., 1956.

5 p. ; 25 cm. — (Cmnd. ; 9715).

1. Title
2. Conference of Privy Councillors on Security

Official communications from heads of government entered under corporate heading for official — 21.4D1. Subheading for head of government acting in official capacity consists of title of office — 24.20C. (Dates and name are not added to subheading, unlike subheading for head of state — 24.20B). Head of government entered subordinately — 24.18(8). Added entry under heading for prominently-named corporate body — 21.30E.

343

UNITED KINGDOM. Royal Air Force. Valley

RAF Valley open day, 1977. — [Anglesey] : RAF Valley, 1977.

24 p. : ill. ; 24 cm.

Cover title.

Flying display programme as insert.

Item which emanates from a corporate body and that records the collectivity activity of an event entered under the heading for the body — 21.1B2(d). Unit of an armed service entered as a direct subheading of the heading of the service of which it is part — 24.24A.

It is appreciated that it would be feasible to catalogue this item as a serial if such open days were successive and were intended to be continued indefinitely.

344

UNITED KINGDOM. Treasury. Organisation and Methods Division

The design of forms in government departments / compiled by the Organisation and Methods Division of Her Majesty's Treasury. — 2nd ed. — London : H.M.S.O., 1962.

173 p. : ill. ; 28 cm.

1. Title

Work of administrative nature emanating from corporate body and dealing with procedures of body itself is entered under heading for body — 21.1B2(a). The fact that it relates to *all* government departments seems immaterial. Entry of a government agency as an *indirect* subheading as name could be used by another agency — 24.19.

UNITED STATES
[Trademark Act]
Trademark laws / U.S., Dept. of
Commerce, Patent Office. — Washington :
G.P.O., 1959.
38 p. ; 24 cm.
Contents: Trademark Act of 1946, as
amended — Notes of other statutes —
Patent Office, establishment, officers,
functions.

1. Title 2. Trademark laws
3. United States. Patent Office

Government Printing Office abbreviated — B.9.

Laws governing one jurisdiction entered under
heading for jurisdiction governed by them —
21.31B1. Uniform title for single law (this item
contains only one act in full, although there are
brief notes on others) is official short title —
25.15A2. Added entry under heading for body
responsible for compiling and issuing the
laws — 21.31B1. In added entry heading, intervening element in hierarchy is omitted, as name
of subordinate body has not been used by another
body entered under same higher body — 24.14.*

346

UNITED STATES. Congress (85th,
  1st session : 1957). House of
  Representatives. Committee on Ways
  and Means. Subcommittee on Foreign
  Trade Policy
Foreign trade policy : hearings before
the Subcommittee on Foreign Trade Policy
of the Committee on Ways and Means . . . —
Washington : G.P.O., 1958.
vi, 865 p. ; 24 cm.
"85th Congress 1st session pursuant
to H. Res. 104, December 2, 3, 4, 5, 6,
9, 10, 11, 12 and 13 1957".

1. Title

If legislature has more than one chamber, each is
entered as subheading of heading for legislature —
24.21A. Committee entered as subheading of
chamber — 24.21B. Legislative subcommittee
entered as subheading of committee to which it
is subordinate — 24.21C. If successive legislatures

are numbered consecutively and if numbered
sessions are involved, these details are added to
the heading for the particular legislature — 24.21D.

347

UNITED STATES. President
Economic report of the President
transmitted to the Congress. — 1947-   . —
Washington : G.P.O., 1947-   .
v. ; 24 cm.
Issued July (1947-1952), required
at the beginning of each regular session
of Congress.

1. Title

Serial which is an official communication from
Head of State entered under the corporate
heading — 21.4D1. Head of state entered
subordinately — 24.18(8). Subheading for a
president consists of the title of the office —
24.20B. Dates and names omitted from heading
which applies to more than one incumbent.

348

UNITED States bicentennial silver
  proof set. — [Philadelphia] : U.S.
Mint, 1976.
3 coins ; in case, 10 x 10 x 1 cm.
Dollar, half-dollar, quarter, 40%
silver, dated 1776-1976.

Description of three-dimensional artefacts — Ch.1
and Ch.10. Coins are not usually intended for
communication and therefore the date would
normally be given first in the publication, etc. area
according to rule 10.4F2. However, in this
instance, they are packaged and issued as a
commemorative set. Physical description — 10.5B1
and 10.5D2. Material named in note — 10.5C1
and 10.7B10. Note on nature of the item —
10.7B1.

349

UNITED States of America, 1776-1976 :
  200th birthday. — Wisconsin : Wisconsin
Tissue Mills, 1974.
1 table mat : paper, col. ; 26 x 36 cm.

It is debatable how this item should be treated. Since it does not fall into any of the categories listed at 8.5B1, it cannot be treated as a graphic material. It has therefore been catalogued as realia, and a specific material designation has been devised — 10.5B1. A possible alternative would be to consider it as a printed sheet as illustrated in example no. 313.

is added to the year in the heading as this is necessary to distinguish between this and other conferments in the same year — 24.7B3.

350

UNIVERSITY CIRCLE (Cleveland)
A map and guide / University Circle, Incorporated. — Scale ca. 1:6,750. — Cleveland, Ohio : Univ. Circle, [1975].
1 map : col. ; 42 x 35 cm. folded to 23 x 11 cm.
On verso : Key and 20 ill.

1. Title

Description of maps — Ch.1 and Ch.3. No scale given on item. Representative fraction computed by comparison with map of known scale. Scale preceded by 'ca.' — 3.3B1.

Work emanating from a corporate body which is of an administrative nature dealing with the operations of the corporate body itself — 21.1B2(a). Entry directly under name — 24.1. Omission of 'Inc' — 24.5C1. Body with name which may be confused with other bodies of the same, or similar names has local place name added — 24.4C3 and, for bodies located outside the British Isles, — 24.4C4.

351

UNIVERSITY OF SHEFFIELD.
Congregation for the Conferment of Degrees (1974 May 3 : University of Sheffield)
University of Sheffield Congregation for the Conferment of Degrees, Firth Hall, Friday 3 May 1974, 7.30 pm. — Sheffield : The University, 1974.
8 p. ; 21 cm.

Meeting with name that has been, or is likely to be, used by another higher body is entered subordinately — 24.13(Type 3). A specific date

352

UNIVERSITY OF SOUTHAMPTON.
Library
MARC at Southampton / designed and presented by Ruth Irvine and other members of Southampton University Library. — Southampton : University Library, [1974].
1 sound cassette (ca. 20 min.) : 1⅞ ips, 2 track, mono.
56 slides : col.
Cassette recorded on 1 track and pulsed for automatic slide change.

1. Title   2. Irvine, Ruth

Description of items made up of more than one material — 1.10. Separate physical descriptions for each class of material recorded on separate lines — 1.10C2(b). Description of sound cassettes — Ch.6. No indication of duration appears on cassette so an approximation is given — 6.5B2. Number of tracks recorded as it is other than standard (i.e. 4) — 6.5C6. (However, cassette is recorded on 1 track only and this is given in a note.) Dimensions of cassette and width of tape are not given because they are standard — 6.5D5. Description of slides — Ch.8. Dimensions of slides not needed because they are standard (i.e. 5 x 5 cm.) — 8.5D5. Important physical details that have not been included in physical description area given in a note — 6.7B10 and 8.7B10.

Work emanates from a corporate body and is of an administrative nature dealing with the procedures and operations of the body itself — 21.1B2(a). A name which includes the entire name of the higher body entered as subheading — 24.13(Type 5). Name of higher body is omitted from subheading — 24.13. Higher body is entered under the name by which it is commonly iden- tified — 24.1.

USING the encyclopedia / Encyclopaedia
Britannica Films, in collaboration
with Jean Lowrie ; producer, Jean E.
Thomson, with the collaboration of the
American Association of School Librarians. —
Toronto : E.B.F., 1963.
1 filmstrip (42 fr.) : col. ; 35 mm. —
(Using the library).
Summary: Designed to show children
what encyclopedias are, why they are
needed and how to use them.

1. Encyclopaedia Britannica Films
2. Lowrie, Jean
3. Thomson, Jean E.
4. American Association of School
    Librarians
5. Series

Description of filmstrips — Ch.1 and Ch.8.
Single statement of responsibility recorded as such
whether persons or bodies named in it perform the
same function or not. Producer named in statement
of responsibility area by analogy with 7.1F1. Brief
summary given — 8.7B17.
Producer named in statement of responsibility
area by analogy with 7.1F1. Brief summary
given — 8.7B17.

This item appears to be the result of collaboration between a person and a corporate body
and should therefore, according to rules
21.6A(6) and 21.6C1, be entered under the one
named first. This appears to indicate that, in
this instance, entry should be under the heading
for the body. However, the work does not fall
within any of the categories listed at 21.1B2
and is therefore entered under title.

VALLEY Forge, Pa. — Longport,
N.J. : Jack Freeman, [19–].
10 pictures : col. ; 8 x 11 cm.
On single piece of card, 74 x 11 cm.
folded to 8 x 11 cm.
Contents: Fort Washington — Major
General Anthony Wayne Statue — National
Memorial Arch — Continental army huts —
Interior, Washington Memorial Chapel —
New Jersey Monument at dogwood blossom
time — Washington's headquarters —
Reception room, Washington's headquarters
— Office and dining room, Washington's
headquarters — Washington's bedroom,
Washington's headquarters.

Description of pictures — Ch.1 and Ch.8.
Additional physical details recorded in note —
8.7B10. Individually named parts listed in note —
8.7B18.

VALUE ENGINEERING ASSOCIATION.
Conference (1st : 1967 : Stratford-
on-Avon)
Proceedings of the 1st Annual Conference, Value Engineering Association,
held at the Shakespeare Hotel, Stratford-
on-Avon, 5-7th October 1967. — Stevenage,
Herts. : Peregrinus, [1969].
73 p. : ill. ; 30 cm.
ISBN 0-901223-01-8.

Conference as corporate body — 21.1B1. Name
that includes the entire name of a higher body
entered subordinately — 24.13(Type 5). Number,
place and date added to heading — 24.7B1.
Added entry under title needed according to
21.30J. However, entry beginning 'Proceedings . . .'
is unhelpful to catalogue-users and so has been
omitted in accordance with 21.29B.

VAN DER PLANK, J.E.
Disease resistance in plants / by J.E.
Van der Plank. — New York ; London :
Academic Press, 1968.
xi, 206 p. : ill. ; 24 cm.
Bibliography: p. 195-201.

1. Title

London would be omitted if item were being catalogued by U.S. agency — 1.4C5.

Surname with prefixes, rules for person's language, i.e. English, followed — 22.5D1.

357

VEN, A.J. van der
Eve / A.J. van der Ven. — Rome, 1841.
1 sculpture : marble, white ; 107 cm. high on base, 144 x 80 x 73 cm.
Presented to Bootle Library and Museum by D.M. Glynn-Morris Nov. 1952.

1.   Title

The term 'art original' is defined (see Appendix D) as 'the original two- or three-dimensional work of art . . . e.g. a painting, a drawing, or sculpture'. 'Art original' is also included as a specific material designation in Ch.8 but obviously this chapter is not appropriate for a sculpture. Indeed, '1 sculpture' is used as an example (p. 227) in Ch.10. — "Three-dimensional artefacts and realia." It follows, therefore that the specific material designation 'Art original' is only used for graphics such as paintings and drawings. A three-dimensional art original, such as a sculpture, must have its specific name given as its designation according to rule 10.5B1. Material added to specific material designation — 10.5C1. Colour added — 10.5C2. Dimensions, with explanatory word if necessary, given — 10.5D1. The dimensions of the base are given by analogy with the rule for recording the dimensions of a container — 10.5D2.

Dutch name containing prefix entered under part following prefix unless prefix is 'ver' — 22.5D1.

358

VISIT to London. — London : Walton, [197-?].
1 film reel (ca. 12 min.) : si., col. ; standard 8 mm. — (Walton home movies).
Available in col. or b&w as standard 8 si. and Super 8 si.

1.   Series

Description of film reels — Ch.1 and Ch.7. Gauge recorded in millimetres; if film is 8 mm., the number is preceded by single, standard, Super, or Maurer as appropriate — 7.5D2. Note on other available formats — 7.7B16.

359

WALES : Holyhead to Great Ormes Head. — New ed. — Scale 1:75,000 : Mercator proj. (W 04° 53'00" –W 03° 48'42"/ N 53° 38'18" –N 53° 13'00"). — London : Admiralty, 1973.
1 hydrographic chart : blue & white ; 63 x 96 cm. — (Admiralty charts ; 1977).
"From Admiralty surveys 1835-1971".

1.   Series

Description of cartographic materials — Ch.1 and Ch.3. Statement of projection recorded if included on the item — 3.3C1. Co-ordinates recorded optionally — 3.3D1. Note on edition and history of item — 3.7B7.

360

WALTERS, Samuel
New Brighton packet / Samuel Walters. — 1835.
1 art original : oil on canvas ; 47 x 68 cm.
Shows the New Brighton with a storm damaged sailing ship in tow.

1.   Title

Description of art originals as graphic materials — Ch.1 and Ch.8. For art originals, only the date of creation is given in the publication area — 8.4A2. Note on the nature of the item — 8.7B1.

Entry under person responsible for artistic content — 21.1A1 and 21.1A2.

WANHALL, Johann Baptist
[Concertos, oboe, strings, F major ; arr.]
Concerto for oboe and strings / J.C. Vanhall ; freely adapted by Vilem Tausky. — London : Oxford University Press, c1957.
1 piano score (18 p.) + 1 part ; 32 cm.
For oboe and piano.
Duration: about 12 min.

1.   Title   2.   Concerto for oboe and strings
3.   Tausky, Vilem

Medium of performance named in note if it does not appear in the rest of the description — 5.7B1. (In this example, the title statement refers to the complete work.) If duration of performance is stated in item, this is given in note in abbreviated form — 5.7B10.

Although the words 'freely adapted' appear on the title page, the musical material appears to be 100% Wanhall. Since there is doubt as to the work's status, it is treated as an arrangement and entered under heading appropriate to original work — 21.18C and 21.18B. Person is known by more than one name. Name by which he is most commonly known or which appears most frequently in his works cannot be determined. Entry is therefore under name appearing most frequently in reference sources — 22.2A(2). Uniform title for work with title consisting solely of one type of composition is the accepted English form of name for that type of composition, given in the plural unless the composer wrote only one work of the type — 25.27B. Medium of performance added — 25.29A1. English term used for individual instrument — 25.29D1. Term selected from list supplied for group of instruments — 25.29E. Statement of key added — 25.31A5. 'arr.' added — 25.31B2.

WASHINGTON MEMORIAL CHAPEL (Valley Forge)
The Washington Memorial Chapel, Valley Forge. — Valley Forge : Wash. Mem. Ch., 1971.
32 p. : col. ill. ; 18 cm.
On endpapers: Brief history of events at Valley Forge, 1777-1778 — Washington's Prayer for the United States of America — Details of Church services.

Work emanates from a corporate body and describes the body and its resources, e.g. the organ, the lectern, the pulpit, a statue of Washington. It also has an administrative function in that it lists and describes services held. It therefore appears to fall within the scope of rule 21.1B2(a) and is entered under the heading for the body. Local church entered directly under its name — 24.1. Location added in parentheses if needed for purposes of identification — 24.10B.

The WATERLOO cannons / Bassett-Lowke Ltd. — Northampton : Bassett-Lowke, [197-].
2 models : hardwood and metal ; approx. 23 and 21 cm. long.
Replicas of the 9 pdr and 6 pdr field guns used by the British at the Battle of Waterloo.

1.   Bassett-Lowke Ltd.

Description of models as three-dimensional artefacts — Ch.1 and Ch.10. Manufacturer is cited in the chief source of information, i.e. the textual material accompanying the items — 10.0B1 and can therefore be given in the statement of responsibility area — 1.1F1. Manufacturer is also distributor and should be shown as such in publication, distribution area — 1.4B2. Physical description — 10.5B1, 10.5C1 and 10.5D1.

Items emanate from a corporate body but they do not fit into any of the categories indicated in 21.1B2; they are therefore treated as if no corporate body were involved and entered under title — 21.1C(3). In added entry heading, 'Ltd' is needed to make clear that name is that of a corporate body — 24.5C1.

WATSON, T.F.
  Making sure of maths. 2 / T.F. Watson, T.A. Quinn. — Edinburgh : Holmes McDougall, 1974.
  24, [24] p. ; 28 cm.
  Twenty-four originals and 24 spirit-masters.
    ISBN 0-7157-1244-6.

  1. Title   2. Quinn, T.A.

If title proper for an item that is a section of another item appears in two parts not grammatically linked, the title of the main work is recorded first, followed by a full stop and the title of the section — 1.1B9. Unnumbered sequence of pages recorded if it constitutes the whole or a substantial part of the publication — 2.5B3. When an item consists of a number of graphics packaged in 'book' format, it could be treated as a printed monograph as shown above and in example no. 246. However, it would seem more useful to describe the item as a graphic. Unfortunately, none of the specific material designations in rule 8.5B1 are appropriate. However, a specific name could be used by analogy with Ch.10. The physical description would then be given as:
  24 spiritmasters ; 28 x 20 cm.
and the note would read:
  Packaged in book format with each master preceded by a print version.

WE, the people : the story of the
  United States Capitol, its past and promise / The United States Capitol Historical Society in cooperation with the National Geographic Society. — 9th ed. — Washington : U.S. Cap. Hist. Soc., 1974.
  144 p. : chiefly ill. (mostly col.) ; 26 cm.
  On endpapers: Constitution and Bill of Rights.

  1. United States Capitol Historical
      Society
  2. National Geographic Society

Work emanating from corporate body but not falling within any of the categories listed at 21.1B2 is entered under title — 21.1C(3).

WHAT every director should know
  about automation : report of a one-day conference at the Connaught Rooms, London, 12 December, 1963. — London : Institute of Directors, 1964.
  71 p. : ill. ; 23 cm.

Conference without name (see definition 21.1B1) entered under title — 21.5A. 'A one-day conference' is not a particular name and 'what every director should know about automation' appears to be a general subject description rather than a specific appellation.

WHITE Star Line R.M.S. "Adriatic" . . . :
  plan of first class accommodation. — Scale ca. 1:250. — Liverpool : [White Star Line?], 1922.
  1 plan in 5 sections ; 57 x 89 cm. folded to 23 x 15 cm.
  Insets: Notes, 4 photos. of interior of ship, 1 drawing of exterior.

Description of plans as cartographic materials — Ch.1 and Ch.3. Mark of omission — 1.0C. Conjectural interpolation (in this case the probable publisher) given in square brackets with question mark added — 1.0C. Scale does not appear on item but has been estimated — 3.3B1. Sections of plan have irregular outlines, so sheet size alone is given — 3.5D1. Sheet contains panel designed to appear on outside when sheet is folded, so sheet size folded is given — 3.5D1. Inset material given in note — 3.7B18.

368

WHY-BECAUSE cards. — Wisbech, Cambridgeshire : Learning Development Aids, 1976.
30 lesson cards : col. ; 11 x 7 cm. in box, 13 x 8 x 2 cm. + 1 leaflet.
Fifteen pairs of picture cards. 1 card in each pair has question on verso, the other has answer.

Item must be treated as graphic material. Strictly speaking, the term 'lesson cards' should not be used as it does not appear in the list of specific material designations for graphics — 8.5B1 — and there is no authority for using an additional term. However, the nearest related term — 'picture' — is inappropriate. This item has therefore been catalogued by analogy with Ch.10 and the specific name of the item given. The example given in rule 1.10C2(a) should also be examined.

369

WILCOCK, H.
Aircraft / by H. Wilcock. — Wakefield, Yorkshire : Educational Productions, 1973.
1 filmstrip (34 fr., 5 title fr.) : col. ; 35 mm. + 1 booklet ([18] p. ; 16 cm.).
"Produced in collaboration with The Hamlyn Group".
Based on: Aircraft / by John W.R. Taylor ; illustrated by Gerry Palmer. 1971. (Hamlyn all-colour paperback series).
Educational Productions: C6870.

1.   Title   2.   Taylor, John W.R.
                     Aircraft

Description of filmstrips as graphic materials — Ch.1 and Ch.8. Name and optionally the physical

description of accompanying material recorded at the end of the physical description — 1.5E1(d) and 8.5E1. Statement of responsibility not recorded in title and statement of responsibility area given in note — 8.7B6. Note relating to history of item — 8.7B7. Important number borne by item recorded in note — 8.7B19.

Name-title added entry under heading for related work — 21.30G.

370

WILLARD, Archibald M.
"Spirit of '76" / Archibald M. Willard. — Hackettstown, N.J. : Scheller, 1973.
1 postcard : col. ; 14 x 9 cm.
Reproduction of original painting: Selectman's Room, Abbot Hall, Marblehead, Mass.
Exact copy, painted by Robert B. Williams: Memorial Building, Washington Crossing State Park, Pa.

1.   Title

Description of postcards as graphic materials — Ch.1 and Ch.8. Postcard is also reproduction of painting; details of original given in note as though for ordinary reproduction — 8.7B8.

Reproduction of art work entered under heading for original work — 21.16B.

371

WILSON, John Rowan
The side of the angels / by John Rowan Wilson. — London : Collins, 1968.
351 p. ; 22 cm.

1.   Title†

Nature of surname uncertain. As person's language is English, entry is under the last part of the name — 22.5C6.

WOODCHUCK puzzle. — Wallop,
Hants. : Pentangle, [19—].
1 game (24 pieces) : wood ; in box,
8 x 9 cm. diam.
Over 20 shapes can be constructed.
Selected for the Design Centre, London.
Registered design no.: 949574.

Description of games as three-dimensional artefacts — Ch.1 and Ch.10. Number of pieces —
10.5B2. Box is cylindrical, so explanatory word
is added to indicate which dimension is being
given — 10.5D1. Important physical details not
included in physical description area are given as
note — 10.7B10. Important number recorded —
10.7B19.

The Open University
Social sciences: a third level course

People and work   Block 1 (Units 1-3)

Work and society

Prepared by the course team

The Open University Press

WORK and society / prepared by the
Course Team [of] The Open
University. — Milton Keynes : Open Univ.
Press, 1976.
120 p. : ill. ; 30 cm. — (Social sciences :
a third level course. People and work ;
Block 1 (Units 1-3)) (DE 351 1-3).
Contents: Unit 1. The sociology of
work / by Graeme Salaman — Unit 2.
Work and social theory / by Peter
Hamilton — Unit 3. Capitalism and
industrial society in social theory / by
Ben Cosin.
ISBN 0-335-07000-0.

1. Open University   2.   Series
3. People and work
4. DE 351 1-3
5. Optionally, author and title
       analytical entries for each part

Word added to make statement of responsibility
clear (by analogy with 1.1F8 and 2.1F3).

Work emanating from corporate body but not
falling within any of categories listed at 21.1B2
is entered under title — 21.1C(3). Where the
added entry for The Open University is concerned,
the name of the Course Team could be included
as a subheading if this were thought necessary by
the particular cataloguing agency, e.g.

Open University. People and Work Course
Team
If one alphabetical sequence of authors and titles
were required within the heading 'Open
University', this subheading would be omitted.

See also example no. 319.

374

WORKSHOP ON THE TEACHING
    OF CLASSIFICATION (<u>1st : 1968 :</u>
<u>Columbia University School of Library</u>
<u>Service</u>)
    The Dewey decimal classification :
outlines and papers presented at a Workshop
on the Teaching of Classification, December
8-10 1966 / edited by Maurice F. Tauber,
Carlyle J. Frarey, Nathalie C. Batts. —
New York : Columbia University School
of Library Service, 1968.
    vi, 121 p. ; 28 cm.

    1.   Title

Workshop as conference, which is treated as
corporate body — 21.1B1 and 21.1B2(d).

375

The WORLD of your hundred best
    tunes : the top ten — London :
Decca, 1970.
    1 sound disc (ca. 45 min.) : 33⅓ rpm,
stereo. ; 12 in.
    Container title.
    Based upon the 10 most frequently
requested tunes from the BBC radio
programme: Your hundred best tunes.
    Contents: Finlandia / Sibelius —
Nuns' chorus from Casanova / Strauss —
Intermezzo from Cavalleria rusticana /
Mascagni — Don't be cross from Der
Obersteiger / Zeller — Final movement
from Symphony no. 6 (Pastoral) /
Beethoven — Piano sonata no. 14
(Moonlight) / Beethoven — Chorus of
the Hebrew Slaves from Nabucco /
Verdi — Violin concerto no. 1 in
G minor / Bruch — Cantata no. 147
(Jesu Joy) / Bach — Nimrod from Enigma
variations / Elgar.
    Decca: SPA 112.

    1.   Optionally, author and title
          analytical entries for each part†

Collective title is on container, i.e. sleeve, only;
this is therefore treated as chief source of
information — 6.0B1. A note of the source
is made — 6.0B1 and 6.7B3. Titles and

statements of responsibility for individual
works contained on a sound recording given
in a contents note — 6.7B18.
Related work under its own heading — 21.28B.
Sound recording containing musical works by
different persons performed by more than three
principal performers (each of the ten tunes is
performed by a different person and/or body)
is entered under title — 21.23D.

376

The WORLD-WIDE encyclopedia
    in colour / edited by Colin Clark. —
[New ed.]. — London : P. Hamlyn for
Golden Pleasure Books, 1966.
    301 p. : ill. (some col.), maps, ports. ;
30 cm.

    1.   Clark, Colin

Work produced under editorial direction entered
under title — 21.7A and 21.7B.

377

WORLOCK, Derek
    You in your parish / by Bishop
Worlock. — London : Living Parish
Pamphlets, [1968].
    20 p. ; 19 cm.

    1.   Title

Statement of responsibility recorded in the
form in which it appears in item — 1.1F1.

Omission of 'Bishop' from heading — 22.15C.
Titles such as Cardinal, Bishop, etc. are only
used in headings when entry is *not* under surname
— 22.8A, *or* when they are required to distinguish
between persons with identical names — 22.19B.

378

YORK / Ordnance Survey. — Scale
    1:50,000. approx. 1¼ in. to 1 mile. —
Southampton : O.S., c1977.
    1 map : col. ; 80 x 80 cm. folded to
23 x 14 cm. — (Ordnance Survey 1:50,000
second series ; sheet 105).
    Part of legend and tourist information
in English, French and German.

    1.   Ordnance Survey   2.   Series

Description of maps — Ch.1 and Ch.3. Optionally, additional scale information that is found on the item may be given following scale expressed as a representative fraction — 3.3B2. Publisher abbreviated as it already appears in statement of responsibility area — 1.4D4. Copyright date given — 1.4F6. More than one series statement given in chief source of information, i.e. the item itself; the variant that identifies the series most adequately and succinctly is used — 1.6B2.

Item is here treated as work which emanates from corporate body but which does not fall within categories listed at 21.1B2 and is therefore entered under title — 21.1C(3). Some map librarians may regret that entry is not under corporate body. It could, perhaps, be argued that the map reflects the corporate thought or activity of the responsible body but as this is a doubtful interpretation according to the wording of 21.1B2, it is treated as if it did not.

It should be noted that it is possible to describe a whole collection of maps rather than to describe each part separately — 3.0J, e.g.

   Ordnance Survey 1:50,000 second series. — Southampton : O.S., [197-] -   .
   204 maps : col. ; 80 x 80 cm.

379

YORKSHIRE REGIONAL LIBRARY SYSTEM
   Yorkshire Regional Library System : organisation and procedure. — Sheffield : Sheffield Central Library, 1958.
   29 p. ; 22 cm.

Work of an administrative nature which emanates from a corporate body and deals with its procedures is entered under the heading for body — 21.1B2(a). Entry directly under name of body — 24.1.

380

YOUNG, Faron
   It's four in the morning / Faron Young. — [London] : Mercury, [197-] .
   1 sound cartridge (ca. 29 min.) : 3¾ ips, stereo.
   Partial contents: After the fire is gone / White — Trip to Tijuana / Harden — I'll take the time / Cochran — It's four in the morning / Chesnut.
   Mercury: 7708-045.

   1.   Title
   2.   Optionally, author and title analytical entries for each part

Description of 8-track stereo sound cartridges — Ch.1 and Ch.6. Number of tracks given only if other than standard (i.e. 8) — 6.5C6. Cartridge is of standard dimensions (i.e. 5¼ x 3⅞in., wrongly cited as 5¼ x 7⅞in. in rule) and tape is of standard width (i.e. ¼ in.) and so this information is also omitted from physical description — 6.5D5.

Sound recording containing works by different persons entered under the person represented as principal performer — 21.23C.

381

YOUNG, I.V.
   An experimental investigation into children's comprehension of school atlas maps / I.V. Young. — Wakefield : Micro Methods, 1962.
   1 microfilm reel ; 35 mm.
   Low reduction.
   Comic mode.
   Thesis (M.A.)—London Institute of Education, 1952.

   1.   Title

Description of microfilms — Ch.1 and Ch.11. 'Cartridge' 'cassette' or 'reel' added to specific material designation as appropriate — 11.5B1. Reel diameter is standard and so is not recorded. Width of microfilm given in millimetres — 11.5D4. Reduction ratio is less than 16x, so 'Low reduction' is the term used — 11.7B10. If item is a dissertation, this is recorded in a note as instructed in rules for printed monographs — 1.7B13, 2.7B13 and 11.7B13.

YOUNG, J.B.

Reprographic principles made easy / J.B. Young. — Godmanchester, Huntingdon : Transart in conjunction with the National Committee for Audio Visual Aids in Education and the Educational Foundation for Visual Aids, 1970.

20 transparencies : b&w ; 22 x 28 cm. + 1 booklet (84 p. : ill. ; 21 cm.). — (Transart flipatrans).

With: Classified list of suppliers.

Instructions for using with multiple-shutter viewer and standard viewer on inside cover.

1.　Title　　2.　Series

Description of transparencies as graphic materials — Ch.1 and Ch.8. These transparencies are in the form of a flipatran (i.e. a book designed to contain transparencies in looseleaf format; it may be used as an entity on a multiple-shutter viewer or the transparencies can be taken out and used separately on a standard viewer). Indication of colour — 8.5C16. Dimensions (height x width) given — 8.5D1. Series statement presented in various forms. It appears inside front cover as "Flipatran visual aid". The series chosen is usually that given in the chief source of information — 1.6B2. In this case, as the chief source of information for a graphic is the whole item, both are given in the chief source. The one given greater prominence has therefore been chosen. The varying form could be given in a note if considered important enough.

382

Place of publication recorded in form in which it appears — 1.4C1.

Constitution entered under heading for jurisdiction — 21.33A. Conventional name of government used, and English form of name of place — 24.3E and 23.2A.* Uniform title is title in original language — 25.4A. Date added in parentheses if considered necessary to distinguish between otherwise identical uniform titles — 25.5C. Language added — 25.5D.

383

YUGOSLAVIA

[Ustav (1962). English]

The Constitution of the Federal Socialist Republic of Yugoslavia : a preliminary draft. — Beograd : Union of Jurists' Associations of Yugoslavia, 1962.

86 p. ; 21 cm.

1.　Title
2.　The Constitution of the Federal Socialist Republic of Yugoslavia

APPENDIX 1
ADDED ENTRIES

AACR 2 is based upon the proposition that one main entry is made for each item described and that this is supplemented by added entries. An added entry is defined as "an entry, additional to the main entry, by which an item is represented in a catalogue; a secondary entry." Although tracings have been given, no added entries as so defined have been included in the main sequence of this work. Such inclusion would have unnecessarily complicated matters, especially as methods of formulating added entries vary from library to library. However, the following notes on possible layouts and examples of added entries will serve to illustrate some of these methods and the form that added entries may take.

THE UNIT ENTRY METHOD

The full main entry, with the addition of appropriate headings, is used for all entries in the catalogue, e.g. from example no. 132

Added entry (collaborator – 21.30B)

> HAWK, Dick
> GONZALES, Pancho
> How to play and win at tennis / by Pancho Gonzales & Dick Hawk ; edited by Gladys Heldman. – 1st British ed. – London : Souvenir Press, 1963.
> 123 p. : 126 ill. ; 23 cm.
> Originally published: New York : Fleet Publishing, 1962.

THE ALTERNATIVE HEADING METHOD

The description is used as a basis for entry and the various required headings are simply added above the title statement, e.g.

> HAWK, Dick
> How to play and win at tennis / by Pancho Gonzales & Dick Hawk ; edited by Gladys Heldman. – 1st British ed. – London : Souvenir Press, 1963.
> 123 p. : 126 ill. ; 23 cm.
> Originally published: New York : Fleet Publishing, 1962.

With this method, filing is simplified. All access points are treated as equal; a full description is included under each heading and, if a tracing is given with each entry, the need to choose a particular heading for a main entry is eliminated.

AACR 2 recognises that many libraries have adopted the alternative heading method. These libraries are recommended to use Chapter 21 as guidance in determining all the entries required in particular instances (see p. 2 of AACR 2).

ABBREVIATED ADDED ENTRIES

The International Conference on Cataloguing Principles of 1961 defined an added entry somewhat differently from AACR 2 as: "any entry giving partial or full information about a particular bibliographical unit, other than the main entry." The word "partial" indicates that the detail given in added entries may be simplified and, from this point, all of the added entries in this appendix are in an abbreviated form. For each example two entries have been prepared. In one, the main entry heading is interposed, where necessary, between the added entry heading and the title statement (as with the unit entry) and, in the other, it is not (as with the alternative heading method), e.g.

> HAWK, Dick
> GONZALES, Pancho
> How to play and win at tennis. – 1st British ed. – 1963.

or

HAWK, Dick
　　How to play and win at tennis / by
Pancho Gonzales & Dick Hawk. — 1st
British ed. — 1963.

The amount of detail to be included in a simplified
added entry will depend upon the policy of the
individual library or cataloguing agency. However,
the minimum requirement would seem to be:
Title / statement of responsibility (if necessary). —
Edition statement (if applicable). — Date. —
Specific material designation (if necessary).

It should also be pointed out that, in certain
instances, references may be employed in lieu
of added entries (see Appendix 2).

In abbreviated added entries, the catalogue user
must be given enough information to enable him
or her to find the main entry so that full details
of an item can be traced if required. In this
connection, there is no great difficulty when the
main entry heading is given after the added entry
heading. When it is not, however, certain
problems are posed. These problems can be
solved, in part, in several ways:

(1)　By indicating the main entry heading in a
note, e.g.

　　Example no. 338　(added title entry)

A DIGEST of the results of the census of
　　England and Wales in 1901 : arranged
in tabular form, together with an explana-
tory introduction / compiled by William
Sanders. — 1903.
　　Full details are entered under:
　　United Kingdom. General Register
Office

(2)　By the use of capitalisation, e.g.

　　Example no. 371　(added title entry)

　　The SIDE of the angels / by John
Rowan WILSON. — 1968

(3)　Another procedure used in some libraries,
either alone or as a supplement to other
methods, is to indicate the main entry heading

following the class number, which is included
in every entry, e.g.

823.91/WILSON or　823.91/WIL

The last two of these methods are problematic
in that their intention may not be clear to the
catalogue user. There must be an adequate
explanation in the guide to the use of the catalogue. But do catalogue users bother to read
such guides? The best solution, therefore, seems
to be the first method but, even here, care must
be taken. A note such as "Main entry is at:
United Kingdom. General Register Office"
could have the user asking two questions: "What
is a main entry?" and "Why do I have to go to
London to find out more about this item?"

ADDED ENTRY EXAMPLES

The following examples are given in the order
of the sections of rule 21.30.

Designations of function are omitted from headings, although it should be noted that AACR 2
optionally allows certain designations such as
comp., ed., ill., tr., and *arr.* to be given in added
entry headings for persons (see rules 21.0D and
21.18B). It must be appreciated that such
omission may necessitate more detail being
supplied in the body of the entry to clarify the
relationship to the publication of the person or
body under which added entry is made. If the
reason for an added entry is not apparent from
the body of the description, then a note must be
provided (see rule 21.29F).

Rules 21.30A and 21.30B

Two or more persons or bodies involved —
Collaborators

From example no. 5

　　FLYE, James Harold
AGEE, James
　　James Agee : a portrait / James Agee
reading [from his work ; Father Flye
reads from Agee's work and reminisces
about the author]. — 1971.
　　2 sound discs.

or

FLYE, James Harold
    James Agee : a portrait / James Agee
reading [from his work ; Father Flye
reads from Agee's work and reminisces
about the author]. — 1971.
    2 sound discs.

From example no. 68

METHODIST CHURCH
CHURCH OF ENGLAND
    Conversations between the Church
of England and the Methodist Church :
an interim statement. — 1958.

or

METHODIST CHURCH
    Conversations between the Church
of England and the Methodist Church :
an interim statement. — 1958.

From example no. 22

AMERICAN LIBRARY ASSOCIATION
ANGLO-AMERICAN cataloguing rules /
    prepared by the American Library
Association . . . [et al.]. — 2nd ed. — 1978.

or

AMERICAN LIBRARY ASSOCIATION
    Anglo-American cataloguing rules /
prepared by the American Library
Association . . . [et al.]. — 2nd ed. — 1978.

Rule 21.30C

Writers

From example no. 221

    MELVILLE, Robert
NOLAN, Sidney
    Ned Kelly : 27 paintings / by Sidney
Nolan ; [text by] Robert Melville. — 1964.

or

MELVILLE, Robert
    Ned Kelly : 27 paintings / by Sidney
Nolan ; [text by] Robert Melville. — 1964.

Rule 21.30D

Editors and compilers

From example no. 106

    SHUGRUE, Michael
FARQUHAR, George
    The recruiting officer / edited by
Michael Shugrue. — 1966.

or

SHUGRUE, Michael
    The recruiting officer / by George
Farquhar ; edited by Michael Shugrue. —
1966.

Rule 21.30E

Prominently named corporate bodies

From example no. 17

    BRITISH COUNCIL OF CHURCHES.
    Education Department
ALVES, Colin
    Religion and the secondary school : a
report undertaken on behalf of the British
Council of Churches. — 1968.

or

BRITISH COUNCIL OF CHURCHES.
    Education Department
    Religion and the secondary school : a
report undertaken on behalf of the British
Council of Churches / by Colin Alves. —
1968.

From example no. 28

    MERSEYSIDE ARTS ASSOCIATION
ARTS alive Merseyside. — No. 1 (Sept.
    1969)-   . — 1969-   .
        v.
    Monthly.

or

MERSEYSIDE ARTS ASSOCIATION
    Arts alive Merseyside. — No. 1 (Sept.
1969)-   . — 1969-   .
        v.
    Monthly.

Rule 21.30F

Other related persons or bodies

From example no. 262

> HAYEK, Friedrich A. von
> ROADS to freedom : essays in honour of
> Friedrich A. von Hayek. — 1969.

or

> HAYEK, Friedrich A. von
>> Roads to freedom : essays in honour
>> of Friedrich A. von Hayek. — 1969.

From example no. 180

> ISAAC, Anthony
> KHACHATURIAN, Aram
>> The "Onedin Line" theme ; Sabre
>> dance / Khachaturian. — 1971
>> 1 sound disc.
>> First item consists of "Music from
>> "Spartacus" as adapted for the BBC-TV
>> series by Anthony Isaac".

or

> ISAAC, Anthony
>> The "Onedin Line" theme ; Sabre
>> dance / Khachaturian. — 1971
>> 1 sound disc.
>> First item consists of "Music from
>> "Spartacus" as adapted for the BBC-TV
>> series by Anthony Isaac".

From example no. 18

> JOECKEL, Carleton Bruns
> AMERICAN LIBRARY ASSOCIATION.
>> Committee on Post-War Planning
>> Post-war standards for public libraries /
>> Carleton Bruns Joeckel, Chairman. — 1943.

or

> JOECKEL, Carleton Bruns
>> Post-war standards for public libraries /
>> prepared by The Committee on Post-War
>> Planning of the American Library Associa-
>> tion ; Carleton Bruns Joeckel, Chairman. —
>> 1943.

Rule 21.30G

Related works

From example no. 128 (Name-title added entry)

> JOYCE, James
>> Ulysses
> GILBERT, Stuart
>> James Joyce's Ulysses : a study. — 1930.

or

> JOYCE, James
>> Ulysses
>> James Joyce's Ulysses : a study / by
>> Stuart Gilbert. — 1930.

From example no. 36

> RADIO times
> B.B.C.
>> Talking points, third series : B.B.C.
>> comments on questions that viewers and
>> listeners ask. — 1969.

or

> RADIO times
>> Talking points, third series : B.B.C.
>> comments on questions that viewers and
>> listeners ask. — 1969.

Rule 21.30H

Other relationships

From example no. 229

> DEVONSHIRE COLLECTION
> PAINTINGS at Chatsworth. — [196-?].
>> 8 postcards.

or

> DEVONSHIRE COLLECTION
>> Paintings at Chatsworth. — [196-?].
>> 8 postcards.

Rule 21.30J

Titles

From example no. 309

BOATS in Whitby Harbour
SUTCLIFFE, Frank Meadow
    Boats in Whitby Harbour. — 1977.
    1 photograph.

or

BOATS in Whitby Harbour / Frank
    Meadow Sutcliffe. — 1977.
    1 photograph.

From example no. 100

POMP and circumstance
ELGAR, Sir Edward
    Pomp and circumstance : military
march no. 1, op. 39. — c1929.
    1 miniature score.

or

POMP and circumstance : military
    march no. 1, op. 39 / Edward
Elgar. — c1929.
    1 miniature score.

From example no. 105

El SOMBRERO de tres picos
FALLA, Manuel de
    El sombrero de tres picos = Le tri-
corne = The three-cornered hat : ballet. —
c1921.
    1 miniature score.

or

El SOMBRERO de tres picos = Le
    tricorne = The three-cornered
hat : ballet / [music by] Manuel de Falla. —
c1921.
    1 miniature score.

Title proper of second item in collection without collective title

From example no. 84

  RUTH
CUNDALL, Arthur E.
    Judges / [Arthur E. Cundall]. Ruth /
[Leon Morris]. — 1968.

or

RUTH / [Leon Morris]. — 1968.
    Full details are entered under:
Cundall, Arthur E.
    Judges / [Arthur E. Cundall]. Ruth /
[Leon Morris]

A name-title added entry under the heading for Morris would also be necessary — see rule 21.7C.

Title proper of an item entered under uniform title — rule 25.2D1.

From example no. 294

    The TALE of the armament of Igor,
      A.D. 1185
[SLOVO o polku Igoreve. English]
    The tale of the armament of Igor,
A.D. 1185 : a Russian historical epic. —
1915.

or

The TALE of the armament of Igor,
    A.D. 1185 : a Russian historical
epic. — 1915.
    Full details are entered under:
[Slovo o polku Igoreve. English]

Rule 21.30J

Uniform titles

From example no. 51

     [L'ADORATION. English]
BOREL, Jacques
    [L'adoration. English]
    The bond. — 1968.

or

[L'ADORATION. English]
    The bond / by Jacques Borel. — 1968.

An added entry under the title proper (see below) and a name-title reference (see Appendix 2) would also be required.

Rule 25.2D2 directs that an added entry be made under the title proper of a work, entered under a personal heading when a uniform title has been used:

    The BOND
BOREL, Jacques
    [L'adoration. English]
    The bond. — 1968.

or

The BOND
    [L'adoration. English]
    The bond / by Jacques Borel. — 1968.

Any title other than the title proper (cover title, caption title, running title, etc.) if it is significantly different from the title proper

Parallel title

From example no. 105

    The THREE-CORNERED hat
FALLA, Manuel de
    El sombrero de tres picos = Le tricorne = The three-cornered hat : ballet. — c1921.
    1 miniature score.

or

The THREE-CORNERED hat : ballet. — c1921.
    1 miniature score.
    Full details are entered under:
    Falla, Manuel de
        El sombrero de tres picos

Container title

From example no. 276

    GREGORIAN chants from Hungary
SCHOLA HUNGARICA ENSEMBLE
    Magyar Gregorianum : a karácsonyi ünnepkör dallamai. — [1976].
    1 sound disc.

or

GREGORIAN chants from Hungary. — [1976].
    1 sound disc.
    Full details are entered under:
    Schola Hungarica Ensemble
        Magyar Gregorianum

Variant title

From example no. 208

    REFORMATION [symphony]
MENDELSSOHN-BARTHOLDY, Felix
    [Symphonies, no. 5, op. 107, D minor]
    Symphony no. 5, D minor (Reformation), op. 107. — [1960?].

or

REFORMATION [symphony]. — [1960?].
    1 miniature score.
    Full details are entered under:
    Mendelssohn-Bartholdy, Felix
        [Symphonies, no. 5, op. 107, D minor]

Some cataloguing agencies might prefer references rather than added entries from titles other than the title proper — see p.177

Rule 21.30K1

Translators

From example no. 173

CAMPBELL, Roy
JOHN, of the Cross, Saint
   Poems / with a translation by Roy
Campbell. — 1968.

or

CAMPBELL, Roy
   Poems / by Saint John of the Cross ;
with a translation by Roy Campbell. —
1968.

Rule 21.30K2

Illustrators

From example no. 121

SCOTT, Peter
GALLICO, Paul
   The snow goose / illustrations by
Peter Scott. — [New] illustrated ed. —
1946.

or

SCOTT, Peter
   The snow goose / by Paul Gallico ;
illustrations by Peter Scott. — [New]
illustrated ed. — 1946.

Rule 21.30L

Series

From example no. 212

ENGLISH linguistics 1500-1800 : a
   collection of facsimile reprints.
MONBODDO, James Burnet, Lord
   Of the origin and progress of language. —
1967.
   6 v.

or

ENGLISH linguistics 1500-1800 : a collection of facsimile reprints.
   Of the origin and progress of language /
by James Burnet. — 1967.
   6 v.

Optionally, the numeric or other designation of
each work in the series can be added.

The above format would be used if arrangement
under the series heading was to be alphabetical
by the authors of the parts of the series. An
alternative arrangement could be numerical by
the number of the part of the series, e.g.

ENGLISH linguistics 1500-1800 : a
   collection of facsimile reprints.
   No. 48: Of the origin and progress of
language / by James Burnet. — 1967.
   6 v.

Rule 21.30M

Analytical entries

From example no. 79 (Name-title added entry)

MAXCY, George
   The motor industry
COOK, P. Lesley
   Effects of mergers : six studies. — 1958.

or

MAXCY, George
   The motor industry
   Effects of mergers : six studies / P.Lesley
Cook with the collaboration of Ruth
Cohen. — 1958.

The above method is appropriate when direct access
to the part is wanted without creating an additional
bibliographic record for the part — see rule 13.4.
Alternatively, the "In" analytic entry may be
considered — see rule 13.5, e.g.

MAXCY, George
    The motor industry / George Maxcy. —
p. 351-393 ; 23 cm.

    In Cook, P. Lesley. Effects of mergers :
six studies. — London : Allen & Unwin,
1958.

or, if an "In" analytic entry is required under the
title:

The MOTOR industry / George Maxcy. —
    p. 351-393 ; 23 cm.

    In Cook, P. Lesley. Effects of mergers :
six studies. — London : Allen & Unwin,
1958.

Further examples of "In" analytic entries are:

From example no. 28

DUNCAN, Ben
    Outward bound / Ben Duncan. —
p. 3-4 ; 30 cm.

    In Arts alive Merseyside. — No. 51
(Mar. 1974)

From example no. 375 (with uniform title used
for part)

BEETHOVEN, Ludwig van
    [Sonatas, piano, no. 14, op. 27, no. 2,
C# minor]
    Moonlight sonata / Ludwig van
Beethoven. — on side B of 1 sound disc
(ca. 6 min.) : 33⅓ rpm, stereo. ; 12 in.

    In The world of your hundred best
tunes : the top ten. — London : Decca,
1970.

ANALYSIS

An analytical added entry is only one of four ways
in which AACR 2 indicates that analysis may be
achieved. The others are described in Ch.13 of
AACR 2 and are:

(i)   A complete bibliographic description
        may be prepared for the part (rule 13.2).
        This is illustrated in examples no. 18,
        78, 123, 168, 177, 319.

(ii)   A contents note may be made in a
        detailed entry for the larger work
        (rule 13.3). This is illustrated in
        examples no. 5, 6, 80, 164, 229, 235,
        321, 323, 331, 345, 354, 373, 375.

(iii)   A multi-level description may be used
        (rule 13.6). This is illustrated in
        examples no. 24, 113, 116, 169, 183,
        186.

APPENDIX 2
REFERENCES

The function of a *see* reference is to direct the user of a catalogue from a form of heading or title that might be sought, but which has not been chosen specifically by the indexer as an access point, to the heading, title or uniform title that has actually been used.

The function of a *see also* reference is to link headings or uniform titles which are related to each other.

When adequate direction cannot be given by a simple *see* or *see also* reference, a more detailed reference, the *explanatory* reference, is made.

See and *see also* references may be made in the form of *name-title* references which refer from or to the personal or corporate heading followed by the title concerned.

AACR 2 summarises the requirements for references in Chapter 26. The rules in Chapters 21 to 25 also indicate particular types of references that are commonly needed in specific situations.

The following are examples of some of the various occasions when references are required. The number of the example in the main entry sequence to which the reference is related is indicated.

SEE REFERENCES

Rule 26.1   Basic rule

This rule states that whenever the name of a person or corporate body or the title of a work is, or may reasonably be, known under a form that is not the one used as a name heading or uniform title, refer from that form to the one that has been used. However, rule 21.30J

stipulates that an *added entry* should be made under any title different from the title proper (see p.174). For those cataloguing agencies that may prefer references, a few examples are given below, but it should be remembered that AACR 2 does not specifically advocate references of this nature.

	Example no.
Alternative title	209

A BIT of a book
   <u>see</u> MILLIGAN, Spike
      A book of bits

Parallel title	105

The THREE-CORNERED hat
   <u>see</u> FALLA, Manuel de
      El sombrero de tres picos

Variant title	207

REFORMATION [symphony]
   <u>see</u> MENDELSSOHN-BARTHOLDY,
     Felix
     [Symphonies, no. 5, op. 107,
   D minor]

A further example of an occasion when a reference would be required is when a title begins with a number and a reference is made necessary by the filing system (see also rule 26.3A5).

ONE thousand makers of the	227

ONE thousand makers of the
   twentieth century
   <u>see</u> 1000 makers of the twentieth
     century

UNITED KINGDOM. Law   188
     Commission
     see LAW COMMISSION

UNITED KINGDOM. Library   191
     Advisory Council (England)
     see LIBRARY ADVISORY COUNCIL
     (England)

WORLD HEALTH ORGANISA-   177
     TION. Joint F.A.O./W.H.O. Expert
     Committee on African Trypanosam-
     iasis
     see JOINT F.A.O./W.H.O. EXPERT
         COMMITTEE ON AFRICAN
         TRYPANOSAMIASIS

(and a similar reference under Food and
Agricultural Organisation. References would
also be required from the initials of the two
organisations).

Name and its variants in the form of subheadings
under the immediately superior body when the
name has been entered under a body higher
than the immediately superior body

UNITED KINGDOM. Board   337
     of Trade. Committee of Inquiry
     into Trawler Safety
     see UNITED KINGDOM. Committee
         of Inquiry into Trawler Safety

UNITED STATES. Department   345
     of Commerce. Patent Office
     see UNITED STATES. Patent Office

For bodies entered subordinately, the name and
its variants in the form of independent headings
whenever the name does not necessarily suggest
subordinate entry

GENERAL REGISTER OFFICE   338
     see UNITED KINGDOM. General
         Register Office

Rule 26.4   Uniform titles

Rule 26.4A1   Different titles or variants of the
title

THOUSAND and one nights   25
     see [ARABIAN nights]

Rule 26.4A3   Titles of parts catalogued under
the title of the whole work

NEW TESTAMENT   46
     see [BIBLE. N.T.]

LUKE (Book of the Bible)   145
     see [BIBLE. N.T. Luke]

SEE REFERENCES — NAME-TITLE REFERENCES

Rule 26.2B   Works of a person entered under
two or more different headings

MARKHAM, Robert   19
     Colonel Sun : a James Bond adventure
     see AMIS, Kingsley

Rule 26.2B2   Initials

B., E.R.P.   98
     Nursery rhymes of Gloucestershire
     see E.R.P.B.

Rule 26.4   Uniform titles

Rule 26.4A1   Different titles or variants of
the title

DICKENS, Charles   90
     The story of David Copperfield
     see DICKENS, Charles
         [David Copperfield]
     Translated titles

BOREL, Jacques   51
     The bond
     see BOREL, Jacques
         [L'adoration. English]

Rules 26.4A2   Titles of parts of a work catalogued separately

JACOB, Naomi   168
     The Gollantz saga. 4. Four generations
     see JACOB, Naomi
         Four generations

SEE ALSO REFERENCES

Rule 26.2   Names of persons

Rule 26.2C1   Works of one person entered under two different headings

KING, Albert   275
    see also SANTEE, Walt

Rule 26.3   Names of corporate bodies and geographic names

Rule 26.3B1   Related corporate headings

INTERNATIONAL LABOUR   166
    ORGANISATION
    see also INTERNATIONAL
              LABOUR OFFICE

EXPLANATORY REFERENCES

Rule 26.2   Names of persons

Rule 26. 2D1   General rule

BLOOM, Ursula   253
    For works of this author written in collaboration with Charles Eade, see PROLE, Lozania

(and a similar reference under Eade)

PROLE, Lozania   253
    The joint pseudonym of Ursula Bloom and Charles Eade. For works written by Bloom under her own name, see BLOOM, Ursula

Rule 26.2D2   Separately written prefixes
(Optional)

VON   262
    Names beginning with this prefix are entered under the part following the prefix when the person's language is Dutch, Flemish, German or Scandinavian. In other cases entry is under the prefix

Rule 26.3   Names of corporate bodies and geographic names

Rule 26.3C1   General rule

Scope of heading

CATHOLIC CHURCH. Pope   174
    (1958-1963 : John XXIII)
    Here are entered works of the Pope acting in his official capacity. For other works, see
JOHN XXIII, Pope

(assuming headings are established for the Pope both as person and religious official)

References applicable to several headings (when appropriate in a catalogue where verbal subject and name-title entries are interfiled)

EXHIBITIONS   165
    Works reporting the collective activity of an exhibition are entered under the name of the exhibition or the title of the publication if the exhibition lacks a name

Headings that supersede one another

Simple situations

SOUTHPORT HIGH SCHOOL   139
    FOR GIRLS
        see also the later heading
GREENBANK HIGH SCHOOL FOR
    GIRLS (Sefton)

Complex situations

SEFTON LIBRARIES AND   82
    ARTS SERVICES
    This heading is used for publications from 1974 onwards. The County Boroughs of Bootle and Southport, the Municipal Borough of Crosby, and parts of the County of Lancashire, i.e. the Urban Districts of Formby and Litherland and parts of West Lancs Rural District, were merged in the local government reorganisation of that year to form the Metropolitan District of Sefton. Works of the previously existing library authorities are entered under the names used at the time of publication

Rule 26.3C2 Acronyms — when the filing system used distinguishes between initials with full stops and initials without full stops

C.A.S.   123
    see CENTRE FOR ADMINI-
            STRATIVE STUDIES
    When these initials occur in a title or other heading without spaces or full stops, they are treated as if constituting a word

CENTRE FOR ADMINISTRATIVE
    STUDIES
    Identified in some publications as CAS. When these initials occur in the form of an acronym at the beginning of titles and other entries, they are treated as constituting a word

26.4   Uniform titles

26.4C2   Titles of parts cataloguing independently (optional)

JACOB, Naomi   168
    The Gollantz saga
    For the separately published parts of this work see
JACOB, Naomi
    Four generations

See also p.179(rule 26.4A2)

REFERENCES INSTEAD OF ADDED ENTRIES

Rule 26.5A   If a number of added entries are required under the same heading, they may be replaced by appropriate references

HAMLET   285
SHAKESPEARE, William
    Editions of this work will be found under SHAKESPEARE, William

Rule 26.5B   Alternative format

HAMLET
SHAKESPEARE, William
    Hamlet. — c1964.
    1 sound disc.
    For other editions, etc., see Shakespeare, William. Hamlet

The above two examples are shown in the 'unit entry' format described in Appendix 1.

AUTHORITY FILES

As references do not appear in tracings, a separate authority file is necessary. This shows, in alphabetical order, the headings used and the references made, and is used to control the provision of references in the catalogue. Examples of entries in the authority file follow.

Barber, Margaret Fairless
    see FAIRLESS, Michael
BIBLE
    ref. from Holy Bible
CAMPBELL, Patrick
    ref. from Glenavy, Patrick Campbell, Baron
CATHOLIC CHURCH
    ref. from Roman Catholic Church
FAIRLESS, Michael
    ref. from Barber, Margaret Fairless
General Register Office
    see UNITED KINGDOM. General Register Office
Glenavy, Patrick Campbell, Baron
    see CAMPBELL, Patrick
GREENBANK HIGH SCHOOL FOR GIRLS
    (Sefton)
    see also the earlier heading
    SOUTHPORT HIGH SCHOOL FOR GIRLS
Holy Bible
    see BIBLE
KING, Albert
    see also SANTEE, Walter
A Lady of Richmond
    see PUTNAM, Sallie
LAW COMMISSION
    ref. from United Kingdom. Law Commission
PUTNAM, Sallie
    ref. from A Lady of Richmond
Roman Catholic Church
    see CATHOLIC CHURCH

SANTEE, Walter
    see also KING, Albert

SOUTHPORT HIGH SCHOOL FOR GIRLS
    see also the later heading
    GREENBANK HIGH SCHOOL FOR
    GIRLS (Sefton)

UNITED KINGDOM. General Register
    Office
    ref. from General Register Office

United Kingdom. Law Commission
    see LAW COMMISSION

The information in the authority file may, of
course, be presented in a different way to that
shown above. For instance, the abbreviations
sa, x and xx could be used, as in the *Library of*
Congress subject headings. This would give
entries such as

FAIRLESS, Michael
    x Barber, Margaret Fairless

which would mean that a *see* reference is to be
made from Barber to Fairless, and

KING, Albert
    sa SANTEE, Walter
    xx SANTEE, Walter

which would indicate that a *see also* reference is
to be made from King to Santee and a reverse
see also reference from Santee to King.

APPENDIX 3
EXAMPLES OF ENTRY LAYOUT WHEN PARAGRAPHING IS NOT EMPLOYED

ABRAHAMS, Gerald
   Trade unions & the law / by Gerald Abrahams. — London : Cassell, 1968. — xix, 254 p. ; 22 cm. — ISBN 0-304-91599-8.

ALANSON, Eric
   A printed catalogue from punched cards / Eric Alanson. — Liverpool : Liverpool Polytechnic, 1978. — 1 program file (70 statements, COBOL). — 75 punched cards : 80 columns. — Not generally available.

BEE GEES
   How deep is your love / Bee Gees. — [London] : RSO Records, 1977. — on 1 side of 1 sound disc (ca. 3 min., 10 sec.) : 45 rpm, stereo. ; 7 in. — "From the Paramount/Robert Stigwood motion picture: Saturday night fever". — RSO: 2090 259. — With: Night fever.

CARTER, Craig J.M.
   Ships of the Mersey / Craig J.M. Carter. — London : Record Books, 1966. — 79 p., 1 leaf of plates : ill. ; 20 cm. + 2 sound discs (33⅓ rpm, mono. ; 7 in.). — (Sound picture series). — Discs, which are recordings of ship's sounds, in pocket.

HOME beer and winemaking. — Vol. 1, no. 1 (Jan. 1970)-   . — Wirral : Foremost Press, 1970-   . v. : ill. ; 28 cm. — Monthly. — Library has v.8, no.3 (Apr. 1977)-   . — ISSN 0041-090X.

LAST, James
   Love must be the reason / James Last [and his orchestra] ; produced and arranged by James Last. — [London] : Polydor, 1972. — 1 sound disc (ca. 40 min.) : 33⅓ rpm, stereo. ; 12 in. — Also available as stereo cassette and 8-track stereo cartridge. — Partial contents: Wedding song / Stookey — Heart of gold / Young — I don't know how to love him / Lloyd Webber — Love must be the reason / Schuman. — Polydor: 2371-281 (disc). — Polydor: 3150-256 (cassette). — Polydor: 3811-152 (cartridge).

PAINTINGS at Chatsworth : colour postcards of paintings in the Devonshire Collection. — Derby : English Life Publications, [196-?]. — 8 postcards : col. ; 15 x 11 cm. — In folder. — Contents: Trial by jury / Landseer — The holy family / Murillo — Georgiano, Duchess of Devonshire, with her daughter Georgiano / Reynolds — The flight into Egypt / Ricci — The Acheson sisters / Sargent — Portrait of an oriental (King Uzzich?) / Van Rijn — Arthur Goodwin, M.P. / Van Dyck — The adoration of the Kings / Veronese.

PHOTOGRAPH and slide classification for western art / Photograph and Slide Collection, Fine Arts Library, Fogg Art Museum. — Cambridge, Mass. : Harvard University Library, Microreproduction Dept., [1973?]. — 1 microfilm reel ; 35 mm. — Low reduction. — Comic mode. — Microreproduction of: Rev. ed., 1973.

RASMUS, Carolyn J.
    Agility / Carolyn J. Rasmus. — Cam-
bridge, Mass. : Ealing, 1969. — 1 film
loop (3 min., 35 sec.) : si., col. ; Super
8 mm. — (Functional fitness). — Consultants: The American Association for Health,
Physical Education and Recreation. —
"Licensed only for direct optical projection
before a viewing audience"—Box. — Notes
on box.